AF587899

Also published by The Film Desk:

François Truffaut by Lillian Ross,
from *The New Yorker*, 1960–1976

John Huston by Lillian Ross,
from *The New Yorker*, 1949–1996

Phillippe Garrel—*L'Enfant secret*

Pasolini in New York

Duras/Godard Dialogues

The World of Jia Zhangke
by Jean-Michel Frodon

Film as a Subversive Art
by Amos Vogel

Facing Blackness
by Ashley Clark

Diary of a Film
by Jean Cocteau

Film Business
by Lillian Ross

Le Depays
by Chris Marker

That Bowling Alley on the Tiber
by Michelangelo Antonioni

Hallelujah Now
by Terence Davies

The Hunger

Melissa Anderson

The Hunger

Film Writing, 2012–2024

THE FiLm DeSK

THE FiLm DeSK

ISBN: 979-8-9864463-8-7
Library of Congress Control Number: 2025944437

1st Edition of 1,500, 2025, Film Desk Books, New York
Jim Colvill and Jake Perlin, publishers

Cover image: Ida Lupino in *The Bigamist* (1953)

The publishers extend their grateful appreciation to
Nancy Handelman, Julia Rose Katz, Laura, and Oliver.

Series design by Brian McMullen
Printed in Michigan

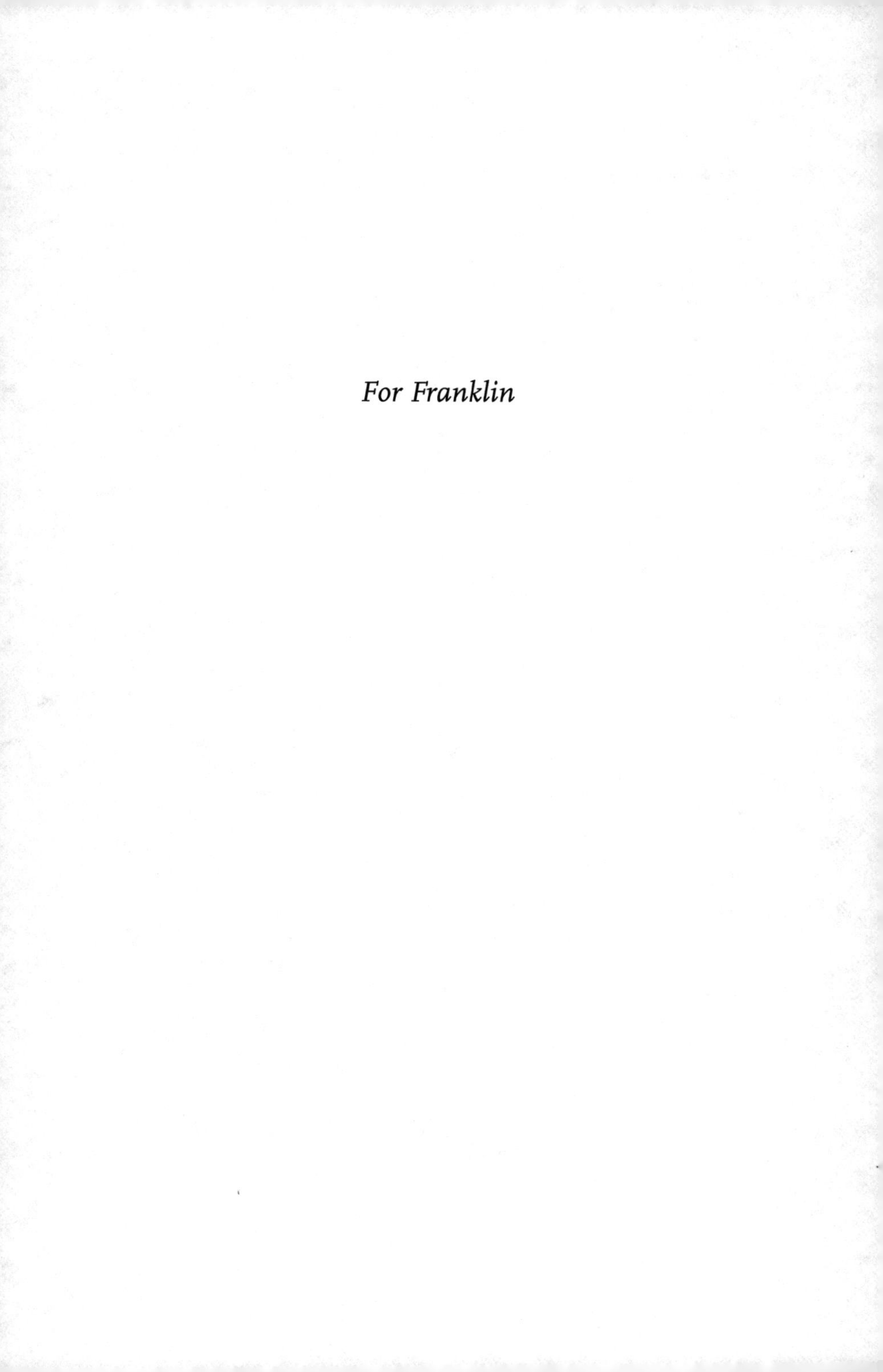

For Franklin

Table of Contents

Introduction

My first formative moviegoing experience involved a film that I could never recommend today. In the fall of 1985, I went to see, for the first of five or six times, Norman Jewison's prestige nunsploitation melodrama *Agnes of God.* It was showing at a twin cinema offset from a mall within walking distance of my family's house in Harrisburg, Pennsylvania. Then a teenager, I always saw the film by myself; this was, I am almost certain, the first instance of my solo moviegoing, a ritual that I still hold sacrosanct. My repeat viewings were mandated by a lust that I, deep in the benighted Reagan era and still years away from coming out, could not fully make sense of at the time. I was besotted with Meg Tilly, who plays the novitiate of the title, about to stand trial for murdering a baby she insists was conceived divinely. Yielding to an erotic pull, however inchoate, that an actress had over me, I felt that my repeat viewings were somehow "wrong," which is why I lied and told my parents that I was going to the public library, located just behind the movie theater.

I am chagrined by the fact that such a middling movie held me in its thrall—and that it was Tilly, and not Jane Fonda, playing the chain-smoking, tweed-blazered and leather-booted psychiatrist assigned to determine Agnes's sanity, whom I ardently responded to (my Jane fascination would come later, after I saw *Klute* on VHS). But my experience with *Agnes of*

God presaged what would later become my profession: trying to articulate a film's effect on me.

As several pieces in this book demonstrate, that articulation often involves analyzing how I responded to a particular performer (usually a female one). I have, to use a helpful term conceived by the film curator Dave Kehr, an "acteurist" bent—a slant that privileges actors when discussing a given movie, that sees them, as Kehr explains, as "vehicles of meaning in their movies." The late, great gay cult critic Boyd McDonald had his own spin on the concept decades before Kehr's coinage, puckishly noting "the importance of the movie star over the movie and thus the importance of star reviews over mere movie reviews, with their constant complaints about plot." (The line is so good that you'll find it twice more in this book.)

McDonald has been a lodestar for me ever since I read the 2015 reissue of his 1985 collection, *Cruising the Movies: A Sexual Guide to Oldies on TV* (my review of which is included here, along with one other book piece, on Cynthia Carr's biography of Candy Darling). In McDonald's volume, which is distinguished by a beautifully elucidated bawdiness and a radical yet nondidactic political point of view, I came across this astounding sentence: "Motion pictures are for people who like to watch women." The observation strikes me as the purest, simplest distillation of cinephilia—or at least one strain of it, mine especially. In McDonald's axiom, liking to watch women on-screen means, on its most fundamental level, to be deeply interested in what they do.

Just as crucial a credo has been this declaration from film scholar Patricia White in her essential 1999 book *Uninvited: Classical Hollywood Cinema and Lesbian Representability*: "Cinema is public fantasy that engages spectators' particular, private scripts of desire and identification." (I've cited that line, and many others from *Uninvited*, frequently over the years.) When I first saw *Agnes of God*, my script was still being written. Scripts can be memorized, refashioned, or abandoned altogether in favor of improvisation. They are multifaceted, ever-mutating things, and the movies that have meant the most to me are those that are similarly complex, that summon a range of responses, that do not preach.

Although the year of the earliest reviews and essays collected here is 2012, I began writing about movies (and about books related to film) more than a decade before, primarily for what was then called the gay press. I date my first significant piece of film criticism to 2000: this was the year—my fourth in New York, where I still live—that I made my debut in the *Village Voice*, having received a message, saved for weeks, on my answering machine from Dennis Lim, the paper's redoubtable film editor until 2006, saying that he liked my clips and inviting me to pitch him. My *Voice* debut consisted of 500 words on a series at the Whitney Museum devoted to women avant-garde filmmakers in the US. That piece, like nearly everything I wrote as a freelancer in the ensuing five years (not only for the *Voice* but also for the *New York Sun* and *Film Comment*, among other publications), is excruciating to revisit. The writing is at once too timid and too moralizing, the sentences too baggy, the adjectives too vague. It was unthinkable to me to include any of those articles here.

In late 2005, I became the film editor of *Time Out New York*, a job that trained me to honor the exigencies, the nonnegotiable deadlines of a weekly print publication. It also taught me how to write haiku-like prose. The standard review length when I started at *TONY* was 250 words; by the time I was let go from the magazine, in January 2009, that already-minuscule length had shrunk to 225 words. Too short to be of much interest, those pieces are also not to be found in this collection.

After *TONY*, I freelanced for many different publications, but my main outlets were the *Voice* and *Artforum* (both the print magazine and its website). During this period, developing a bit more confidence, I concentrated on honing my voice, which I would describe as queer but undoctrinaire—homophilic yet heterodox. I tried to make my language more specific and vivid; at the same time, I tried to loosen up. (It wasn't until 2012 that I began to feel that I was doing this adequately.)

In late 2015, I became a staff film critic at the forever-being-revived *Voice*, which had just been bought by a billionaire. In addition to writing about new releases, I had a column that was devoted to repertory programming in New York City, then in a period of great re-efflorescence. It was an extremely rewarding, if occasionally destabilizing, job. With its multiple weekly deadlines, with so many current releases that I felt wholly indifferent to but had to say something about, my nearly two-year tenure as a *Voice* staffer so often brought to mind Renata Adler's description of her year-plus as the chief film critic for the *New York Times*. She remembers the position, which she held from 1968 to 1969, as "a particular kind of adventure—with time ... with the peculiar experience it always is to write in one's own name something that is never exactly what one would have wanted to say." I can usually recognize myself in these pieces. Just as often, I can detect the ticking clock that loomed over me as I wrote them.

By the summer of 2017, the rich man who had been hailed as the *Voice*'s savior would begin the yearlong process of overseeing its demise, first shutting down the print version and then abandoning the website. It was during this grim time that I met with Margaret Sundell, the founder and editor in chief of *4Columns*, a weekly online magazine devoted to arts criticism, which she had launched in 2016. She was looking to expand the site's film coverage; I was hired as the film editor and lead film critic. It remains the best job I have ever had and the one I have held the longest. The position has not only provided more time to research and compose a piece—I write two 1,000-word reviews (of films new and old) a month, as opposed to the one to three (or more), of varying word counts, I would previously often write in a week—but also given me the opportunity to commission work from the most talented writers I know.

One of those immensely gifted writers, Erika Balsom, graciously agreed to talk with me about this collection; our conversation serves as the afterword. And another came up with the book's title. I struggled for months over what to call this volume, having tried all kinds of wearying puns with *out* or *dark*, then thought that "Shadowlands," a nod to a term that Kenneth Anger uses in *Hollywood Babylon II*, might work. My friend Ed Halter—a brilliant critic and programmer and, with the equally formidable Thomas Beard, the founder of Light Industry, New York City's most vital micro-cinema—rightly dismissed the Anger homage as "too goth." Minutes later, he came up with what I knew instantly was the perfect title. *The Hunger*, of course, is the name of Tony Scott's stylish, ludicrous ode to bicuriosity from 1983, starring Catherine Deneuve as a soignée vampiress who seduces Susan Sarandon. I didn't see the film until sometime in my 20s, at least a decade after its release. (Did *The Hunger* ever play at the cinema where I saw *Agnes of God*? If it had, would the R rating have prevented me, then under 17, from seeing it by myself? But I'm still puzzled as to why I didn't somehow manage to see the film in '83, the year that my ardor for David Bowie, another of the movie's stars, peaked. Was the explicitly sapphic plotline simply too terrifying to my proto-lesbo adolescent self?)

In addition to signaling a dyke touchstone, the book's title also implies—both more broadly and more evocatively—craving, desire. It conjures these lines from the narration of Terence Davies's acidulous, rueful documentary-memoir *Of Time and the City* (2008): "At seven, I discovered the movies, loved them, and swallowed them whole. ... I gorged myself with a regularity that would shame a sinner." Delivered with orotund crispness by the director himself, the declaration acutely captures cinephilia's deranging power, its ability to whet an appetite that can never fully be sated. I was a cinephile long before I was a film critic, and I hope to never lose that sense of open-minded curiosity, of hopefulness, of a keen willingness to be transported, all essential elements of cine-love.

But having an appetite does not mean having indiscriminate taste. I've been quite fortunate not to have to weigh in on the kind of cinema that I find most enervating and soul-crushing: superhero franchise films. The sole exception is *Wonder Woman*, my review of which is included here. In that piece, as in everything else you'll find in this book, the goal was always the same: to express, as precisely as possible, my pleasure or displeasure.

Looking Back

A Bigger Splash

(Jack Hazan, 1974)

SEXY. David Hockney luxuriates in the word, adding extra sibilance to the adjective, one he applies to a friend, the American model Joe MacDonald, who sits with him in a hotel room in Geneva in June 1973. Their flirty conversation occurs early on in Jack Hazan's *A Bigger Splash*, a partly scripted, partly improvised quasi-documentary about the English painter, then at the height of his fame and recently broken up with Peter Schlesinger, the subject of some of Hockney's best-known works. Fact embellished by fiction (and vice versa), *A Bigger Splash*, protean in structure, explores fluid connections: within Hockney's milieu are onetime lovers who are now friends, friends who are not yet lovers, and ex-lovers who have yet to become friends. The film—whose central figure has never not been out (at least since his Royal College of Art days in the early 1960s, several years before homosexuality was decriminalized in the UK)—is effulgently yet casually gay, replete with cocks in various stages of tumescence and alabaster butts contrasting starkly with otherwise sun-kissed flesh. Recently reissued in a coruscating 4K restoration, it is also beautiful to behold.

Hazan's first feature, *A Bigger Splash* was made with the reluctant participation of Hockney—a reluctance belied by his ease and abundant charm before the camera. The filmmaker conceived the project after seeing Hockney's 1970 retrospective at the Whitechapel Gallery in London; particularly inspiring were the exhibition's double portraits. (At that point, Hazan was known mainly for his short 1969 documentary on the

Liverpudlian nature painter and sculptor Keith Grant.) "I got very excited because the subjects were alive, and I could possibly gain access to them, and maybe ... I could film them in the same poses," he explained in 2011 to Christopher Simon Sykes, the author of a two-volume Hockney biography. "The film was never intended to be a documentary. I wanted to make something cinematic."

After repeatedly but politely declining Hazan, Hockney finally relented in the spring of 1971. ("I agreed to do it to get rid of him," the artist told Sykes.) It was around this time that Hockney's relationship with Schlesinger—begun in 1966 when the San Fernando Valley native, then 18, took a UCLA drawing class taught by the rapidly ascending painter, then 28—was starting to unravel. Filming over the next two-plus years, primarily in London though with detours to New York and Los Angeles (scenes from the "Geneva resort," which the director later admitted were actually shot in Hockney's London apartment, bookend the movie), Hazan used the termination of this romance and its repercussions as the throughline of *A Bigger Splash*. To assuage his heartache, Hockney spent long hours in his studio. The masterwork that animates Hazan's movie isn't the 1967 painting with which it shares a title, the most famous of Hockney's depopulated California-pool canvases (which nonetheless has a cameo during the opening-credit sequence and at the film's midpoint). Instead, this nimble docufiction chronicles the creation, destruction, and re-creation of *Portrait of an Artist (Pool with Two Figures)*, 1972, Hockney's homage to the young man, struggling to be recognized for his own talents, who had left him.

The split affects not only Hockney. "When love goes wrong, there's more than two people suffer," Mo McDermott, the artist's studio assistant, says in a rueful voice-over, among the many stylized components of *A Bigger Splash*. (Hazan, who also served as cinematographer, shooting on 35mm, cowrote the movie with David Mingay, its editor.) McDermott, part of Hockney's circle since 1962, is one of a number of the artist's closest associates to appear in the film, all playing slightly heightened versions of themselves. Variously avoiding, comforting, upbraiding, or advising him, the members of this charismatic coterie also include the couturier Ossie Clark (a former lover of Hockney's) and his spouse, the fabric and textile designer Celia Birtwell; John Kasmin, Hockney's gallerist; and curator–bon vivant–daddy nonpareil Henry Geldzahler, the artist's New York bestie, who's filmed at one point as if in a tableau, replicating the pose he had struck for Hockney's *Henry Geldzahler and Christopher Scott*, 1969.

But thanks to his tobacco-deepened, impassioned off-screen narration, McDermott—who recalls an older, loucher, "Rocket Man"-era Elton John (and whose boyfriend Mike Sida shows up intermittently as a mute, expressionless rocker dutifully sharpening drawing pencils)—emerges as the project's preeminent romantic, voicing vulnerabilities that Hockney mostly keeps to himself. First seen in a sequence filmed in June 1973, per one of the intertitles used throughout to establish time and place, McDermott sits solemnly at a large table in Hockney's live-work space in Notting Hill (which Hockney had shared with Schlesinger), located next to an establishment with the intriguing slogan PLAYER'S PLEASE emblazoned on its window. McDermott drifts into reverie, recalling a time between the couple before they separated for good.

That reminiscence leads into a bit of fabulous footage from two years prior, showing Hockney slumped in the front row of Clark's fashion show at the Royal Court Theatre. He's flanked by Birtwell and Schlesinger—delighted by the action and sporting both a cute candy necklace and a Tadzio sailor top. In contrast to Schlesinger's ebullience (and that of most of the crowd), the usually cheerful Hockney seems subdued. Though Hockney and Birtwell are seen exchanging comments, neither man talks to the other. Love is going wrong.

After the couple's rupture, Schlesinger, a budding painter and photographer, moved into his own studio, which was just around the corner from Hockney's place. In a staged moment, we see the young American, clad only in white briefs, dancing with himself in front of an easel, reveling in a night alone at his tiny pad. (Schlesinger agreed to take part in *A Bigger Splash* only if Hazan paid him.) Earlier in the film, we witness Schlesinger in another contrived domestic episode, though this time with naked company: he gets it on with a friend, the actor Eddie Kalinski. (IRL, Schlesinger's boyfriend immediately after Hockney was the photographer Eric Boman, who never appears in *A Bigger Splash*; they remain together today.) In another segment, constructed as a SoCal fantasia, Schlesinger skinny-dips in a pool with a trio of brunet twinks. One of them delivers the (off-screen) come-on "Would you like to play with us?" Another is Gregory Evans, who, by 1975, would be Hockney's boyfriend and, later, his manager. (Players please.)

No longer Hockney's lover and far from being a pal, Schlesinger is still Hockney's occasional silent, sullen model in *A Bigger Splash*. With his peroxided mop grown a bit too shaggy, Hockney sketches and paints Schlesinger from the back—a study for *Sur la terrasse*, 1971, a nearly completed canvas that rests behind the artist as he squints through his Mr. Peabody and Sherman specs at his ex's perfect, V-shaped torso. That's one of several works in progress we watch Hockney contemplate, meticulously add to, then examine again. Unembellished vérité, the episodes in the studio stand out as this sensuous film's most mesmerizing: they offer unrushed glimpses of the artist's credo—"I paint what I like when I like, and where I like"—in action.

Could a corollary to that guiding principle be: When love goes wrong, art—eventually, painstakingly—goes right? That's what happens in Hazan's film, especially as Hockney completes *Portrait of an Artist (Pool with Two Figures)*, a painting, featuring a pink-jacketed Schlesinger standing on the edge of a *piscine*, that he labored over off and on, with increasing frustration, for six months. After realizing the angle of the pool was wrong, Hockney cut up the canvas and started anew, finishing the piece—with the help of Schlesinger, who poses for his onetime boyfriend very early one morning in Kensington Gardens—in an astonishing two weeks.

The painting made headlines last November for the price it took at auction, though this datum doesn't interest me. More significant is the return of the too-little-revived film that documents *Portrait of an Artist*'s charged iterations and the circumstances surrounding them. After watching *A Bigger Splash* a few weeks before its premiere at Cannes in 1974, Hockney said he was "utterly shattered" by it, his anguish spiked further by a film-director friend who likened it favorably—if somewhat incongruously—to "a real *Sunday Bloody Sunday*," John Schlesinger's astute, London-set, big-studio-backed 1971 drama about a love triangle (two men, one woman). More felicitous comparisons might include Wakefield Poole's *Boys in the Sand* (1971), a gay XXX landmark in which a Fire Island natatorium becomes a pleasure palace, not to mention Robert Kramer's *Milestones* (1975), an epic dirge for the failed dreams of the New Left in the US, which was also devised as a docufiction. (Hazan and Mingay would return to this genre with 1980's *Rude Boy*, centering on the

Clash.) But as for movies about making (art) and unmaking (a relationship), I can think of none better, or more sinuous—as serpentine as Hockney's enunciation of a favorite descriptor.

—*Artforum*, Summer 2019

La Piscine

(Jacques Deray, 1969)

Sunstroked and sex-soaked, Jacques Deray's *La Piscine*, a French Riviera–set tale of high-stakes hedonism originally released in 1969, offers, among its many sensuous pleasures, multiple studies of blue. There is the cerulean of the Mediterranean and the aqua of the swimming pool of the title, part of a luxe villa high up in the hills overlooking Saint-Tropez, where most of the film's action takes place. Most voluptuously, there are the hues of the eyes of Alain Delon (sapphire) and Romy Schneider (beryl), who play Jean-Paul and Marianne, the central couple of a sybaritic foursome. Blue is the hottest color.

Obscenely beautiful, Jean-Paul and Marianne, together for two years, are spending their summer holidays at the opulent estate, lent to them by friends traveling in India. We learn, about halfway through this two-hour movie, that they are members of the creative class. She's a journalist; he's an advertising executive, a profession he took up after too many years as a failed novelist. It's impossible, though, to imagine them devoting even one minute to anything besides their true vocation: arousing lust, jealousy, and other extreme emotions in each other.

Half-naked, fully turned on, the two generate so much erotic heat that the Côte d'Azur, during the weeks of filming, must have seen record-high temperatures. (Delon and Schneider, lovers from 1958 to 1963, likely relied on sense memories for their intimate scenes. They remained close after they split; Delon insisted to Deray that his ex be cast opposite him.) As they bake in the sun or lounge in bed, the camera besottedly rests on each actor, slowly zooming in on Delon as he lies supine poolside in the movie's opening scene or, later, panning languorously up Schneider's body. The couple's sexcation is interrupted—or, more accurately, complicated—by the unexpected arrival of two guests: music producer Harry (Maurice Ronet), a friend of Jean-Paul's since their adolescence and a former flame of Marianne's, and Harry's 18-year-old university-student daughter, Penelope (Jane Birkin).

The second they emerge from Harry's Maserati Ghibli—his flashy car merely one example of his pathetic attempts to deny his encroaching middle age—father and daughter add a sinister element to the lubricious ambience. Contests of one-up(wo)manship are waged. Harry and Marianne outrageously flirt. Jean-Paul is determined to seduce Penelope, not only to even the score with Marianne but also to cuckold Harry, who perversely treats his offspring, whom he neglected for her entire life until recently, more like his girlfriend.

These narcissists love to watch and be watched. Marianne thrills at the thought of Penelope observing her hosts doing it alfresco; the teenager becomes transfixed as she witnesses her goatish dad ogle Marianne. The fierce competition, which inevitably leads to violence, between the two men over the two women has tinges of displaced homoeroticism, a dynamic not too dissimilar from that shared by the characters Delon and Ronet played in *Purple Noon*, René Clément's 1960 adaptation of Patricia Highsmith's *The Talented Mr. Ripley*.

Although Marianne and Penelope regrettably ignite no sapphic sparks, the stark contrast between the actresses portraying them exerts its own libidinal fascination. Schneider, an Austro-Gallic superstar then at about the midpoint of her career (which ended with her death, at age 43, in 1982), exudes such feline, slinky amour propre that any of her actions, such as a costume change from bikini to maillot, constitutes a major event. A Swinging London scenester, Birkin enhances Penelope's feyness with her aggressively Anglo-accented French and gangly movements. Twenty-one at the time of filming, Birkin, like Sissy Spacek in 1976's *Carrie*, possesses the supernatural gift of appearing simultaneously much younger and much older than the age of her character.

Deray's best-known film, *La Piscine* was remade in 2015 by Luca Guadagnino as *A Bigger Splash* (a title that evinces another kind of repurposing, lifting the name of both a 1967 David Hockney painting and a 1974 quasi-documentary about the artist). Guadagnino ditched Saint-Tropez for Pantelleria, a volcanic island off the coast of Italy, but closely re-created the original's febrile, intergenerational love quadrangle. Yet he marred his pulpy sex thriller with a tonally disastrous bid at topical relevance, inserting a plot thread indicting Europe's response to the migrant crisis.

No such gravid grandstanding taints Deray's version. Filmed in August, September, and October 1968, *La Piscine* so seductively presents a microcosm of pampered egocentrics that the demonstrations that had nearly brought France to a halt a few months prior seem as distant as the trial of Joan of Arc. But real-life events—contemporaneous, or nearly so, with the making of *La Piscine*—involving two of its principal cast members heighten the movie's licentious appeal. On October 3, police arrived on the set to question Delon about the murder, still unsolved today, of his bodyguard Stefan Marković, whose corpse had been found in a dump outside Paris two days before. The "Marković affair" would soon include allegations of sex parties attended by the actor and Claude Pompidou, the wife of the soon-to-be-elected president. (More tarnishing infamy resulted in 2013 when Delon announced his support for France's far-right party, now called the National Rally. Dubbed the "male Brigitte Bardot" in the '60s, Delon and that former sex symbol are still linked, well into their senescence, by their shared ardor for Marine Le Pen, the National Rally's leader.)

Earlier in '68, Birkin filmed *Slogan* with Serge Gainsbourg, a project that marked the beginning of their creative and romantic partnership; for a decade-plus they reigned as France's premier libertine couple. The month after *La Piscine* opened in France, Birkin and Gainsbourg released their two most salacious singles, "Je t'aime ... moi non plus," punctuated by her orgasmic sighs, and "69 année érotique." Neither song is heard in *La Piscine,* which is scored by Michel Legrand and features two square pop numbers with lyrics by Alan and Marilyn Bergman. But they nonetheless echoed in my head as I watched Deray's movie, providing a phantom soundtrack to this carnal feast.

—*4Columns,* May 21, 2021

Losing Ground

(Kathleen Collins, 1982)

During the past six miserable, movie theater–shuttered months, no algorithm, no "what to watch" listicle, no recommendations from friends, not my own trawling for rarities in the deceptive plenitude of film-streaming services has come even close to matching the inspired choices and connections made by repertory-cinema programmers, especially those in New York City. More than five years ago, genius curators at Film at Lincoln Center made it possible for me and many lucky others to see *Losing Ground*, the only feature-length work by Kathleen Collins, who died of breast cancer at age 46 in 1988. Beautifully restored by the indispensable Milestone Films, Collins's movie screened as part of FLC's "Tell It Like It Is: Black Independents in New York, 1968–1986," a phenomenal series that brought together some of the most underrecognized movies, of varying lengths and genres, by a collection of filmmakers too long overlooked.

Collins—whose name was unknown to me at the time—is often cited as one of the first Black women to write and direct a feature-length movie, with *Losing Ground* preceding Julie Dash's lush, oneiric *Daughters of the Dust* (1991) by nearly a decade. Receiving just a scant number of screenings in the years after it was made, *Losing Ground*, which had a proper theatrical release in 2015, kicked off by that FLC retrospective, can finally be appreciated as an essential work of American independent cinema. Defined by a nimble élan and piercing wit, Collins's movie ranks as one of the best about a marriage between two ambitious members of the creative class. Possibly cinema's first Black-female-intellectual protagonist, Sara (Seret Scott), a beloved philosophy professor, reads *Saint Genet* in her downtime and is assiduously researching "the ecstatic experience"—a concept she fears that her too-analytical, ordered mind forecloses in her own life. Her spouse, Victor (Bill Gunn), a supremely self-assured (as his name implies) abstract painter, makes this boast to Sara after one of his paintings is purchased for a museum's permanent collection: "I'm a genuine success! Your husband is a genuine Black success!"

The line has a sharp bite, Victor drolly mocking the qualifying *Black* in his exultation. This piquant moment exemplifies Collins's keen observations about race in *Losing Ground*, a film that calls attention to the sentimentality that too often attaches to narratives about Black life, a mawkishness that obscures and dishonors complex humans. Sara's mother, a self-savoring stage actress played by Billie Allen, for example, offers this wry description of her latest production to her daughter and son-in-law over dinner: "Oh, it's one of those family dramas. I play someone's mother ... a beacon of strength and humility. It's a thoroughly colored play." (Collins also remains ever alert to the pieties and clichés surrounding race in *Whatever Happened to Interracial Love?*, a collection of undated, previously unpublished short stories issued in 2016; in the book's title story, racial categories are consistently enclosed in scare quotes, as if to suggest their absurdity or inadequacy as descriptors.)

Just as astutely, Collins assays the strains that inevitably arise in a long-term relationship, no matter how electric it may seem. Married for a decade, Sara and Victor are still clearly in love; their long, lusty kiss after he crows about the sale of his painting reveals a carnal heat nowhere close to being dampened. Their conversations, with each other and with those in their larger orbit, are about art and ideas, loamy talk that further evinces a dyad not in danger of growing stale. But his selfishness stings: Victor's proposal that they leave their Manhattan apartment for the summer to rent a bigger place in Rockland County where he can paint landscapes doesn't take into account Sara's need to be close to a well-stocked library for her research purposes. "If I did something artistic, like write or act, would that get me a little more consideration?" she snaps. Victor's chilly response: "If you were any good."

Though she's furious at Victor and achingly envious of the "private ecstasy" his work provides him, Sara—once she gets a look at the stone manor set amid pastoral splendor that a real estate agent shows them—ultimately can't say no to relocating for a few months to a hamlet outside the city. The change of scenery, in fact, seems to have loosened something in her—so much so that she finally agrees to act in the thesis film of one of her especially boisterous, persistent students, the monocle-sporting George (Gary Bolling). He's cast Sara as the female lead in his reimagining of the love-triangle folk ballad "Frankie and Johnny"; playing opposite her is George's debonair uncle Duke (Duane Jones), who, unlike Victor, finds Sara's scholarly pursuits fascinating.

While Sara stays in the city for a few days for the film's shoot—an ecstatic experience finally within reach—Victor remains upstate, distracting himself with Celia (Maritza Rivera), a local woman who agrees to sit for him. Sara has long inured herself to her husband's philandering—"There have always been women," she tells her mother during a heart-to-heart—but she cannot countenance his hypocrisy and cruelty when she brings Duke for a visit to their country digs.

Even during the scenes of *Losing Ground* that most closely adhere to marital melodrama—moments, that is, between Sara and Victor that seem to mirror the outsize emotions of George's interpretation of "Frankie and Johnny"—the film remains loose and agile, largely owing to the magnetism of the performers. Playing a character who, like many of the female protagonists in Collins's fiction, is frustrated, occasionally inconsolable, but never self-pitying, Scott entrances with an understated grandeur. Victor's most abhorrent traits—solipsism chief among them—are softened by Gunn's duende, a bewitching amour propre shared by Jones.

Losing Ground also benefits from a long-established camaraderie among the principal cast and crew. Jones and Gunn had acted together before, in *Ganja & Hess* (1973), a seductive, wildly disjunctive vampire movie and the second of three films directed by the multihyphenate Gunn, who also wrote for the stage and screen and published two novels (and who, like Collins, died much too young, at age 54 in 1989). *Losing Ground* also marked the second collaboration between Gunn and Collins: in 1975, she was the assistant director for *Black Picture Show*, a play he wrote and directed. Centering on a playwright-filmmaker father and his movie-director son—both stand-ins for Gunn—who are driven mad by the artistic compromises demanded of them, *Black Picture Show* was just one of many autobiographically informed projects by a man who tried to expand, if not trouble, the meaning of "genuine Black success."

As for *Losing Ground*'s other key catchphrase, "the ecstatic experience": even when watched in the least ideal circumstances—in my case, on a whirring four-year-old laptop that has been my puny makeshift cinema since mid-March—Collins's movie still elates.

—*4Columns*, September 25, 2020

New York, New York

(Martin Scorsese, 1977)

A film of otherworldly artifice and emotional ravaging, Martin Scorsese's doleful musical *New York, New York* forms a fascinating diptych with *Taxi Driver*, released the year before. The earlier movie, perhaps the definitive totem of Abe Beame–era Gotham and a signature work of the New American Cinema, hypnotizes and repels with its sordid, stygian portrayal of a suppurating metropolis. With *New York, New York*, Scorsese, a Little Italy native, created a far rosier tribute to his hometown by saluting the Hollywood musicals of the 1940s and '50s that he had so loved during his movie-mad youth.

The city here is a neon-bathed fantasia, re-created mostly on backlots and sets in Los Angeles. Despite its sumptuousness, *New York, New York* throbs with an anguish nearly as raw as that found in its predecessor. Scorsese likened this lavish production to "a $10 million home movie," its plot reflecting the real-life discord the director himself was facing. The look and sound of *New York, New York*, which screens for a week at Metrograph in a swoony new 35mm print, may rapturously bring to mind any number of postwar MGM marvels. But its mood suggests outtakes from a scorching psychodrama, rushes from a documentary of a couple imploding.

New York, New York begins with a scene of superbly orchestrated mass revelry, as hundreds celebrate V-J Day at a Times Square ballroom, swinging, drinking, and necking while Tommy Dorsey's band plays. One of those carousers is ex-GI Jimmy Doyle (an overwhelmingly beautiful Robert De

Niro, in his third movie with Scorsese). Decked out in spectator shoes and a garish Hawaiian shirt imprinted with Big Apple landmarks, Jimmy circuits the dance hall like a jittery horndog, his pinballing intensity recalling the lusty energy of the sailors on 24-hour shore leave in New York in Gene Kelly and Stanley Donen's exuberant *On the Town* (1949). He delivers a fusillade of terrible pickup lines ("Can I meet ya in Central Park?") at Francine Evans (Liza Minnelli), who's handsomely attired in her USO uniform, her lips and nails matching the maraschino cherry that she fishes out of her cocktail.

Francine's snubs of Jimmy's pathetic come-ons—in uttering a simple "no" more than a dozen times, Minnelli deftly handles the monosyllable like a rubber ball—typify the kineticism of *New York, New York,* which went into production without a finished script and was largely improvised. But despite her initial flat-out rejections, Francine finds the Brylcreemed live wire alluring enough that she ends up tagging along with Jimmy, a tenor sax player, to his audition at a Flatbush Avenue club. About to be eighty-sixed for one of his tantrums during the tryout, Jimmy is saved by Francine, who launches into "You Brought a New Kind of Love to Me," one of several standards Minnelli sings in *New York, New York,* in addition to tracks written for the film—including the title anthem—by her frequent collaborators John Kander and Fred Ebb. Jimmy and Francine go on the road together, fall in love, and wed, but their romantic and professional partnership cannot withstand his jealousy of her success, behavior that leaves Francine increasingly isolated.

The couple's candid talk often takes place in settings of exquisite make-believe; a scene of Jimmy and Francine deep in conversation on a winter day features an art nouveau copse that could have been designed by Aubrey Beardsley. The lush decor, rather than distracting from or diminishing the feelings laid bare, serves to heighten them. As the director himself explained in the book-length interview *Scorsese on Scorsese* (1989), his '40s-set musical is animated by Me Decade concerns about parity in relationships: "It's about two people in love with each other who are both creative. That was the idea: to see if the marriage would work. We didn't know if this marriage was going to work, because we didn't know if our own marriages were working."

In fact, Scorsese's marriage to Julia Cameron, a journalist who did script-doctoring on both *Taxi Driver* and *New York, New York,* was floundering: they wed in 1976 and divorced the following year. While his musical was in production, months that coincided with Cameron's pregnancy, Scorsese carried on an open affair with Minnelli, mirroring Jimmy's caddish treatment of Francine. (As the author of 1992's "creative recovery" guide *The Artist's Way,* Cameron now enjoys a fame that may be just as enduring as, if less high-profile than, her ex-spouse's.)

The casting of Liza, the monstrously talented only child of Vincente Minnelli and Judy Garland—two of the greatest luminaries of the movie genre Scorsese was deifying—ensures that *New York, New York* can ingeniously blur film fiction and off-screen reality and seamlessly inhabit two time frames at once. Liza, who became a '70s icon largely owing to her work with Bob Fosse early in the decade—*Cabaret* and the TV concert *Liza with a "Z"*, both from 1972—signals au courant superstardom and a throwback to the cherished song-and-dance movies her father directed or her mother starred in. Late in *New York, New York,* as Francine, now a single mother, records her first album for Decca, Liza tears into the Kander and Ebb composition "But the World Goes 'Round"—

an atavistic performance that summons not only Sally Bowles (the plaintive track is reminiscent of *Cabaret*'s "Maybe This Time") but also, thanks to Liza's beseeching gestures, Mama Judy belting out the torchy "The Man That Got Away" in *A Star Is Born* (1954).

Scorsese's bold experiment, which did poorly both critically and commercially, was released on June 21, 1977—less than a month after George Lucas's *Star Wars*, the juggernaut that irrevocably, irreparably changed the film industry. Marcia Lucas, George's wife at the time and an editor on both *New York, New York* and *Star Wars*, was one among many Hollywood insiders who predicted that the two movies would meet with opposite fates: "*New York, New York* is a film for grown-ups, yours is just a kids' movie, and nobody's going to take it seriously," she reportedly told her husband.

While *New York, New York* was still being edited, George advised Scorsese that his film could gross an extra $10 million if he gave the musical a happy ending. The counsel chilled him. "When I heard him say that, I knew I was doomed, that I would not make it in this business," Scorsese told Peter Biskind, author of the New American Cinema chronicle *Easy Riders, Raging Bulls* (1998). "I knew that what the two characters had gone through in that film, I had gone through in my own life, and I knew I wouldn't be able to face myself or them if Bob and Liza were to go off together." It would be absurd to say that the man who went on to direct, among so many other lauded movies, *Goodfellas, The Departed*, and *The Irishman* hasn't made it in the business. But his kind of cinema—films for grown-ups—remains ever imperiled.

—*4Columns*, January 31, 2020

Play Misty for Me

(Clint Eastwood, 1971)

The opening sequence of *Play Misty for Me,* a film from 1971 that marks the directorial debut of Clint Eastwood, who also stars, may be the most beautiful I have ever seen. Swooping aerial photography captures the majestic coastline of central California's Carmel-by-the-Sea, enormous whitecaps crashing against the rocks. Within this awesome natural splendor, a lone figure first appears as a speck, then comes into sharper focus. It's Eastwood, 40 at the time of filming, and nearly as beautiful as the setting that engulfs him. Playing a local jazz deejay named Dave Garver, he stands forlornly on the deck of his former girlfriend's temporarily vacated cliffside house in the Carmel Highlands. He stares below at the Pacific's ceaseless swirl, walks up some steps, and peers inside, noticing a not especially accurate or flattering portrait of himself on an easel, the work of the woman whose absence he finds, though he can't bring himself to admit it, unbearable.

This scene segues to one that counters what we have just seen: the ruggedly handsome man, initially so vulnerable, so small, transforms into a virile free spirit. Dave gets into his Jaguar XK150 and zooms down Highway 1, the car radio blasting a jazz-fusion instrumental called "Dirty Boogie." He's a lone wolf in black wraparound sunglasses. He can detour 26 miles south, crossing Big Sur's Bixby Creek Bridge, before turning back to clock in for his 8 p.m. to 1 a.m. slot at radio station KRML. He can do whatever he wants.

But a complication enters Dave's unfettered life: Evelyn

(Jessica Walter), a fan of his show—her call-in request for the Erroll Garner jazz standard provides the film's title—with whom he has a one-night stand. Breezily in accord at first with Dave's insistence on a no-strings-attached arrangement, Evelyn is quickly revealed to be a stalker, a psychopathic prototype for other single, sexually active women unhinged by their all-consuming possessiveness, like Glenn Close's Alex Forrest in Adrian Lyne's *Fatal Attraction* (1987) and other female crazies in movies far inferior to Eastwood's.

Evelyn's machinations become more diabolical once she discovers that Dave has reunited with his ex, Tobie (Donna Mills), who returns to Carmel after four months in Sausalito, a sojourn undertaken mainly to recover from Dave's philandering. "The thing I hate the most in the whole world is a jealous female. And that's what I was starting to be," she tells him during one of their many beachside walks, as Dave delicately broaches the possibility of getting back together. And thus Evelyn isn't repellent or dangerous simply because she's mentally ill. Her repugnant qualities are gendered: she represents female neediness in extremis. To paraphrase one of Susan Sontag's more celebrated lines: I am strongly drawn to *Play Misty for Me*, and almost as strongly offended by it. That is why I want to talk about it.

Like most movies that imprint themselves on me, that I can't shake, *Play Misty for Me* is a tangle of contradictions—a quality shared by many studio-backed movies from the '70s, that confounding decade that saw as many advancements as retreats in the US for women's rights (not to mention civil rights and LGBTQ liberation). I think of Eastwood's movie as the bizarre fraternal twin of, or the gender inverse of, another film released the same year and one that evinces similar anxiety around second-wave feminism, then cresting, and women's sexuality more generally: Alan J. Pakula's *Klute*. That movie was as crucial a project for star Jane Fonda, who won an Academy Award for her performance as the boho-chic sex worker Bree Daniels, as *Play Misty for Me* was for Eastwood, who was not only directing for the first time but also playing a part far removed from the cowboys and bounty hunters that had established his reputation.

Like Eastwood's movie, *Klute* is structured by a perverse triangle, consisting of a loving couple and a maniac who menaces the principal character: in Pakula's film, Bree grows emotionally attached to the eponymous private detective played by Donald Sutherland, who's protecting her from a serial killer who was once her client. Both films are punctuated by the terrifying peal of a rotary phone, a lunatic on the other end. Each boasts incredible footage of its respective locales. With its shots of Hell's Kitchen, where Bree lives, *Klute* could almost be a city-symphony; abounding not only with littoral landscapes but also the flora of the Monterey Peninsula, *Play Misty for Me* doubles as a nature documentary. (Eastwood was so devoted to Carmel that he would serve as mayor of the town from 1986 to 1988.) One other link, which I didn't notice until revisiting Eastwood's movie last week: Walter and Mills both sport shag haircuts, variants of the coiffure indelibly associated with Fonda during the early '70s.

In *Klute*, Bree works through her irreconcilable feelings—about sex work, about her acting aspirations, about her affection for the PI—in her analyst's office. Bree, an imperfect but enduring emblem of women's liberation—played by the most left-leaning, politically outspoken star of the time—is quite literally rescued by a man. The traditional roles of savior and saved obtain, as they do in *Play Misty for Me*; Dave must protect Tobie, in addition to himself, from Evelyn. But the image of

Dave as macho defender—or of Eastwood as a paragon of masculinity—isn't so clear-cut. Twice the actor is filmed in various states of undress, once without a shirt, another time in nothing but white briefs. His body is sexualized, fetishized, subject to a lubricious scrutiny usually reserved for actresses.

Here I should note that in addition to the fascinating, generative paradoxes found within *Play Misty for Me*, the film also stirs up my own roiling incongruities. A staunch lesbian supremacist, I find Eastwood's duende undeniable. My deep indifference to heterosexuality vanishes during an alfresco love scene between Dave and Tobie, scored to Roberta Flack's empyreal rendition of "The First Time Ever I Saw Your Face," which plays in its entirety.

But now I must admit to other conflicting, overwhelming feelings, prompted by writing this piece. My initial viewing of *Play Misty for Me*, almost three years ago to the day, took place at Manhattan's Metrograph theater, where the film was projected on 35mm and where I sat surrounded by at least 50 other people. The film has remained so alive in my mind largely owing to the conditions in which I first saw it. While rewatching it, at my dining room table as an audience of one, I couldn't stop thinking about those strangers I'd convened with on Ludlow Street on that April day of 2017. I hope they're all okay. I hope you are, too.

—*4Columns*, April 17, 2020

Room at the Top

(Jack Clayton, 1959)

One of the bleakest movies I know, Jack Clayton's *Room at the Top* also ranks among the sultriest: a wildfire smoldering in a desolate landscape. The film—often cited as the first in the British New Wave movement, which centered on stories about the struggles and miseries of the working class—follows the angles, acute and obtuse, of a trigon.

Joe Lampton (Laurence Harvey), a lowly civil servant newly arrived to the Northern town of Warnley from the even gloomier burg of Dufton (both places are fictional; location shots were filmed mainly in West Yorkshire), is determined to win over Susan Brown (Heather Sears), the chaste daughter of Warnley's biggest baron. But while the striver aggressively pitches woo—Joe's hounding of Susan motivated as much by ladder climbing as by genuine attraction—he begins a passionate affair, one untainted by mercenary motives of any sort, with Alice Aisgill (Simone Signoret), a Frenchwoman a decade his senior stuck in a dismal marriage to a man who takes sick pleasure in humiliating her with his own philandering. During their stolen afternoons and evenings together, Joe and Alice experience carnal and spiritual bliss—they are perhaps the only two people in Warnley relieved, however fleetingly, of the town's pervasive grimness. Of course, their ecstasy cannot last; their transporting love must be crushed by not only the might of the UK's caste system but also the garroting codes of gender roles and their attendant misogyny.

Based on a 1957 best-selling novel of the same name by John Braine, a second-tier member of the "angry young men" writers who ascended in Great Britain in the '50s, *Room at the Top* marked the feature directing debut of Clayton, who would go on to helm *The Innocents* (1961), a supple adaptation of Henry James's *The Turn of the Screw*, and a taxidermic screen-transfer of *The Great Gatsby* (1974). *Room at the Top* remains Clayton's top, largely owing to the way that the director, working with cinematographer Freddie Francis, deftly showcases the lust-drunk faces and entangled bodies of Joe and Alice. The critic Andrew Sarris once wrote that Elizabeth Taylor and Montgomery Clift, the stars of George Stevens's *A Place in the Sun* (1951), were "the most beautiful couple in the history of cinema" and that watching "those gigantic close-ups of them kissing was unnerving—sybaritic—like gorging on chocolate sundaes." To gaze at Harvey and Signoret, each possessed of an unconventional allure, in the same frame proves a much less cloying experience—more akin to slurping down oysters from a bed of rapidly melting ice than a sugar rush. (Perhaps the best food analogy for Harvey can be found in the title of a film he headlined in 1968: *A Dandy in Aspic*.)

Both Harvey and Signoret had been making movies for more than a decade by the time of *Room at the Top*'s release. But the film was a breakthrough for each. For Harvey, Joe Lampton served as the rough draft for his signature character, the nattily attired lothario. Harvey's posh executive Weston Liggett in *BUtterfield 8* (1960) and louche advertising magnate Miles Brand in *Darling* (1965) are Joe with a plummier accent and a fatter checking account. For Signoret, the movie gave the French performer her widest international audience and a Best Actress Oscar, an award rarely given to those for whom English is not their native tongue.

Harvey wasn't always a generous screen partner; Jane Fonda, who costarred with him in the lurid Big Easy melodrama *Walk on the Wild Side* (1962), said of the experience: "There are actors and actors—and then there are the Laurence Harveys. With them, it's like acting by yourself." But he and Signoret have a galvanic connection, an alternating current of tenderness, understanding, and desire. Joe likes to think of his relationship with Alice as that of "loving friends"; a similar sense of comity informs Harvey and Signoret's dynamic.

Further deepening their roles are traces of autobiography, even if proleptic. Joe's rabid desire for reinvention, his refusal to resign himself to the class he was born into—"I'm entitled to be in love with any girl," he says to all those who scoff at his pursuit of Susan—recall the vigorous efforts by which Larushka Mischa Skikne, born in Lithuania in 1928, became Laurence Harvey, the epitome of Brit suavity. Only 37 when *Room at the Top* opened, Signoret easily looks ten years older; the actress's self-possessed mien, her gloriously heavy-lidded face enhance the sense that Alice has inured herself to any hurt. In 1975 Signoret published one of the most superbly titled memoirs, *Nostalgia Isn't What It Used to Be*, a world-weary line that I could imagine Alice murmuring to Joe. Even more powerful is her retort to Joe after he erupts in a jealous rage upon learning that she once modeled nude for an artist. Castigating him for his "beastly little provincial mind," she declares, "I own my own body." But however indomitable she appears, Alice is crushed when Joe tells her he is marrying Susan; might her crumpled reaction have been mirrored by Signoret herself a year later when her beloved spouse, Yves Montand, had a very public affair with Marilyn Monroe?

"There is always something vulgar about a triangle," Elizabeth Hardwick wrote in an essay on Henrik Ibsen—a piece composed in 1971, shortly after her husband, Robert Lowell, left her for Caroline Blackwood. "The victors are degraded by slyness, corruption, and greediness; the loser by weakness and humiliation." But the victors in *Room at the Top* are indistinguishable from the losers. Joe is forced to wed Susan, who's carrying his child, by her father or face utter ruin by the tycoon; what's more, Joe must now work for the man. Walking down the aisle, Joe marches to his death; Alice, referred to by various Warnley residents as "all woman" or "an old whore," has already met her actual demise. The concluding line of Hardwick's essay is the perfect coda for this gutting movie: "In the end, nothing will turn out to have been worth the destruction of others and of oneself."

—*4Columns*, November 12, 2020

Rosebud

(Otto Preminger, 1975)

In the first half of his five-decade career, the director and producer Otto Preminger helmed several touchstones in a wide variety of genres: noir (*Laura*, 1944), the musical (*Carmen Jones*, 1954), the courtroom drama (*Anatomy of a Murder*, 1959). He launched the star trajectories of soon-to-be icons, like Jean Seberg, a native Iowan chosen by Preminger from among 18,000 aspirants for the title role in his *Saint Joan* (1957). He cast the already famous in unexpected parts, as he did with Frank Sinatra, who played a heroin addict in *The Man with the Golden Arm* (1955)—one of many projects with taboo themes that Preminger took on, helping to render the priggish Production Code obsolete.

I am drawn not to the heights of Preminger's oeuvre but to the oddities and misfires that clot his late-period output. These flops include *Bunny Lake Is Missing* (1965), a bizarre London-set mystery featuring a cast consisting of not only the blank, blandly attractive American actors Keir Dullea and Carol Lynley as orphaned siblings with a byzantine backstory but also fruity British eminences in supporting roles, such as Noël Coward as a landlord accessorized with a Chihuahua named Samantha and a vast collection of S-M accoutrements. That curiosity was followed three years later by the even more outlandish *Skidoo*, the squarest head-movie ever made, one partially inspired by Preminger's own experimentation with LSD.

But Preminger's penultimate movie, *Rosebud*, rarely revived, had long eluded my viewing; that gap is now blessedly filled, thanks to Kino Lorber's release of the film, in a brand-new 2K master, on home video. Dense with often incomprehensible plot, this international suspense epic centers on British CIA agent Larry Martin (Peter O'Toole) and his quest to rescue five young women—all from highly influential families in politics or business—who have been kidnapped from the yacht of the title by the Palestine Liberation Army.

The element that has always fascinated me about *Rosebud* is that two members of this imperiled quintet are portrayed by actresses I've loved for decades, each a titaness in her own right: Kim Cattrall, who made her screen debut in Preminger's movie and was only 17 at the time of filming (and 23 years away from being part of *Sex and the City*'s famous quartet), and Isabelle Huppert, three years older and with more credits than her costar but still shockingly baby-faced, almost impossible to imagine as the she-deity of auteurist Continental cinema that she would become. To see them together, in their only shared project to date, so early in their careers provides both the film's purest delight and its greatest frustration; there aren't enough scenes devoted to them, though Huppert's Helene, the first of the pentad to be set free, has the most screen time of the sister-hostages. (The other three are played by Brigitte Ariel, Debra Berger, and Lalla Ward.)

Yet *Rosebud* offers other thrills, too, especially for those who cherish incongruities. First among them: several members of the PLA—who gather at a safe house in Corsica, the cellar of which serves as the holding pen of the five daughters of fortune after they are abducted, black hoods over their heads, from the pleasure craft—seem to have been plucked from the discotheque or Yves Saint Laurent's atelier. Cattrall's character, Joyce, is the child of a US senator, played by John Lindsay, the mayor of New York City from 1966 through 1973, in his first—and, understandably, last—screen appearance. Similarly, *Rosebud* is the lone film script credited to Erik Lee Preminger, Otto's son, who was born in 1944 and is the product of Dad's adulterous relationship with the burlesque performer Gypsy Rose Lee; sworn to silence by the striptease artist, Otto didn't meet Erik until 1966. (Distinguished lineages also mark *Rosebud*'s source, the 1974 novel of the same name by Joan Hemingway and Paul Bonnecarrère: the former is the granddaughter of Ernest and the older sister of actresses Margaux and Mariel; the latter, a French writer and journalist who died in 1977, was the maternal grandfather of the filmmaker Mia Hansen-Løve, who directed Huppert in 2016's *Things to Come*.)

Several real-life people, events, and groups from the early '70s are invoked throughout *Rosebud*, namely the Palestinian militant organization Black September, which here supports the PLA and is led by a roly-poly megalomaniac Brit named Sloat (Richard Attenborough), who insists that he has been chosen to "eliminate Israel" and "regain Arabia." The mention of King Hussein and Lufthansa hijackings may ground the viewer in the film's convoluted geopolitics, but it's frequently impossible to tell just where, exactly, globe-trotting Larry Martin has landed. (Yet he will reliably declare, within seconds of leaving the airport, that he must get back to Paris.) And even when his coordinates are legible, his activities baffle: a detour to Hamburg, as best I could gather, is necessary to track down the anti-Semitic cartoons of an outfit called the Franco-Belgian Society for Graphic Arts, sleuthing that entails threatening to out an uncooperative photo-shop proprietress with a predilection for bedding her teen-girl employees.

However ludicrous, Preminger's movie benefits too from coincidental timing, reflecting actual, contemporaneous episodes that were themselves deranging in an already turbulent epoch. *Rosebud* went into production the same year that 19-year-old Patty Hearst, granddaughter of the outsize newspaper tycoon William Randolph Hearst, was kidnapped in her Berkeley apartment by the Symbionese Liberation Army, its acronym only one letter away from PLA. (More odd concurrences: Granddaddy Hearst is, of course, the partial inspiration for *Citizen Kane*, the film whose famous, cryptic uttered word gives Preminger's movie its name.) At one point Huppert's Helene dons a dark wig not too dissimilar from the one that Patty Hearst, under the SLA nom de guerre Tania, wears in the famous surveillance photo depicting her robbing a San Francisco bank. Cattrall's Joyce, the lone American among the five captives, may be Patty's closest analogue—but the fictional privileged daughter, blithely doing sit-ups and singing Harry Nilsson's "I Guess the Lord Must Be in New York City" to keep her body and mind fit during her Corsican imprisonment, enjoys an internment closer to Outward Bound, while the real heiress endured unimaginable trauma.

During *Rosebud*'s making, Cattrall and Huppert suffered the abuses of a genuine terrorist: Preminger himself, an on-set tyrant who proudly boasted, "I don't get ulcers, I cause them." On a 2014 episode of the *Talkhouse* podcast, they recount the director's volcanic temper. The unpleasant experience forged a friendship between the two young actresses, who remain close to this day. Unlike Patty Hearst, they did not fall victim to Stockholm syndrome—never bonding with Preminger, their captor, but only with each other.

—*4Columns*, March 26, 2021

Saturday Night Fever

(John Badham, 1977)

Disco isn't dead and never has been—not even the mass psychosis evinced during the grotesque spectacle known as "Disco Demolition Night," held in Chicago's Comiskey Park in the summer of 1979, could snuff the music out. (Or, put less charitably: DISCO DIDN'T DIE. HOUSE MURDERED IT, per a T-shirt worn by a celebrant at a dance party deep in Prospect Park that I stumbled across a decade ago.) But one of its totems now officially enters middle age: John Badham's *Saturday Night Fever*, first released 40 years ago, returns to theaters nationwide on May 10 with an updated sound mix and four minutes added to the original 118. With this revival comes the opportunity to consider anew—or to choose or switch sides in—a partisan battle that's been fought since December 1977, the month *Saturday Night Fever* premiered: Did this resolutely straight, white movie about a musical idiom and subculture that was predominantly gay and Black betray and banalize disco or democratize it?

By the time *Saturday Night Fever* began filming in mid-March 1977, disco had been ascendant for at least three years; some of its early top-ten singles include the instrumental "Love's Theme" by Barry White and the Love Unlimited Orchestra, from 1973, and Gloria Gaynor's Jackson 5 cover "Never Can Say Goodbye," from '74. *Saturday Night Fever*'s producer, Robert Stigwood, the Australian-born music grandee who had been crucial to bringing the rock operas *Jesus Christ Superstar* and *Tommy* to the screen in 1973 and 1975, was eager to make a disco movie. In Nik Cohn's "Tribal Rites of the New Saturday Night," the cover story for the June 7, 1976, issue of *New York* magazine, the mogul had found a promising source text: "I see a $100 million movie here," Stigwood said. (The film would gross almost two and a half times that.) Cohn's article, a chronicle (largely fabricated, as the journalist admitted years later) of 2001 Odyssey, a real-life Bay Ridge disco, was reworked by screenwriter Norman Wexler, whose earlier credits included scripting two other New York stories, 1970's *Joe* and *Serpico*, from '73. *Saturday Night Fever* was to be the first star vehicle for the actor Stigwood had recently signed a three-film deal with: John Travolta, eager to expand beyond the confinements of Vinnie Barbarino, the dim Italian stallion he played on *Welcome Back, Kotter*, the Bensonhurst high school sitcom that had made him an object of pinup lust.

As Tony Manero, the peacocking 19-year-old prince of Bay Ridge in *Saturday Night Fever*, Travolta remains one of the most intriguingly irreconcilable icons of the '70s. His intro, no matter how many times you may have seen the film, still thrills: below the elevated tracks where a B train is roaring past, Tony struts down the street while on a midday work errand, the rumble of the subway adding to the percussion of "Stayin' Alive"—one of six songs on the *SNF* soundtrack by the Bee Gees, the falsetto-favoring trio (signed to Stigwood's RSO Records) that had made the move to disco in '75 with "Jive Talkin'."

During Tony's sidewalk swagger, he wolfishly ogles two women, just one instance of the backward behavior he and his sexist, racist, and homophobic buddies regularly exhibit. Their entire lives are limited to deepest southwest Kings County, miles and light-years away from Manhattan, which looms, in the very first shot of *SNF*, like the Emerald City across the

East River. A chasm also gapes, as disco scholars like Tim Lawrence have pointed out, between the 2001 Odyssey, where Tony rules the dance floor among the uniformly heterosexual and predominantly Italian American habitués, and the more intimate Manhattan discotheques where an almost exclusively gay clientele gathered—nightspots such as the Loft, Flamingo, and the Tenth Floor, clubs that boasted varying levels of racial diversity.

In a 2011 essay, "Disco and the Queering of the Dance Floor," Lawrence censures *SNF* for "enact[ing] the reappropriation of the dance floor by straight male culture inasmuch as it became a space for straight men to display their prowess and hunt for a partner of the opposite sex." As the 2001 Odyssey patrons clear the light-pulsating floor so Tony can swivel and thrust while the Bee Gees shriek "You Should Be Dancing," his spectacular solo gyrating—choreographed, as all of Travolta's numbers were, by Lester Wilson, a gay African American—epitomizes what Lawrence detests.

Tony's solitary hustling and grapevining contrasts wildly with the ecstatic "oneness" promised by disco, as throngs of gay guys yield to the rhythm en masse, a scenario unforgettably described in Andrew Holleran's 1978 novel of homo nightlife, *Dancer from the Dance*. He writes of his revelers, "Now of all the bonds between homosexual friends, none was greater than that between friends who danced together. The friend you danced with, when you had no lover, was the most important person in your life."

Also insupportable for Lawrence is *SNF*'s Bee Gees–heavy soundtrack, "which threatened to leave viewers with the impression that disco amounted to a new incarnation of shrill white pop." But some first-responder disco devotees, notably the longtime *Village Voice* writer and editor Vince Aletti, loved the sound of the Gibb brothers. "Their phrasing is tight, each word clipped, precise, compressed into a brittle squeal, often underlined by twitching guitar and pumping percussion but offset by strings hung like a silken curtain in the background," Aletti wrote in the February 13, 1978, issue of the *Voice*, near the beginning of the *SNF* soundtrack's 24-week reign as the number one album in the country.

Among latter-day appreciations of *SNF*, Alice Echols, author of *Hot Stuff: Disco and the Remaking of American Culture* (2010), makes a solid case for saluting, rather than reviling, the film, arguing, contrary to Lawrence, that it tries "to expand, not constrict, the parameters of masculinity." Echols scrutinizes the homoerotic voltage of the scenes in which Tony, *a casa* Manero, is filmed in nothing but tight black briefs. In the first of these, the camera slowly, adoringly pans up Tony's near-naked body as he lies prone in bed. *SNF*'s director wanted the segment to go even further, but Travolta said no, sort of. "As a movie star, he turned down Badham's request to get out of bed with no pants on," Frank Rose wrote in his waggish profile of the actor, "Travolta Puts Out," which ran in the *Voice* dated December 19, 1977. The idol "did offer a compromise, however: he would sit up in bed in his black bikini briefs and, you know, 'adjust himself.'" Four decades later, the time is right for *this* image of Travolta to replace that white-suited, finger-pointing, grim-looking dance-floor martinet.

—*Village Voice*, May 9, 2017

Smithereens

(Susan Seidelman, 1982)

"See what's there and make a film about what's there, rather than trying to re-create a script that calls for specific locations. Go out and see what's available," Susan Seidelman told *American Cinematographer* in 1983, a year after her first feature, *Smithereens*, premiered at Cannes (the first American independent film ever to play in competition at the festival). Set primarily in the East Village, *Smithereens*, like many of the micro-budgeted New York–based movies from that fertile decade—Jim Jarmusch's *Permanent Vacation* (1980), Lizzie Borden's *Born in Flames* (1983), and Spike Lee's *She's Gotta Have It* (1986), among scores of others—is made especially vivid by its specific sense of place and time.

Seidelman's imperative chimes with an observation once made by Jacques Rivette: "Every film is a documentary of its own making." Though a work of fiction, *Smithereens* is also a detail-rich chronicle of one iteration of the city: the mid–Koch era, before the gentrification of large swaths of downtown, on the cusp of the AIDS pandemic (the disease that would claim underground multihyphenate Cookie Mueller, who has a small part in Seidelman's film). Some of the storied spots Seidelman captured still exist, like the Orpheum Theatre on Second Avenue and Cafe Orlin on St. Marks Place. Others, such as the Peppermint Lounge, were shuttered decades ago. Thanks to the luster of the brand-new 35mm print of *Smithereens* screening at Metrograph for a weeklong run, these landmarks take on an even more romantic glory. Yet while *Smithereens* fascinates in part as a document of our metropolis's recent past, the story it tells—which Seidelman developed with coscreenwriter Ron Nyswaner (who would later script the 1993 gay weepie *Philadelphia*)—reflects a perennial New York narrative: an adrift young person feels entitled to fame even though her only apparent talent is for aggressive self-promotion.

That russet-haired hustler, Wren, is played by Susan Berman, one of several in the cast making her screen debut. As her name suggests, she is constantly in flight. *Smithereens*' fantastic opening scene establishes the tempo of her stop-start rhythm: in slo-mo, a woman with mirrored sunglasses with checkerboard frames dangling from her right hand is approached from behind on a subway platform by Wren, adorned in fishnet stockings and a vinyl shepherd's-check miniskirt. After she snatches the eyewear, the action assumes normal speed, as the camera tracks the string-bean antiheroine tearing down the station steps and leaping into a train that has just pulled in. Wren flirts with the guy sitting across from her, though she's most besotted with herself, getting up to wheat-paste Xeroxes of her face throughout the subway car.

Her brash confidence proves irresistible to that fellow commuter, Paul (Brad Rijn), a recent penniless arrival from Montana whose sweet face and strapping build instantly signal guilelessness. Paul's paint-flecked white tees and the floridly decorated exterior of his van (designs courtesy of graffiti godhead Lee Quiñones), which doubles as his home, suggest artistic aspirations, but they are never articulated. Most of his energy is devoted to Wren, who returns the Big Sky Country hunk's affections only when it's to her advantage—after being evicted from her apartment, say, or after being spurned by rocker Eric (the rakishly handsome punk frontman Richard Hell), a go-getter even more unscrupulous and self-serving than she is.

The interior decoration of Eric's crash pad typifies *Smithereens*' agile, askew humor: among the enormous posters featuring his lithe, contorted body and his band's name, which gives Seidelman's film its title, is one of George Benson, then at the apex of his easy-listening R&B fame. One of the sex workers who visits Paul in his vehicle, which is usually parked along the West Side Highway, splits her brown-bag lunch with him—"It's chicken salad with mayonnaise. My mother made it"—before offering to let him see her scar for $5. This inveterate scene-stealer is played by Katherine Riley, a performer unknown to me, who died the same year *Smithereens* was released. Glimpsed later in the film, one of her flesh-peddling colleagues is portrayed by Chris Noth, who'd reteam with Seidelman in 1998 when she directed the pilot and two other episodes of *Sex and the City*. The quartet of aspirational women of that HBO touchstone, along with Noth's Mr. Big, exist in a Manhattan that Wren and her circle would have found unrecognizable and despicable.

But Seidelman's movie is canny enough to forestall facile nostalgia for those pre-Giuliani years, no matter how much we, 30-some years on, may pine for (or fetishize) the chain-store-free city blocks Wren trudges, the rubble she navigates. For all the film's wit and verve, the latter quality manifest in the variety of musical idioms heard (reggae, new wave, postpunk), *Smithereens* has an inescapable dolorousness. "You know, Paul, I'm really rotten. I'm disgusting," Wren, in a rare moment of self-reckoning, tells her friend, who tries to coax her into traveling to New Hampshire with him. Delusional with ambition—and determined never to return to her birth state of New Jersey, where her older sister spends her days eating Beefaroni with her miserable family—Wren might be thought of as a descendant of an Edith Wharton protagonist, an Undine Spragg of Alphabet City who ends up with nowhere to go. But she is also a predecessor of another flamboyantly styled vagabond circulating below 14th Street: Madonna in *Desperately Seeking Susan* (1985), Seidelman's follow-up film, one of the most buoyant ever made in—and about—the city.

—*Village Voice*, July 26, 2016

The Group

(Sidney Lumet, 1966)

The prose of Mary McCarthy, whether fiction, essays, or criticism, dazzles with pinpoint satire and piety-puncturing. The title of one of her early novels, *Cast a Cold Eye* (1950), easily doubles as her lifelong mandate. The introduction to *Sights and Spectacles, 1937–1956*, a collection of McCarthy's theater reviews, most of which first appeared in *Partisan Review*, includes this fabulously venomous assessment: "People who go to the theatre today are divided into two classes—those who know how bad it is and those who have no inkling."

She spared no one from her mordant scrutiny, least of all herself and her circle. By far her most successful book, *The Group* (1963) epitomizes McCarthy's talents for mining—better yet, fracking—her autobiography to create a pungent, precisely detailed portrait of her milieu. Tracing the postgraduate lives of eight women from the Vassar class of 1933—the same year McCarthy received her BA from that Seven Sisters institution—the book functions as both a lampoon and a novel of ideas. *The Group* recounts upper-middle-class folly; political divisions among the left; and the binds and blind spots of McCarthy's Greatest Generation heroines, doomed to repeat their parents' patterns, no matter how much they abjure them: "The worst fate, they utterly agreed, would be to become like Mother and Dad, stuffy and frightened. Not one of them, if she could help it, was going to marry a broker or a banker or a coldfish corporation lawyer. ... They would rather be wildly poor and live on salmon wiggle than be forced to marry one of those dull purplish young men of their own set." Densely plotted and populated, the book never falters in tone or temperature. Served from a constant low simmer, McCarthy's witty, caustic observations still singe.

But in Sidney Lumet's 1966 adaptation of *The Group*, the heat—and the volume—is turned way up. Several members of the central octet deliver their lines as if in the throes of delirium. The clamor repels and fascinates me equally. Lumet's febrile movie, which was scripted by Sidney Buchman, has barely been in rotation on the repertory-cinema circuit; in New York, I can recall only one screening from the past decade, when Hilton Als presented *The Group* in 2009 as part of the ongoing "Queer | Art | Film" series. The near absence has surprised me. *The Group*, Lumet's tenth feature, may seem a curio even in the long, wide-ranging career of the director, who died in 2011 and is usually remembered for his work with a florid Al Pacino in the Fun City diptych *Serpico* (1973) and *Dog Day Afternoon* (1975). But Lumet's overwrought Vassar alumnae seem to anticipate his most outsize and best-known female protagonist: Faye Dunaway's frenzied, calculating Diana Christensen in *Network* (1976).

Adding to the allure of this strange artifact, now available on Blu-ray, is the cast. *The Group* marked the screen debut of Candice Bergen, playing the sapphic, Europhilic beauty Lakey (more on her later). It was the second film of Jessica Walter, here as Libby, a catty, nattering publishing-house aspirant, who shares some of the same malice and self-regard exhibited by Lucille Bluth, the dipso, manipulative matriarch the actress portrays on *Arrested Development*.

Other performers, far more obscure (and/or long since retired or dead), intrigue, if only to ultimately exhaust, with their maximalist, unmodulated acting, particularly Joanna

Pettet. She plays Kay, the character who seems to have the most overlap with McCarthy's own history. Kay, like her creator, was wed a week after college graduation to an actor and would-be playwright, called Harald in both the book and the film (he's played by Larry Hagman)—and Harold in real life. And, in an episode likely sourced from McCarthy's second, fractious marriage, to the prodigious writer and critic Edmund Wilson, Kay is committed to a psych ward by the boozing, philandering, failing Harald. In McCarthy's book, that scene is chilling but rendered dispassionately; in Lumet's film, Pettet wildly palpates the walls of the hospital room, as if trapped in a Tennessee Williams tryout. (Considering how much McCarthy hated Williams's work—*Sights and Spectacles* contains her eminent evisceration of *A Streetcar Named Desire*—the histrionic segment registers all the more jarringly.)

During these discordant moments—which also include the high-pitched giggle Walter appends to nearly every one of Libby's pronouncements and the distracting, orotund elocution of Joan Hackett as Dottie, tragically in love with the debauchee who has deflowered and forgotten her—I recall, and agree with, the appraisal of Elizabeth Bishop, McCarthy's friend since their Vassar days (the poet was class of '34). In a 1967 letter from Rio de Janeiro to Robert Lowell, Bishop writes: "A rainy Saturday afternoon with nothing to do we went to the local cinema to see O GRUPO—my it is dreadful; one of the worst films I've ever seen. Surely Mary had nothing at all to do with it." (Mary didn't.)

And yet much of the din in the movie, which runs just over two and a half hours, results from an admirable, maybe foolish, act of fealty: to replicate most of the novel's abundant storylines. Nearly every incident, whether major (save for a detailed sex scene early in the novel, coyly handled in the film by a cut to the morning after) or minor, is recapitulated. Some even take place in the actual New York locations where they occur in the book, such as Dottie's pivotal wait, for a suitor who never shows, on a Washington Square Park bench. While the movie couldn't hope to reproduce McCarthy's disquisitions on epoch-defining events, *The Group* is likely the only film of 1966 to feature characters uttering "Loyalist Spain," "Moscow Trials," and "Trotsky."

There's something else in Lumet's movie that's found in few others from that year, that decade, the past half century: a glamorous, unrepentant lesbian supremacist. As with the novel, Lakey, who departs for the Continent shortly after graduation and returns to New York after the outbreak of World War II, is absent for most of the film. To the shock of her schoolmates, who are meeting Lakey's boat, she comes back not just with steamer trunks but with a lover: an older, tweedy-butch baroness. "It occurred to them all that Lakey, who had always been frightening and superior, would now look down on them for not being Lesbians," McCarthy writes. But Lakey's most reproachful glare is reserved for—and demolishes—Harald, *The Group*'s most villainous man. Bergen is unsteady in the part, but she excels in carrying out her character's most crucial action: casting a cold eye.

—*4Columns*, February 8, 2019

To Sleep with Anger

(Charles Burnett, 1990)

Whether by design or pure serendipity, 2016 has turned out to be a celebratory year for three of the most distinguished alums of the LA Rebellion movement, a constellation of Black auteurs who studied at UCLA film school between the late 1960s and the late '80s. In February, *And When I Die, I Won't Stay Dead*—the first completed work by Billy Woodberry since his gutting debut, *Bless Their Little Hearts* (1983)—opened MoMA's "Documentary Fortnight" showcase. Now a quarter-century old, Julie Dash's oneiric *Daughters of the Dust*, a key influence on many of the set pieces in Beyoncé's *Lemonade*, will be rereleased, in a 2K restoration, in theaters in November. And for a week beginning this Friday, the Film Society at Lincoln Center hosts a revival run of Charles Burnett's digitally restored third feature, *To Sleep with Anger*, one of the finest films to explore city versus country, old ways versus new, kin versus kin.

Born in Vicksburg, Mississippi, in 1944 and a resident of South Central Los Angeles (where many of his films take place) for most of his life, Burnett, in his first three films especially, is ever astute about the complexity of families, highlighting the strain of obligations to blood ties. His UCLA thesis film, *Killer of Sheep* (1977), a remarkable evocation of daily hardship and joy, revolves around an abattoir worker whose family is just barely eking out a marginally comfortable existence in Watts. The droller *My Brother's Wedding* (1983) tracks a 30-year-old man who's still living at home with (and working for) Mom and

Dad and is consumed with disdain for his sibling's upwardly mobile fiancée. Some of these familial fissures recur in *To Sleep with Anger*, though here the ensemble is larger and the domestic drama is entwined with the supernatural.

Burnett's flawless blending of impeccably observed realism and the fantastic animates the opening scene. Gideon (Paul Butler), the stout patriarch of the central clan, sits, weary-looking and sweat-soaked, at a table, facing the audience as Sister Rosetta Tharpe's "Precious Memories" plays on the soundtrack. Nearly motionless save for the twiddling of his thumbs, he becomes part of a bizarre still life: a bowl of fruit by his elbow soon sprouts flames, the mini-conflagration later dancing on the tops of Gideon's white loafers.

No explanation is given for these micro-infernos, and none is needed. They presage the appearance of Harry (Danny Glover, in his best performance), a charismatic—and malevolent—bumpkin from "down home" whose arrival at Gideon's solidly middle-class, two-story South Central residence upends the lives of his family and friends. Angelenos for three decades, Gideon and his spouse, Suzie (Mary Alice), a midwife who teaches Lamaze classes to Black and white couples in their living room, haven't entirely shed their Southern, "country" customs—an attachment that their houseguest will insidiously exploit to his advantage.

"I always make me a pallet on the floor," Harry tells Suzie on his first night in her home, insisting he doesn't want to be any trouble. Soon, though, he's commanding Gideon and Suzie's younger son—a grown man, with his own family, burdened with the infantilizing nickname Babe Brother (Richard Brooks)—to turn off the tap for him and clean the tub. The younger man doesn't balk at the orderts; Babe Brother has become entranced by Harry and starts to emulate the old head's masculinist prerogative, which puts further strain on his relationship with his parents, wife (Sheryl Lee Ralph), and older sibling (Carl Lumbly). The down-home drifter's arrival also puts a strain on Gideon's heart: he suffers mysterious strokelike symptoms and is bedridden for three weeks.

As Harry begins to overstay his welcome, one former Southerner, Hattie (Ethel Ayler)—superbly drawn, like all of the film's primary and secondary characters—perfectly articulates his dual nature: "Back home, Harry always did try to act like the colored gentleman. But he's evil." He is, but Burnett has sympathy for this devil, a trickster who creates chaos that forces those in its wake to confront long-simmering resentments and still-raw wounds.

Dusted with paranormal activity, *To Sleep with Anger* is foremost a film dedicated to capturing the nuances of real-world intimacy. "Why don't you shut the door and come on over here?" Gideon, smiling wide and patting the bed, says to Suzie. She stares at him silently and exits the room to tend to their grandson—but softens her rebuff with a knowing wink. This brief scene communicates, better than many films devoted solely to the subject, the delights and disappointments of enduring unions, dyads that require the constant balance of desires and duties.

The film is also, of course, a reflection on reconciling the past—specifically, the Second Great Migration, in which millions of African Americans from the South, from roughly World War II through 1970, relocated to, among other areas, large cities in the West—with the present. It's difficult to watch *To Sleep with Anger* without thinking about its maker's own past, and his future. Burnett followed up this movie with *The Glass Shield* (1994), a scorching, intricate look at racism and police corruption, which will screen at the Walter Reade on

35mm on September 10. This singular filmmaker has never stopped working, but this has been the last of his movies to date to have been picked up for theatrical distribution. When I covered MoMA's complete Burnett retrospective for this paper in 2011, I wrote that he was slated to direct a documentary on Stanley Ann Dunham, President Obama's mother. No one is better qualified to helm this project, though I'm not sure of its current status. You can ask the filmmaker himself: Burnett will be at the Film Society for the opening weekend of *To Sleep with Anger*.

—*Village Voice*, September 7, 2016

Town Bloody Hall

(Chris Hegedus and D. A. Pennebaker, 1979)

Chris Hegedus and D. A. Pennebaker's restless, captivating Direct Cinema triumph *Town Bloody Hall* is a work of oceanography, documenting one splashy moment in the cresting and crashing of American feminism's second wave. The film chronicles the "Dialogue on Women's Liberation," held on April 30, 1971, at Manhattan's Town Hall, the hallowed performance venue and meeting space for activists on West 43rd Street. The event was sponsored by the Theatre for Ideas, an organization founded in 1961 by dancer and choreographer Shirley Broughton; by 1969, *New York* magazine was hailing it as "the forum for [the city's] intellectual elite."

Occasioning the colloquy was the appearance, in the March 1971 issue of *Harper's*, of Norman Mailer's unhinged, incendiary essay "The Prisoner of Sex," his rebuttal to his drubbing by Kate Millett in her landmark feminist treatise *Sexual Politics* (1970), in which she devotes an entire chapter to analyzing the work of the novelist, whom she lambastes as "a prisoner of the virility cult." This passage from his *Harper's* piece typifies Mailer's bluster: "[Millett's] lack of fidelity to the material she read was going to be equaled only by her authority in characterizing it ... and the yaws of her distortion were nicely hidden by the smudge pots of her indignation. ... Everywhere were signs that men were guilty and women must win."

Broughton rightly thought the furor caused by the *Harper's* article would make for a high-profile event, one that—featuring

Mailer in conversation with prominent women selected for their varying positions within or toward feminism—could also serve as a fundraiser for her organization. As seen in *Town Bloody Hall*, moderating in a suit jacket and striped tie, Mailer never eases up on his pugnacity during the symposium. He alternately provokes further outrage from, flirts with, and fulminates against the panelists, who speak in alphabetical order, each allotted ten minutes at the microphone: Jacqueline Ceballos, president of the New York chapter of the National Organization for Women, which, with its emphasis on attaining equality through political and legal reform, she nervously acknowledges as the "'square' organization of women's liberation"; the more radical Germaine Greer, author of *The Female Eunuch* (1970), an international bestseller that lays out the harm done to women by the nuclear family as an institution; Jill Johnston, the gonzo dance and cultural critic for the *Village Voice* and unrepentant lesbian supremacist; and Diana Trilling, the literary-critic doyenne, who, unwilling to forge common cause with her cospeakers, seems at best skeptical of feminism itself. (Conspicuous by her absence, Millett, who turned down an invitation to appear on the panel, is mentioned throughout the evening. The same year that *Town Bloody Hall* was shot, Millett released her own documentary, *Three Lives*, a triptych of autobiographical accounts by women.)

A highly self-conscious consciousness-raising, *Town Bloody Hall* demonstrates that, for these discussants and the literati-glutted audience—several members of which have their own star turns in the documentary—the personal is not only political but also voluble. The film abounds with loamy, invigorating talk, even if on occasion an argument is hard to follow, if not outright incoherent. True to the name of the event's promoting institution, the conversation manifests both theater and ideas, with the former more in evidence, onstage and off. The dramatics start before the panelists even assemble. In the theater's lobby, as a throng of attendees—almost exclusively white, their average age between 35 and 40—pick up tickets, a bespectacled woman in a poncho mounts a protest: "Women's lib betrays the poor!" she yells, then calls out Mailer and the speakers as fellow traitors of the indigent. A nattily attired man and woman stare at her with contempt and ask, "Why?"

We never hear her answer—perhaps she didn't have one—but the exchange crisply establishes the fractiousness to follow, the verbal sparring so emblematic of an era when public intellectuals wrangling on television (as Gore Vidal and William F. Buckley Jr. had infamously done on ABC in 1968) was not an uncommon sight. The ponchoed dissenter reappears about halfway through *Town Bloody Hall*, heckling Mailer et al. from the audience before storming out. Perhaps in the lobby she encountered the Beat eminence Gregory Corso, who had likewise marched off in high dudgeon earlier, yelling, "All of humanity! Not just half of humanity!" while Ceballos was outlining NOW's agenda for the compensation of women's domestic labor and other liberal proposals.

The histrionics, the preening, the bombast, the mesmerizing stage presence: all are elements that were singularly suited to Pennebaker, who had established himself prior to *Town Bloody Hall* as one of Direct Cinema's nimblest chroniclers of performers and performance. Having captured Jane Fonda in the infancy of her career in *Jane* (1962); Bob Dylan at the peak of his superstardom in *Dont Look Back* (1967); Janis Joplin's raw, hungry cover of "Ball and Chain" and Otis Redding's third-rail electricity while singing "Shake" in *Monterey Pop* (1968); and Elaine Stritch's rage in *Original Cast Album: "Company"* (1970), Pennebaker was an excellent choice to record the peacocking and posturing—and outright lunacy—certain to take place that late-April night in '71. In fact, it was the event's most excitable participant, Mailer himself, who had suggested to Pennebaker that he film it. The two men knew each other well: Pennebaker was a cinematographer on the first three films Mailer had directed, between 1968 and 1970: *Wild 90*, *Beyond the Law*, and *Maidstone*. Mailer acts in all three; by the time of *Town Bloody Hall*, Pennebaker was an adept at spotlighting the writer's twitchy, hectoring demeanor.

But, as he explained to the *New York Times* in 2017, Pennebaker never got the official okay from the Town Hall management to film the event, a constraint that led him and his fellow camera operators (Jim Desmond and Mark Woodcock) to spend much of the night evading security, finally finding refuge onstage. Deeming the rushes unusable after an initial viewing, Pennebaker stashed away the footage. Hegedus, who was already working with Pennebaker and would begin codirecting with him in 1976, started editing the material, which she has called "incredibly rough," in the mid-'70s. An avowed feminist and an admirer of several of the symposium's participants, she adroitly condensed the rollicking three-and-a half-hour event to 85 minutes. The film premiered theatrically in 1979. (Pennebaker and Hegedus would marry in 1982 and go on to make 1993's *The War Room*, among other notable documentaries.)

The occasional shakiness of the camera aptly mirrors the frenetic energy of the evening. While Mailer's overweening outbursts—"Hey, cunty, I've been threatened all my life," he yells at one heckler; "You are all singularly without wit," he castigates the audience at large—make for dynamite footage, his perverse charisma is often eclipsed by Greer's aloof duende. Resplendent in fur stole, sleeveless maxi-dress, feminist-fist pendant, and shaggy, luxuriant brunette mane, the Australian writer—whose exasperated utterance supplies the film with its title—abounds in glam-rock allure, her poise perhaps the result of her earlier stints as an actor. (A week after the Town Hall symposium, Greer appeared on the cover of *Life*, which called her the "saucy feminist that even men like." The copy typifies the condescending language deployed by the mainstream press in its reporting on feminism at the time; in 1970, *Time* had labeled Millett, whose portrait by Alice Neel graced its cover, the "Mao Tse-tung of Women's Liberation.")

Striding to the rostrum, Greer proclaims that she is a political movement of one: "I do not represent any organization in this country," she begins. "And I daresay the most powerful representation I can make is of myself as a writer, for better or worse. I'm also a feminist. And for me the significance of this moment is that I'm having to confront one of the most powerful figures in my own imagination, the being I think most privileged in male elitist society—namely, the masculine artist, the pinnacle of the masculine elite." The film immediately cuts to Mailer; he laughs, perhaps at the dis or at something off-screen.

All on the panel—save one—seem mesmerized, if not starstruck, by Greer. Johnston sticks out her hand to clasp Greer's in sisterly solidarity as the tall antipodean author makes her way to the podium. At the very end of *Town Bloody Hall*, Ceballos—who has been quiet for most of the evening, clearly aware that she is outmatched by the brio of her fellow speakers—gushes to the author of *The Female Eunuch*, "It was worth being on this panel with you!" For all his combativeness with Greer, Mailer is clearly smitten with her. ("There was so much sexual tension going on between Norman and Germaine," Hegedus has said. "I almost edited it as a love story, in a certain way.")

Trilling, however, remains unimpressed. After delivering her own disquisition—a difficult one to parse, skipping, among a host of other points, from developmental psychologist Erik Erikson to vaginal orgasms, both topics raised by Mailer in his *Harper's* screed—the éminence grise upbraids "Miss Greer" for her purported misreading of Freud. Greer tartly halts the rebuke: "One of the characteristics of oppressed people is that they fight among themselves." The retort echoes this dire assessment from a year earlier by Ti-Grace Atkinson, a prominent radical feminist (who also declined to participate in the Town Hall debate), of the movement's internecine battles: "Sisterhood is powerful. It kills. Mostly sisters."

But between Greer's and Trilling's presentations—and before their dustup and the tumultuous queries from the audience—comes the evening's most insurrectionist speaker, and a legendary moment of sapphic sabotage. Introduced by Mailer as "that master of free-associational prose in the *Village Voice*," Johnston immediately lives up to the description. "I think Germaine was born in Australia, and I was born in England," she begins loopily, a big grin on her face. (A minute or so later, the camera makes her seeming non sequitur less disjunctive by zooming in on a Union Jack patch on her denim jacket.) Removing her aviator frames, Johnston starts her oration in earnest: "The title of this episode is 'New Approach.' All women are lesbians except those who don't know it naturally. They are but don't know it yet. I am a woman and therefore a lesbian. I am a woman who is a lesbian because I am a woman." Her sermon, Seussian and Steinian in equal measure and peppered with puns ("Some women want to have their cock and eat it too"), is frequently interrupted by delighted laughter, both the audience's and Johnston's own. Yet her plan of action for the uprising—"Until all women are lesbians, there will be no true political revolution"—wasn't in jest; two years after the Town Hall colloquium, she would publish *Lesbian Nation: The Feminist Solution*, which unequivocally endorses lesbian separatism.

And Johnston is all too willing to close the gap between theory and praxis. As her womanifesto exceeds her allotted time and Mailer demands she wrap things up, Johnston is joined onstage by two ardent female admirers; this threesome soon collapses onto the platform in a tangle of groping limbs. The guerrilla same-sex make-out session prompts Mailer's best line of the night, alluding to Town Hall's proximity to Times Square: "Hey, you know, it's great you paid 25 bucks to see three dirty overalls on the floor when you could see lots of cock and cunt for four dollars just down the street."

After this spectacular performance, Johnston and her lez conspirators simply leave the stage, and the *Voice* writer never returns. But the subject of homosexuality isn't banished; it lingers, whether overtly or covertly. Gay activist Peter Fisher asks from the audience whether the female panelists believe there's a "connection between the women's liberation movement and the gay liberation movement." Greer's response lays bare more fissures within the feminist struggle: "I always thought it was part and parcel of the same movement. I know this means some of my sisters part company with me on this issue." One of those sisters was Betty Friedan, also in attendance at Town Hall that night and seen, just a few minutes before Fisher speaks, railing at Mailer. In 1969, while president of NOW, Friedan had warned members of that group that a "lavender menace"—that is, lesbians active within the women's movement—would destroy the credibility of feminists, who, as she imagined it, could easily be dismissed as misandrists.

Another luminary in the audience, Susan Sontag, was never officially out during her lifetime, though her same-sex relationships, even in 1971, were largely an open secret. Microphone in hand, Sontag announces that she has a "very quiet question" for Mailer about his condescending use of the word *lady*. (A little while later, Cynthia Ozick poses the evening's most uproarious query: "Mr. Mailer, when you dip your balls in ink, what color ink is it?") Seated immediately to Sontag's left is the fleetingly glimpsed Adrienne Rich—who would declare her lesbianism five years later in a collection of poems, and would go on to write some of lesbian feminism's most foundational essays. Perhaps unsurprisingly, Sontag and Rich would engage in their own intramural skirmish about feminism in an exchange published in the *New York Review of Books* in 1975.

The verbal combat highlighted in *Town Bloody Hall* was just one episode in an ongoing argument, an ever-changing movement. The symposium's illustrious participants themselves continued to develop their stances on feminism over the decades, sometimes ignominiously. At 81, Greer, the film's swashbuckling shero, for instance, is now notorious for her transphobic positions.

But nearly 50 years after the event it documents, *Town Bloody Hall* has lost none of its power to entrance—and enrage—with its manic, stimulating, polyvocal energy. Starting in the mid-2010s, the documentary became popular on the repertory circuit; those who had grown weary of a feminism articulated via hashtag or hot take surely found *Town Bloody Hall*'s bracing IRL discourse a tonic. The documentary itself was "remade," in a way, courtesy of the Wooster Group, whose wan stage production *The Town Hall Affair* diluted the dynamism of the debate into austere slapstick. The play opened in New York just two weeks after the Women's March of January 2017—an enormous, wildly imperfect, yet ultimately revitalizing gathering that may be the worthiest sequel to that unforgettable night in April 1971.

—Criterion Collection Blu-ray/DVD liner notes,
August 2020

Madonna: Truth or Dare

(Alek Keshishian, 1991)

Outliving Michael Jackson and Prince, Madonna is the sole survivor of the holy triad of pop superstars born in 1958. She turned 58 last week; also celebrating a (milestone) birthday is Alek Keshishian's immensely pleasurable vérité backstager/concert doc *Madonna: Truth or Dare,* now 25 years old. Reviewing the film in the May 14, 1991, issue of the *Voice,* J. Hoberman praised *Truth or Dare* as "a remarkable portrait of a sacred monster in her prime." The description remains unassailable—and is now all the more poignant, considering Madonna's diminished stature today. Though she is still active in a variety of fields and endures as one of the most famous people on the planet, she has, of course, been eclipsed by others in the past quarter century; Queen Bey has for several years worn the crown that once sat atop the head of Her Madgeness. Nor has Madonna, an artist in the decadent phase of her career, been immune to the ignominious imperatives of portfolio-diversifying: she repurposed the name of Keshishian's documentary for a "lifestyle brand" that she launched in 2011 specializing in handbags, footwear, and fragrance.

And yet for this Gen X critic, the experience of revisiting *Truth or Dare*—which I returned to repeatedly in theaters during the spring and summer of 1991—for the first time since its initial release prompted a flood of memories about

Madonna's enormous influence on American culture, and, by extension, on my life: nearly every conversation (public or private), academic essay, and broadsheet op-ed about race, gender, and/or sexuality from roughly the mid-'80s through the mid-'90s inevitably involved the Material Girl. During these peak years of postmodernism, Madonna, unparalleled provocatrice and recycler of high and low iconography, operated, per Hoberman, "as a sign system" unto herself. She was excoriated in bell hooks's 1992 essay collection *Black Looks: Race and Representation* for her cannibalizing of African American culture and lauded in 1990 by Camille Paglia in the *New York Times* as "the future of feminism."

At the D.C. law firm where I had a miserable entry-level job, Madonna's '92 coffee-table book *Sex* was passed around like smutty samizdat among the senior partners, paralegals, and support staff; among my coworkers, she was either dismissed by the uptight and obtuse as narcissistic or looked to, primarily by secretaries living in the suburbs, as a model of aspirational bedroom practices. For a not-quite-out teen and young adult, as I was then, Madonna's role as sapphic signifier—whether covert (as the object of Rosanna Arquette's fascination in Susan Seidelman's *Desperately Seeking Susan* from 1985; whatever she was up to with Sandra Bernhard on David Letterman's show in 1988) or overt (evidenced in the infamous Steven Meisel photos that ran in *Rolling Stone* shortly after *Truth or Dare*'s release; several tableaux in *Sex*)—functioned as both lure and repellent.

The Madonna captured in *Truth or Dare* is all and none of these things, a tiny, hard body bearing the weight of the symbols and symbolism ascribed to her (by herself, by others, by me), personae that she shrewdly dons or sheds at will. Keshishian's documentary tracks Madonna in several different cities around the globe during her 1990 "Blond Ambition" tour, her third, mounted in support of her albums *Like a Prayer* and *I'm Breathless*, the soundtrack to *Dick Tracy*. (The 1990 Warren Beatty–directed project is one of seven titles showcasing the singer's thespian skills—and limitations—that will screen in "Body of Work: A Madonna Retrospective," which runs concurrently with Metrograph's revival of *Truth or Dare*. Beatty, Madonna's romantic partner during the "Blond Ambition" tour, smugly skulks in the background in Keshishian's film, the old guy getting his comeuppance when his girlfriend demands, "Get over here, you pussy.")

In dressing rooms, hotel suites, and ladies' lavatories, among other intimate locations, Madonna and her crew are filmed in black-and-white 16mm; onstage, their pulse-quickening numbers ("Express Yourself," "Like a Virgin," "Holiday," and others) are rendered in effulgent, almost garish, color. Madonna is a machine; an ever-yammering, saucy mouth; and, most queasily, a "mother," a self-designated role she remarks on several times in voice-over (and for which she was especially rebuked in hooks's book). "I think I've chosen people who are emotionally crippled or need mothering in some way," says the superstar, who lost her own mom at age five—and whose *Truth or Dare* visit to Ma's gravesite, scored to "Promise to Try," reveals the singer's talent for the unbearably maudlin.

Among those "crippled" people are her seven backup dancers, mostly gay Black and Latino men, all of whom, along with supporting singers Niki Haris and Donna De Lory, first reached wide visibility in Madonna's "Vogue" video from 1990. (That septet is the focus of *Strike a Pose*, a doc that screened at the Tribeca Film Festival in April and that will open in theaters early next year.) Auditioning for the singer at a nightclub to land the "Blond Ambition" gig, two of the dancers, Luis Camacho and Jose Gutierez, were members of the House of Xtravaganza, one of the ballroom clans immortalized in Jennie Livingston's documentary *Paris Is Burning*, released the same year as *Truth or Dare*, with which it forms a crucial diptych. Livingston's film, like Keshishian's, is an essential investigation of queerness, race, and stardom—as lived by those whom Madonna flagrantly cribbed from and who, in turn, have achieved a kind of immortality that may forever elude her.

—*Village Voice*, August 23, 2016

Women in Love

(Ken Russell, 1969)

I always think I've misremembered the title, or that the name itself is a red herring: Why is it *Women in Love* when the most infamous scene from Ken Russell's 1969 film—an adaptation of D. H. Lawrence's 1920 novel—features Alan Bates and Oliver Reed, both nude and sweat-slicked, their dongs jouncing, wrestling in front of a roaring fire? The lusty grapple lasts three minutes and feels like 30. "Was it ... too much for you?" one man asks the other, panting.

The query could apply to nearly any segment of Russell's third movie, his breakthrough. (Within the next ten years, the English director would advance his immoderate style with a film about witchcraft, several florid biopics of artist-geniuses, and, most ostentatious of all, a screen version of the Who's rock opera *Tommy*.) The film *is* too much. But is it—was it—enough?

Yes, there are women in *Women in Love*, set in the Midlands in the years immediately after World War I: the Brangwen sisters, Ursula (Jennie Linden), a teacher, and Gudrun (Glenda Jackson), a "sculptress." And they may be in love—Ursula with Rupert Birkin (Bates), a school inspector and wearisome intellectual, and Gudrun with Gerald Crich (Reed), the sulky scion of a benevolent coal-mining magnate. Bearded like Lawrence, Rupert is the author's surrogate. He gives voice to and enacts the writer's incoherent libidinal doctrines, which include a proto-poly platform, some version of dendrophilia, and what Susan Sontag once disdainfully called, in a 1961 essay, Lawrence's "mystique of male separateness." In that same piece,

Sontag also decried the British novelist's "puritanical insistence on genital sexuality." Yet it is to the film's great credit that, in its depiction of that "puritanical insistence," heterosexuality is revealed to be the most unnatural form of coupling—never more so than during a scene of frenzied rutting between Gudrun and Gerald in an alpine chalet, the camera wildly zooming in and out as the grimacing industrialist pounds away.

Some of this straight-bashing was likely unintentional, simply an expression of the hysteria common to Lawrence adaptations of the era (cf. Mark Rydell's *The Fox,* from 1967)—or, more accurately, an amplification of the lunacy found in the originals. But it might also have resulted from a generative tension felt by at least one member of the principal cast. In a 1976 TV interview with Glenda Jackson included in the Criterion Collection's new home-video release of *Women in Love,* the actress recounts her extreme reliance on the source text, no matter how much she repudiated it: "I never had that book out of my hand on one day that we were shooting. I found it quite difficult because I tend to discount—well, I *do* discount—most of Lawrence's philosophy and certainly his view of the male-female battle." Jackson, here in the first of five films she would make with Russell, evinces slinky hints of misandry in an early scene, as her character explains the etymology of her given name to Gerald: "In a Norse myth, Gudrun was a sinner who murdered her husband." (Jackson won an Oscar for her performance.)

However foolish it may be to assign talismanic significance to the date that *Women in Love* premiered, 1969 was, of course, year zero of the LGBTQ intifada. Can we call the man who wrote the script (and also served as producer) an insurrectionist? Seeing Larry Kramer in 1968, during a brief on-location interview featured in another of the disc's extras, proves supremely (but not unpleasantly) disorienting: How is it possible that the galvanic éminence grise of gay activism was ever this young or mild-mannered? Standing on a sloped patch of grass in Derby, Kramer, who is preppily dressed and sports a thick mane of side-parted dark hair, nervously smiles and rarely looks his interlocutor in the eye as he explains why he thinks "Lawrence would be proud" of his page-to-screen transfer.

Ultimately, *Women in Love*'s greatest claim to sexual sedition stems from what its success made possible almost a decade later. Kramer, as detailed in a *New Yorker* profile in 2002, was next asked to write the script for a project that bombed (a musical version of *Lost Horizon*) but for which he was paid the then-exorbitant sum of nearly $300,000—money that, owing to his brother's wise investing, guaranteed his financial independence. He could write what he wanted. In 1978, he published a book that inspired another kind of uprising and that will likely never be made into a movie: *Faggots*.

—*Artforum*, March 2018

II.

The Homosexual Agenda and Trans Missions

The Royal Road

(Jenni Olson, 2015)

Suffused with melancholy, longing, and chagrin, Jenni Olson's supple cine-essay *The Royal Road* is, above all, a film against forgetting. In its densely packed but fleet 64 minutes, this discursive documentary considers topics as disparate as the Spanish colonization of California, the Mexican-American War, *Vertigo* (and other celluloid touchstones), and the director's own "lifelong pursuit of women." As personal as it is political, Olson's meditative project offers a profound lesson on intimacy and history—and the ways in which both are distorted and remade by memory.

The documentary's title is the English translation of "El Camino Real," the name of the 600-mile path, running from Sonoma in the north to San Diego in the south, that connects California's 21 Spanish missions. Olson focuses on the stretch between San Francisco, where she has lived since 1992 and where her earlier nimble essay film *The Joy of Life* (2005) takes place, and Los Angeles, home of "Juliet," one of her unconsummated crushes. The complex adoration the movie-besotted filmmaker feels for this inamorata extends to her place of dwelling; Juliet's Spanish Colonial Revival lodging is compared with the one that shelters Barbara Stanwyck in *Double Indemnity* (1944), one of several titles from Hollywood's golden age that Olson discusses eloquently.

The Royal Road opens, in fact, with Olson citing another Billy Wilder classic, *Sunset Boulevard* (1950), a film that famously begins with the posthumous voice-over of its protagonist, first seen floating face-down in a pool. Though of course very much alive, Olson, a bodiless presence, hovers like a specter throughout the film, her fluid narration—delivered in a voice that is steady, low, impassive, and still somehow impassioned—evoking all kinds of ghosts. The images are beautiful yet haunting: simple, static urban-landscape compositions—showcasing San Francisco's Drydock, or the Church of the Good Shepherd in Beverly Hills, or, more often, mundane buildings and homes—that are entirely devoid of people.

That these city tableaux were shot, by Olson's cinematographer Sophie Constantinou, on 16mm Kodak film underscores the director's affection for the physical, the analog, the old and perhaps soon-to-be-obsolete. "To this day, I suffer from a compulsion to defend my overly intense attachment to the past," Olson, born in 1962, confesses. "The past" here can refer to still contentious events from hundreds of years ago, as in the filmmaker's elucidation of the uglier side of the legacy of Father Junípero Serra (canonized by Pope Francis last month), who forced the conversion (and worse) of California's Native population in the 18th century. Or it can imply interactions between two people that transpired just a day or hours before: "I cherish these aftermaths, these reminiscences," the director says of her fondness for replaying in her mind the minutiae of every moment spent with a woman she's been trying to woo.

In segueing so seamlessly from broad overviews of American history—at one point an animated map is deployed to illustrate the territory Mexico had to cede after its defeat by the US in 1847, in our nation's largely forgotten "first foreign war"—to candid first-person disclosures, Olson reveals a great talent for shaping a narrative and arriving at fruitful detours. Her gift for storytelling is rooted in her cinema-glutted childhood, her memories of which are worth quoting at length: "Growing up in the Midwest as a gender-dysphoric tomboy, watching movies was a cherished relief from the awkward realities of daily life. Emulating the actors in my favorite classic Hollywood films, I happily acquired a new borrowed masculine persona. Experiencing myself as a fictional character has been a mode of survival for me ever since."

Those elegant sentiments reminded me of this pithy observation by Patricia White in her critical study *Uninvited: Classical Hollywood Cinema and Lesbian Representability* (1999), a work I can never recommend highly or often enough: "Cinema is public fantasy that engages spectators' particular, private scripts of desire and identification." Though *Uninvited* isn't mentioned in *The Royal Road*, Olson's film shares a deep affinity with White's book in that both are invested in mapping out lesbian cinephilia. It's no surprise, then, that reflections on another film—*Vertigo*—should serve as *The Royal Road*'s most illuminating through line.

Olson has mined Alfred Hitchcock's 1958 Fog City–set masterpiece before: *The Joy of Life* devotes part of its psychogeographical ruminations to the rescuing of Madeleine (Kim Novak) by Scottie (James Stewart) after she jumps into the San Francisco Bay. But it is *Vertigo*'s overarching theme, "about the pull of the past," that most interests Olson in *The Royal Road* and amplifies her larger points about the pleasures and pitfalls of nostalgia, whether evidenced in California architecture movements (the Mission Revival style that emerged in the late 1800s) or in the director's pining for someone completely unavailable. Olson astutely notes that Scottie is "caught up in his own travelogue of desire" as he pursues the soignée

Madeleine, the woman he will be so desperate to re-create, throughout the city; later in Hitchcock's film, they will drive 90 miles south along El Camino Real to Mission San Juan Bautista, the site of *Vertigo*'s climactic moment. In her own unforgettable travelogue of desire, Olson voyages even farther down this historic route for a woman who consumes her. "I continue to search for inspiration in the movies, just like I did when I was little," she says in the closing minutes of *The Royal Road*, a film that richly rewards its viewers with the very thing she has spent her life seeking.

—*Village Voice*, October 28, 2015

A Fantastic Woman

(Sebastián Lelio, 2017)

A true star, of any vintage, can make the small seem grand. In her first major screen role, Daniela Vega, who plays Marina Vidal, the beleaguered central character in Chilean director Sebastián Lelio's *A Fantastic Woman*, elevates even the most mundane action—petting a dog, lifting an arm to activate a motion-sensor hallway light—into a gesture of minor majesty. With every pause or look, the actress ennobles an unsteady melodrama.

Marina, like Vega, is a trans woman, and, when we first see her, instantly bears out the description in the title, a direct translation of the original *Una mujer fantástica*. (Or at least one denotation; the film's name will later prove to be feebly punning.) She dazzles, singing the salsa classic "Periódico de ayer" at what appears to be a one-off gig at an upscale hotel while her boyfriend, Orlando (Francisco Reyes), looks on besottedly. They are an age- and class-discordant couple. He is 57, at least 25 years Marina's senior, and owns his own textile company; she earns her living as a waitress. (The opera lessons she takes convey the scope of her ambitions.) Yet the tenderness and lust they display over the course of an evening spent celebrating Marina's birthday—at a favorite Chinese restaurant, on a dance floor, against a wall in Orlando's elegant Santiago apartment—suggest an enviable match.

But later that night—and before the movie's 20-minute mark—Marina, racing to get a panting and disoriented Orlando to the hospital, will be widowed. She will also be humiliated:

by a physician who treats Marina like a criminal, by a cop who flagrantly misgenders her. Further degradation awaits her.

In fact, *A Fantastic Woman*, which Lelio cowrote with Gonzalo Maza, a frequent collaborator, can at times seem too invested in defining Marina not by what she does but by what is done to her. She will stoically endure the increasingly contemptible behavior of Orlando's family, especially his wastrel adult son, Bruno (Nicolás Saavedra), and his splenetic ex-wife, Sonia (Aline Küppenheim), both of whom Marina meets for the first time only after her partner's death. "When I look at you, I don't know what I'm seeing," Sonia all but spits at Marina during their initial encounter. After a pause, she lands on a wounding, repellent word: "A chimera, that's what I see."

The way Marina responds to this barb typifies Vega's talent for communicating her character's ineradicable core of dignity with the tiniest of movements, the slightest change in posture. After softly repeating the injurious term back to Sonia, Marina shrugs a shoulder almost imperceptibly before offering this assessment of the woman who's just diminished her: "You're normal. You're fine." But Marina injects lethal droplets of venom into each of those banal adjectives, knowing full well that their recipient will be too absorbed in her cis-superiority to register the disparagement—at least at first. Marina's hushed comeback is a slow-release drug.

This exchange is one of many in which Vega, whose character arc is shaped by tragedy and tribulations, demonstrates Marina's unfailing, if subdued, self-respect. Whether with a scene partner or alone—there are several segments in *A Fantastic Woman* that depict Marina in silent solitude—Vega unerringly calibrates the emotions roiling beneath a serene surface. Watching Marina do anything, like walking home solo in the wee hours in the rain after a long night at a club, where she's indulged in a bit of debauchery to assuage her grief, proves as absorbing as watching the sun rise or set.

Vega is consistently excellent, even as *A Fantastic Woman* becomes increasingly sentimental, or worse. Late in the film, Marina whispers a Nietzschean pop-psych mantra to herself: "What doesn't kill you makes you stronger." (Lelio's previous movie, 2013's *Gloria*, a pleasant, anodyne drift through the dating and family travails of a middle-aged divorcée, is largely devoid of such bromides. He's currently filming an English-language remake of it.) The most obtuse soundtrack choice imaginable—Aretha Franklin's "(You Make Me Feel Like) A Natural Woman"—is used here as a kind of go-girl anthem: it plays as Marina is driving to that fractious appointment with Sonia. And though we are meant, rightfully, to recoil at the slur Orlando's ex-wife directs at Marina, occasionally Lelio evinces his own queasy-making, retrograde notion that his protagonist is a mythical creature made up of unknown, perhaps "incongruous" parts.

The fixation on Marina's body is all the more glaring considering that Lelio includes one scene that establishes, at least superficially, the irrelevance and insensitivity of questions about anatomy and genitals. To Bruno's blunt inquiry "Did you get the operation?" Marina replies, "You don't ask that." Yet Lelio all but contravenes his heroine's sage counsel in segments that follow. Called in for a physical exam by the police, to rule out foul play in Orlando's death, Marina is shown naked from the waist up. When she is asked to uncover her lower half, the camera lingers on the downward gaze of the inspectors. Nothing is revealed, except for Lelio's attachment to such cheap ploys to build "suspense." The gambit repeats in the movie's final minutes, as Marina, first seen in profile naked on her bed, looks down at a reflection of herself, a round looking glass placed strategically over her crotch. (Mirrors abound in *A Fantastic Woman,* as if Douglas Sirk went on a tear through Bed Bath & Beyond.)

Also dispiriting is the dopey double meaning of the film's title: Marina is a woman prone to flights of fancy, seeing the ghost of her lover everywhere. At one point Marina imagines herself the captain of a gyrating pom-pom squad, capable of defying gravity. The whimsy grates. Superfluous, the frippery interferes with the more riveting drama of watching Vega's micro-movements: we are spellbound as she glances sidewise in one instant and then trains a steely gaze on someone in the next. Lelio should have realized that his star is already as big as life—in other words, fantastic enough.

—*4Columns,* January 26, 2018

Before Stonewall

(Greta Schiller, 1984)

Gay USA

(Arthur J. Bressan Jr., 1977)

Even this cranky lesbian has been delighted, if not moved, by the sheer number of cultural redoubts in New York City that are currently hosting, have already mounted, or will soon showcase programming, events, or exhibitions commemorating the 50th anniversary of the insurrection at the Stonewall Inn. I am touched by the scope of these tributes, which range from the grand, gravid, two-gallery-spanning show "Art After Stonewall, 1969–1989" to the more idiosyncratic, solo salute, evidenced in the handbill I picked up at the New York Public Library for the Performing Arts earlier this week announcing a free performance by Jacqueline Jonée, "the world's premiere concert pianist drag diva," part of the ongoing, NYPL-wide Stonewall celebration.

Filmwise, several of the city's repertory and independent cinemas this month are presenting a vast assortment of LGBTQ movies, many (but not all) made after the intifada of June 28, 1969. These offerings encompass the canonical (Jennie Livingston's *Paris Is Burning*, from 1990, now at Film Forum through June 27) and the recherché (Brooklyn's essential micro-cinema Light Industry hosts a program on June 25 of waggish shorts made in the early 1960s by a group of LA-based fag friends calling themselves the Gay Girls Riding Club). Among this fantastic array of lavender cinema are two newly restored documentaries playing at the Quad, neither of which I had seen before: Greta Schiller's *Before Stonewall*, a lively chronicle, commencing with the 1920s, of queer life in the decades prior to the pivotal Christopher Street rebellion; and Arthur J. Bressan Jr.'s *Gay USA*, an effulgent portrait of the homo movement assembled from interviews all conducted on one day—June 26, 1977—during Pride parades in several different cities. Both films rouse with their first-person testimony, their pleasing polyvocality.

Narrated by Rita Mae Brown, author of the legendary lez opus *Rubyfruit Jungle* (1973), *Before Stonewall* begins with a declaration and a query, affecting in their didactic earnestness: "Today the lesbian and gay community is a highly visible aspect of American society. How did this come about?" To partly answer that question, Schiller's documentary incorporates archival footage and clips from several pre-'69 Hollywood productions of varying levels of overtly queer content, such as the Clara Bow–starring vehicle *Call Her Savage*, from 1932. (In its cine-selections, *Before Stonewall* recalls Vito Russo's crucial compendium *The Celluloid Closet*, first published in 1981.)

But the most indelible history lessons in *Before Stonewall* are those articulated by the film's 30 or so interlocutors, most of whom recapitulate their own autobiographies. A few of these interviewees are LGBTQ luminaries: Audre Lorde recounts the racism of Greenwich Village lesbian bars in the '50s; Martin Duberman discusses his regimen of extreme self-abnegation—breaking up with a boyfriend, no sex for two years—to rid himself of his homosexuality (topics later discussed in his 1991 memoir, *Cures: A Gay Man's Odyssey*). Just as mesmerizing are those on-camera speakers of more rarefied celebrity, such as the Harlem Renaissance personage Richard Bruce Nugent, charmingly recollecting the gay clubs and dyke entertainers of that uptown neighborhood—memories that overlap with those of Mabel Hampton, identified on-screen as "former domestic worker/dancer," and resplendent in a red T-shirt with the logo for SAGE, the organization whose acronym then stood for Senior Action in a Gay Environment. Hampton belongs to the group of interviewees in *Before Stonewall* whose stories enthralled me the most: the everyday s/heroes, the glorious working-stiff butches and femmes of all genders—the printers, publishers, former secretaries, onetime government employees, World War II vets, bar owners and habitués, archivists, and bookstore owners vividly reminiscing about the indignities of the closet, courageous actions against hate, the risks and thrills of same-sex loving and lusting.

Culminating in a flurry of still and moving images from the Stonewall riots, Schiller's documentary ends on a triumphant note, the final words going to Ted Rolfs, ID'd as a retired merchant marine and one of the film's many gray-haired participants: "By joining and uniting, all of us, we have really gained power. ... And from the time of Stonehenge to Stonewall, this has been the struggle. And we're winning." Audiences taking in that statement 35 years after it was uttered may be especially struck, perhaps perplexed, by its buoyancy; *Before Stonewall*, made during Reagan's first term, premiered three years after the first cases of AIDS were reported in the US. By the end of the '80s, Rolfs's jubilant cry would be replaced with "And we're dying."

This is one of the painful privileges of retrospective viewing: having knowledge of a past that, to the person you're watching on-screen, is an unfathomable future. That destabilizing collision of temporalities is especially pronounced in *Gay*

USA, which the Quad is copresenting with NewFest on June 26 as part of the semiregular series "Coming Out Again," devoted to reviving underseen titles in the queer kino-corpus. This dense, exhilarating collage of sights (throngs of Pride revelers primarily in San Francisco but also in New York and Chicago, among other metropolises) and sounds (so much spirited talk, both on-screen and off-, and—trigger warning—some of the gooiest gay/lez folk love songs I've ever heard) reflects the liberationist fervor of the '70s, utopian hopes not yet extinguished. Or, at the very least, not yet co-opted and marketed: no ghastly rainbow-hued merchandise, no corporate slogans soil these festivities. A typical gay-power banner in '77 carries a message unlikely to be emblazoned on any Starbucks commemorative Pride tumbler in 2019: DOWN WITH THE NUCLEAR FAMILY—ROOT OF ALL SEXUAL OPPRESSION.

And yet, for all the furiously, ecstatically alive people in *Gay USA*, the film is inescapably haunted by death. The great Black lesbian poet Pat Parker appears here, reciting some puckish verse about the hypocrisy of squeamish heterosexuals; by 1989, she would die, at age 45, of breast cancer. Arthur J. Bressan Jr. perished, also in his mid-40s, from AIDS-related illness a decade after *Gay USA* was shot. Watching the documentary, I was consumed with morbid thoughts, wondering how many other young guys seen and/or interviewed (but never named) in Bressan's documentary—the chevron-mustached clones, the nursery school teacher, the ballet-trained dancer, the twink who fled Kansas for the hedonistic promise of California—would also not live beyond early middle age.

Both *Before Stonewall* and *Gay USA* present vital chapters in a history still being made, revised, corrected. And they are being shown in a theater located less than a ten-minute walk from several long-standing, still-thriving landmarks: the indispensable LGBT Community Center, where ACT UP first met in 1987; Julius', New York's oldest gay bar; the Cubbyhole, a sapphic boîte open since 1994; the Stonewall Inn itself. See these films, go to one of these places: sites of a psychogeography more vibrant than any varicolored WorldPride tie-in trinket.

—*4Columns*, June 21, 2019

Behind the Candelabra

(Steven Soderbergh, 2013)

Caftans, poodles, poppers, toupees, face peels, glory holes, diamonds, and furs: *Behind the Candelabra*, Steven Soderbergh's terrific Liberace biopic, shows just what a spectacle the closet could be.

Spanning 1977, the year that Liberace (Michael Douglas) began his relationship with Scott Thorson (Matt Damon), through 1987, when the outré pianist died of complications from AIDS at age 67, *Behind the Candelabra* anatomizes not just a love affair but a specific cultural condition. (With its sharp yet never didactic observations, *Behind the Candelabra* continues the immensely pleasurable social studies that dominate two of Soderbergh's other recent triumphs, last summer's *Magic Mike* and *Side Effects*, released in February.) The final decade of Liberace's life marked a paradoxical era when flaming queerness was seemingly everywhere—1977 was also the year the Village People formed—but could never be called out as such. Throughout his career, Liberace sued (and won against) those who insinuated he was homosexual; his management at first tried to insist that his cause of death was cardiac arrest, somehow related to "anemia caused by a watermelon diet." The folie à deux that Liberace and Thorson, 40 years the entertainer's junior, enacted in private was echoed in the bizarre pact between the flamboyant musician and his fans, all too willing to overlook the obvious.

Based on Thorson's 1988 memoir and scripted by Richard LaGravenese, *Behind the Candelabra* quickly establishes the skills Liberace needed for such seduction, whether performing for thousands or just one teenage hunk. "It's funny that this crowd would like something this gay," a starstruck Scott, surrounded by even more agog middle-aged women, tells his friend Bob (Scott Bakula), who's taken the peroxided cutie to the Las Vegas Hilton for his first Liberace show. "They have no idea he's gay," says Bob—who earlier cruised Scott in a West Hollywood bar with Tom of Finland tableaux on the walls and "I Feel Love" playing at eardrum-puncturing volume, in the film's perfect opening scene—before introducing him to Mr. Showmanship himself after the concert.

Scott, who's spent most of his life in and out of foster homes, quickly falls for the entertainer's promises to take care of him. (The 42-year-old Damon convincingly passes as someone two decades younger, if not quite the 18 Thorson was when he first met Liberace.) "I want to be everything to you, Scott: father, brother, lover, best friend," Lee, as he is known to his intimates, declares to his callow lover—a pledge made all too grotesquely literal when Scott obeys Liberace's request that he get a chin implant to look like the pianist in his youth.

The couple's adventures in plastic surgery—procedures performed by a hilarious Rob Lowe, here an amalgam of Dr. Fredric Brandt and Andy Gibb—are merely one manifestation of the ermine-draped showman's perverse penchant for excess. Yet as appetites—not just Liberace's lust for new flesh but also Scott's for drugs—and emotions grow ever more unmanageable, neither the movie nor its main actors ever lose control, refusing to succumb to easy, flaccid camp. "Nobody ever took care of me the way he does," a panicky, sweaty Scott confesses to an indifferent cokehead after a blow binge. This is a film (which may or may not be Soderbergh's last) about need: for love, for sex, for control, for lies—for more.

—*Artforum* online, May 22, 2013

Blue Is the Warmest Color

(Abdellatif Kechiche, 2013)

A high-water mark in cinematic lesberation or, as a *New York Times* headline put it, a "slutty impostor"? Examining the reception of Abdellatif Kechiche's fifth feature, *Blue Is the Warmest Color*—a sexually explicit but often fatuous tale of a sapphic sentimental education—since its premiere in May at the Cannes Film Festival, where it won the Palme d'Or, has proven more stimulating than the film itself.

In the first of the director's many interventions in this loose adaptation, cowritten by Kechiche and Ghalia Lacroix, of Julie Maroh's graphic novel *Le Bleu est une couleur chaude* (2010), he changes the name of the original's teenage protagonist, Clémentine, to match that of the actress who plays her: Adèle Exarchopoulos, a little-known 19-year-old performer whose mien, particularly her ripe, full mouth, evokes both Brigitte Bardot and Jean-Luc Godard regular Anne Wiazemsky. (The film's original title is *La Vie d'Adèle—Chapitre 1 & 2*.)

That *bouche* appears incapable of ever fully closing. Adèle is frequently shown, often in extreme close-up, with her mouth agape: while asleep; during classroom discussions of Pierre de Marivaux's *Life of Marianne* (Adèle and her fellow Lille high-school juniors talk of "predestination" and "love at first sight," just one example of Kechiche's blunt telegraphing); and after sex with a male classmate, for whom she feels little physical attraction. This constantly ajar orifice suggests, again too obviously, Adèle's ravenous hunger—she slurps down multiple plates of spaghetti Bolognese—and carnality, her sexual curiosity piqued when she first sees Emma (Léa Seydoux), a slightly older, soft-butch, turquoise-haired beaux-arts university student, who cruises her back.

After they reencounter each other at a dyke club—Adèle has ended up there after tiring of the boy bar a gay male friend took her to; maybe it was the tattooed old queen who slurred, "Love has no gender. Take whoever loves you," who scared her off—the teenager later asks her crush about her own appetites: "When was the first time you tasted a girl?" Shortly after this besotting fact-finding mission—one of the film's best scenes—and with Emma's previously mentioned girlfriend mysteriously eliminated from the plot, the two rapaciously devour each other, kissing, licking, sucking, fingering, scissoring, ass-slapping, sixty-nining, and moaning.

Adèle and Emma's three scenes of hot lez lust, which add up to roughly ten minutes of screen time in a three-hour-long film, were the focal point of nearly every review, most of them rapturous, after the film's Cannes debut. This breathless dispatch from *The Guardian*'s Peter Bradshaw typifies the praise: "The extended sex scenes have an explicitness and candour which can only be called magnificent; in fact they make the sex in famous movies like, say, *Last Tango in Paris* look supercilious and dated." Yet in a prominent dissent, Manohla Dargis of the *New York Times* lambasted the director, writing that "the movie feels far more about Mr. Kechiche's desires than anything else," later adding that he "seems so unaware or maybe just uninterested in the tough questions about the representation of the female body that feminists have engaged for decades." Most damning were comments that Maroh posted on her blog the day after *Blue* won the Palme d'Or. "It appears to me that this was what was missing on the set: lesbians," the 27-year-old author observed, calling Adèle and Emma's intimate scenes "a brutal and surgical display, exuberant and cold, of so-called lesbian sex, which turned into porn, and made me feel very ill at ease. ... As a feminist and lesbian spectator, I cannot endorse the direction Kechiche took on these matters."

Though I, another feminist and lesbian spectator, cannot entirely endorse these scenes, either—they strike me more as athletic endurance tests than expressions of pure erotic abandon—I also feel compelled to defend them. As Patricia White, a professor at Swarthmore, argues in her brilliant book *Uninvited: Classical Hollywood Cinema and Lesbian Representability* (1999), "Feminist film theory has been unable to envision women who looked at women with desire"; it is this persistent blind spot that Dargis's critique seems not to consider. And though Maroh, crucially, makes sure to stress that she is expressing only her opinion and is "looking forward to hearing what other women will think about [the film]," her suggestion that the director's and lead actresses' (presumed) heterosexuality automatically makes the sex scenes inauthentic and "pornographic" is queer politicking at its most reductive.

What *is* indefensible, or at least risible, about *Blue Is the Warmest Color,* though, is what happens when Adèle and Emma aren't in bed. The class differences—and attendant career ambitions—that mark and ultimately sunder Adèle, who is training to be a nursery-school teacher, and Emma, fiercely determined to land her first painting exhibition, are highlighted in a staggeringly trite party scene. The younger lover, who in dutiful wifey mode has prepared vats of her signature pasta, uncomprehendingly listens as Emma argues heatedly with an art-historian friend about the relative merits of Gustav Klimt and Egon Schiele. More egregious banalities, which we are meant to ponder seriously, emerge from Lille's most prominent gallerist, a man who yaps on about the "mystical" nature of female orgasm and insists that "art by women never tackles female pleasure." Kechiche tackles female pleasure, but he has no art to show for it.

—*Artforum*, October 2013

Cruising the Movies

(Boyd McDonald, reissued in 2015)

Nearly 20 years ago, Susan Sontag, in "The Decay of Cinema," lamented, "No amount of mourning will revive the vanished rituals—erotic, ruminative—of the darkened theater." But a decade before this dirge was written, Boyd McDonald, who had largely abandoned going out to the movies in 1969 (for reasons never explained), proved that some of the most ecstatic cinephilic—and carnal—delights could be found sitting alone at home. McDonald lustily, discursively wrote about the films that aired at all hours on television, which he viewed in his single-room apartment on the Upper West Side, often focusing on minor or supporting actors, as in this tribute to Steve Cochran, a second-billed performer in *White Heat* (1949): "But I have digressed from my topic, and digressed so far that it may be necessary to remind the reader what my topic is: the size of Cochran's meat." Between 1983 and 1985, his lubricious cultural criticism ran as a column in the gay magazine *Christopher Street*; those pieces, along with others written for *New York Native*, *Connection*, and *Philadelphia Gay News*, were published in 1985 by the Gay Presses of New York as *Cruising the Movies: A Sexual Guide to Oldies on TV*. McDonald's essential but under-recognized book, reissued by Semiotext(e) in an expanded edition with previously uncollected articles, offers, in its beautifully articulated bawdiness, perverse pleasures and a radical, though nondidactic, political view. It is, in other words, a model critical text.

The expansive introduction to *Cruising the Movies*, by experimental filmmaker William E. Jones, provides a helpful biographical sketch of McDonald and places this singular writer in a larger homo-cultural context. The "declassed Ivy Leaguer and film fan" was born in 1925 in South Dakota, served in World War II, and graduated from Harvard. He wrote and edited copy for *Time* and IBM for 20 years and drank excessively. He sobered up, went on public assistance, and moved to his spartan Manhattan lodging, which served as his primary screening room until his death in 1993. McDonald would write of his cherished piece of equipment: "I have confined my studies to pictures which are available on commercial TV. I watched them on a GE b/w receiver. It cost $80 and has brought me an estimated $80 million worth of ecstasy." Before he began writing his piquant film analyses, McDonald founded the zine *Straight to Hell*, composed mainly of readers' submissions of their own homosexual experiences—contributions that, as Jones notes, were "rigorously edited for style but never diluted or censored"; no less a lavender authority than Gore Vidal called *STH* "one of the best radical papers in the country."

McDonald's sinuous style, at once caustic and charitable, animates what he refers to as the "sermonettes" collected in *Cruising the Movies*. In addition to his XXX disquisitions on mostly forgotten B (and lower-letter) movies from Hollywood's golden age, the volume includes book reviews (of Joan Collins's *Past Imperfect*, for example) and the brilliant, abecedarian found poem "When Words Fail," a three-page list of movie performers, many of them lesser-known character actors, that starts with Nick Adams and ends with George Zucco. This catalogue-*cum*-salute points to McDonald's fondness for the plebeian rather than the aristocratic, whether on-screen or off-.

Jones's assessment of *Cruising the Movies* as that "rare thing: a book of popular film criticism that is both unabashedly sexual and unapologetically political" is indisputable; yet what distinguishes McDonald's prose even further is that his digs at, say, Katharine Hepburn, the Reagans, or Reagan Republicans manage to be both piercing and hilarious without ever becoming strident or nasty.

Though McDonald does not shy away from pointing out the homophobic idiocies of someone like Bob Hope—"He is Hollywood's senior sissy and fag-baiter"—his aim in *Cruising the Movies* is not to classify or police movies, as Vito Russo does in *The Celluloid Closet* (1981), a key predecessor, as "good" versus "bad" portrayals of gays. Such Manichaeanism held little appeal for the man who wrote, "The spoken word is at least 10% of the charm of 'talkies' (the other 90% of course is the groins and butts of the actors)"; that "other 90%" comes under particular scrutiny in McDonald's appraisal of Gregory Harrison in the 1981 made-for-TV movie *For Ladies Only*. In his mischievousness and deftness at setting up Wildean paradoxes ("She is a principal beneficiary of a perversion inherent in the picture business, to wit, that bad pictures are better than good pictures"), McDonald hews closer in style to that deployed by Parker Tyler in his witty and recherché *Screening the Sexes* (1972), another significant precursor. But though Tyler is not averse to using the first-person-singular pronoun, his *I* isn't as irrepressible as McDonald's, as evidenced by this declaration in *Cruising the Movies*: "Just as for sex I find a hot piece of meat preferable to a wonderful human being, so in show biz I enjoy a star more than someone who's merely a great actor."

Or, as Jones memorably puts it: "[McDonald] holds that talent is not only irrelevant, but a distraction from the main point of movies, the exhibition of beautiful and exceptional people simply being rather than acting. A star is above all a person millions of spectators want to rim, suck, and fuck." (And it is always the people in front of, not behind, the camera who interest McDonald; he rarely mentions directors.) McDonald's is always a cogent concupiscence, utilized to elevate semi-luminaries like David Nelson (Ricky's older brother) to the exalted position of "one of Hollywood's premier suck objects," an honorific bestowed on the actor largely thanks to his role as a white-clad trapeze artist in *The Big Circus* (1959). Michael Callan, who played a similar role in *The Flying Fontaines* (from the same year), likewise receives high praise for the bulges revealed by his big-top costume.

While the most gloriously ribald passages of *Cruising the Movies* concern the men McDonald sees, and lusts after, on his TV screen—those who fall into "one of [his] 55 or 60 types"—his paeans to actresses, even if platonic, are no less impassioned. In a piece written for a 1983 issue of *Straight to Hell* excerpted in Jones's introduction, McDonald underscores a key element of his cinephilia: "Motion pictures are for people who like to watch women." (A corollary to that aesthetic principle might be this more personal avowal: "May I say that I like women better than men, but not for cock.") His veneration of Gloria Grahame, the incomparable noir seductress, is worth quoting at length:

> Gloria Grahame is a high school boy's dream of cool, of real, effortless masculinity as opposed to the effort to act masculine made by her co-star in *In a Lonely Place* (1950), a poseur named "Humphrey Bogart." She had the sullen, bored walk and talk of someone who can't be shocked, isn't afraid and just doesn't give a shit. But she was perfectly feminine; the badge of her

> femininity was the fantastically sharp outline of her lips, or, more precisely, her lipstick. ... I never take my eyes off her lips, but just sit waiting for her to open them and say something.

McDonald, we discover, is often drawn to actresses who display a subtle butch bravado; in singling out the performance of Jane Russell in 1952's *Macao* (in which, coincidentally, Grahame has a supporting role), he writes: "Anyone who treasures cool virility cannot fail to be favorably impressed by Russell; her easy masculine style is more admirable than the more showy machismo of men, for, unlike them, she does not prey upon the vulnerable but merely counterattacks when men prey upon her." McDonald's sharp dissections of masculinity's absurdity—that is, when practiced by men—amplifies his sly feminism, announced at the end of the preface: "I have, finally, no wife to thank for typing my manuscript. Unlike 'straight' writers, if I had a wife I'd want her to do something that's more fun than typing my manuscript."

As my copious citations of McDonald prove, he honed a kind of cultural criticism—personal but outward-looking, raunchy yet brainy, funny and furious—rare in his era and barely in evidence today, when we are overrun with professional (and paraprofessional) opinionators whose writing rarely rises above plot synopses with some adjectives and adverbs thrown in. Throughout *Cruising the Movies*, McDonald archly points out the deficiencies of what he dubs "pack journalism," of those arbiters who had far more readers than he; Leonard Maltin's movie-review vernacular is aptly described as "Tarzan-like English." He presents, without commentary, an instance of flagrant plagiarism found in the *New York Times*' obituary for director Henry Hathaway and aims a well-turned barb at Janet Maslin, that paper's fixture. Halfway through the book, in an ode to actor Richard Widmark, McDonald states his frustrations with "film criticism" in general: "[Widmark] demonstrates the importance of the movie star over the movie and thus the importance of star reviews over mere movie reviews, with their constant complaints about plot." McDonald is especially "unmoved" by any critical stance taken by Pauline Kael, among the most powerful critics at the time of *Cruising the Movies*' original publication and one whose influence remains outsize today. Like Kael's, McDonald's sensibility was resolutely uncompromised. But his writing, even if for a very specific audience, teems with qualities—generosity, curiosity, wit, raillery, and, of course, lust—lacking in hers and that of most other critics, then or now. The columns collected in *Cruising the Movies* reflect the best that criticism can do—they are, as Oscar Wilde would have it, a record of McDonald's soul.

—*Bookforum*, December 2015/January 2016

BPM (Beats per Minute)

(Robin Campillo, 2017)

The original French title of Robin Campillo's *BPM (Beats per Minute)*, a bracing drama about the Paris branch of the direct-action advocacy group ACT UP in the early 1990s, includes a specific number: *120 battements par minute*. That's the average heart rate of a body engaged, as many of *BPM*'s ensemble are, in high-adrenaline activities, like sex, like the civil resistance that members of ACT UP (the call-to-arms acronym for AIDS Coalition to Unleash Power) engaged in to target those who did nothing to stop the disease. The figure is also the typical rhythm of house music, the hypnotic, post-disco genre that dominates *BPM*'s soundtrack, heavy on hi-hat cymbals and bass lines. The number sets the tempo for a film that pulsates equally with rage, grief, desire, and debate.

BPM, which Campillo cowrote with Philippe Mangeot, is partially rooted in the director's own biography: born in 1962, Campillo joined ACT UP–Paris in 1992. Although *BPM* is technically fiction, it has the rawness and immediacy of an eyewitness account, qualities often lacking in dramatized tales of LGBTQ history (Roland Emmerich's ghastly *Stonewall*, from 2015, quickly comes to mind). Campillo's movie forms a dialogue with two crucial 2012 documentaries about ACT UP in New York, where the inaugural chapter of the activist group was founded, in 1987: Jim Hubbard's *United in Anger: A*

History of ACT UP and David France's *How to Survive a Plague*. (The Paris division, modeled on the one in New York, was formed in 1989.) Both of those impassioned nonfiction films combine archival footage with present-day interviews with ACT UP vets, who look back not only on the coalition's guerrilla protests but on their much younger selves. In *BPM*, Campillo also recollects memories from a quarter century ago—but he conjugates the past tense into a form of the present perfect.

While *BPM* has the urgency of a communiqué, even if one from a not-so-distant era, it also seamlessly breaks free of a standard narrative arc: there are oneiric elements in the film and time doesn't always move in a straight line. (Time, you might say, is queered.) We are immersed in the middle of the action—or, more specifically, of a demonstration about to happen—in *BPM*'s opening scene. Several ACT UP members are backstage at a conference, whispering, conspiring, placing whistles in their mouths, waiting for just the right moment to disrupt a speaker from AFLS, a French anti-AIDS agency that the direct-action group finds unconscionably laggard in its response to the epidemic. They storm the stage, air horns blaring, signs raised (COLERE = ACTION). The scene ends abruptly amid this cacophony and is followed by one set in the university lecture hall where ACT UP's weekly meeting takes place. With their T-shirts and faces still smeared with the fake blood they tossed, those ACT UP members who took part in the AFLS protest explain to their comrades what happened. No two flashbacks, some of which are rendered in slo-mo, are alike; they shift, in camera placement, in details recalled, with the recounting of each speaker, a few of whom are still upset by the on-the-fly tactics of their confreres at the demo.

That scene beautifully establishes the polyvocal energy that animates the drab, fluorescent-lit classroom where several segments of *BPM* take place. Campillo's film is dense with talk: planning, analyzing, arguing, apologizing, inciting. (An oblique forerunner to *BPM* is Laurent Cantet's similarly voluble *The Class*, from 2008, about a junior-high teacher in the 20th arrondissement and his African, Asian, and Arab students; Campillo cowrote the script with Cantet, with whom he frequently collaborates.) Meetings have rarely seemed so riveting; the words come alive thanks to Campillo's ferociously committed ensemble cast, most in their 20s and early 30s. Several performers make their screen debut in *BPM*. Only one actor in Campillo's film is well-known in France: Adèle Haenel, superb, as she is in every film of hers I've seen that's been released stateside, in the role of Sophie, a dyke member of ACT UP who ranks among its most headstrong members. Campillo's coalition comrades are largely, but by no means exclusively, young gay white men. As was the case in real-life ACT UP meetings, *BPM*'s include attendees of different genders, races, generations, sexualities, serostatuses, and abilities (about half a dozen activists seated in the lecture hall are deaf)—a heterogeneity that's organic, unforced. (That diversity is evidenced in Hubbard's and France's documentaries, too.)

One of the interviewees in Hubbard's chronicle memorably calls ACT UP a "cauldron of political anger, flirting, and cruising"; that libidinal intensity suffuses *BPM*. An ACT UP newcomer, Nathan (Arnaud Valois), is greeted by wolf whistles when he stands up to introduce himself. The shy, HIV-negative hunk is drawn to Sean (Nahuel Pérez Biscayart), a fervent member of the group whose T-cell count is rapidly diminishing. Though their love story, and Sean's perilous health, provides the main through line of *BPM*, especially in the film's second half, this dyad doesn't exist in isolation; the two men are always part of a collective, a cause, something larger than themselves.

Through die-ins on cold Paris streets, the storming of pharmaceutical companies, heated discussions in that cavernous classroom and cozier apartments, and ecstatic gyrating on the dance floor, *BPM* reminds us again and again of the kinetic power of the group, of the tremendous vitality that results from so many disparate, ardent individuals united in fight. And here, of course, united exclusively IRL: one of my favorite moments in *BPM* is a fleeting scene shot from the back of the lecture hall during a 15-minute break in the weekly meeting, showing members talking in pairs or in larger groups, or sitting alone, absorbed in their own thoughts. No devices distract anyone.

Campillo's film rousingly captures the vigor of those surrounded by death, many of whom were dying themselves. *BPM* makes vivid these potent remarks from the art historian, critic, and ACT UP vet Douglas Crimp, who, in a 2007 interview for the coalition's Oral History Project, discussed "the kind of pleasures that can be associated with political activism, even in the face of truly gruesome problems and truly terrible things happening in our midst. ... I think it was lifesaving in more ways than one. Even for people who weren't dying, it was lifesaving to be able to stand up against the kind of vilification that we were experiencing." However specific its time frame and focus, *BPM* is not a narrow nostalgia piece, nor will it ever be as long as people are still dying, still being vilified. An odd coincidence: the title of Campillo's film is only one letter removed from the abbreviation for Black Lives Matter. The beats go on.

—*4Columns*, October 20, 2017

Carol

(Todd Haynes, 2015

Their eyes met at the same instant, Therese glancing up from a box she was opening, and the woman just turning her head so she looked directly at Therese. She was tall and fair, her long figure graceful in the loose fur coat that she held open with a hand on her waist. Her eyes were gray, colorless, yet dominant as light or fire, and caught by them, Therese could not look away.

—Patricia Highsmith, *The Price of Salt*

Published in 1952, when sapphic couplings depicted in high and low culture commonly ended in misery, ignominy, or suicide—and when same-sexing itself was a criminal offense—Patricia Highsmith's second novel, *The Price of Salt*, was nearly unprecedented in the happy ending it imagined for its lesbian couple. Sixty-three years later, *Carol*, Todd Haynes's simultaneously controlled and rapturous adaptation of Highsmith's book, arrives at a moment of inexorable homonormativity. (I happened to see *Carol* the night before the Supreme Court delivered its landmark ruling on gay marriage.) The latest work by one of the pioneers of New Queer Cinema doesn't romanticize the closet but passionately salutes lovers who exist outside the law.

"Identity and its pathologies have always been interests of mine," Haynes remarked to Amy Taubin in an interview published in the March 2011 issue of this magazine, occasioned by the HBO premiere of *Mildred Pierce*, the filmmaker's highly faithful page-to-small-screen transfer of James M. Cain's 1941 novel. That theme is especially pronounced in *Mildred Pierce*, a sharp dissection of motherhood and martyrdom, as it is in Haynes's other interventions into the "woman's picture," notably *Safe* (1995) and *Far from Heaven* (2002), "woman" perhaps being the most fraught identity of them all. *Carol* continues Haynes's exploration of that film genre, though the notion of identity here is less fixed: in both the book and the movie, the words *lesbian*, *gay*, and *homosexual* are never uttered. In a romance unfolding 17 years before Stonewall, the central lovers—the soignée, 30-ish, upper-middle-class New Jersey wife and mother Carol Aird and the guileless 19-year-old Manhattan shop clerk Therese Belivet, who is indifferent to and often annoyed by the boyfriend who's keen on marrying her—attach no labels to their desire.

But even if theirs is the love that dare not speak its name, neither protagonist feels any shame about her erotic inclinations. Crucially, though, both are pathologized by others, most poisonously by Carol's soon-to-be ex-husband, who hires a private detective to tail his spouse, gathering evidence as to why she should not be allowed near their four-year-old daughter. (As Manohla Dargis of the *New York Times* pointed out in an interview with Haynes in May at the Cannes Film Festival, where *Carol* had its world premiere, Highsmith's novel was published the same year the American Psychiatric Association labeled homosexuality a "sociopathic personality disturbance.") In refusing to demonize its same-sex couple, Highsmith's novel was a progressive work in a benighted era. Conversely, one of the many perverse pleasures of Haynes's period piece lies in teasing out its subtle intimations of what queer culture—and identity—has irretrievably lost in the decade or so in which attaining the right to wed came to define it.

It is instructive to note, though, that the publishing history of the novel that inspired Haynes's film is filled with its own incongruities. Highsmith was an accomplished serial seducer of women (her conquests and relationships, most of which flamed out disastrously, are detailed in Joan Schenkar's lively 2009 biography of the writer). But the butch bravado that marked her private life wasn't necessarily matched in her public one. Taking precautions to ensure that her career wasn't derailed by societal—or, more specifically, the literary establishment's—abhorrence of lavender life, Highsmith published *The Price of Salt*, which sold nearly a million copies when released in paperback in 1953, under a pseudonym, Claire Morgan, and did not publicly acknowledge the book until 1984. (Highsmith died in 1995, at the age of 74.)

As the author herself details in the afterword to later editions of *The Price of Salt*, the initial meeting that inspired the story was followed by an actual fever—a delirium that Haynes's film so beautifully translates to the screen. In 1948, a year before the publication of her first novel, *Strangers on a Train*, Highsmith worked in the toy section at Bloomingdale's for a few weeks during the Christmas rush. One morning, she noticed "a blondish woman in a fur coat" who "seemed to give off light." After this elegant client bought a doll and left, Highsmith writes, "I felt odd and swimmy in the head, near to fainting, yet at the same time uplifted, as if I had seen a vision." She went home and wrote eight pages sparked by this encounter, producing in two hours a complete synopsis of the narrative that would become *The Price of Salt*. She woke up the next day with a 104-degree temperature, the beginnings of chicken pox.

Carol, the source of this department-store luminescence, is played in Haynes's movie by Cate Blanchett; Therese, the young woman who is woozily deranged by her, by Rooney Mara. They meet in circumstances almost identical to those of Highsmith's real-life scenario, with Bloomingdale's renamed Frankenberg's. *Carol* marks Blanchett's second collaboration with Haynes. In their first, *I'm Not There* (2007), the filmmaker's brilliant antibiopic of Bob Dylan, the actress plays, in a triumph of gender-blind casting, the folk-music sage in his most iconic, mid-'60s incarnation. The role seemed to shake something loose in Blanchett, whose most prominent films at that time included the airless historical costume drama *Elizabeth* (1998) and the *Lord of the Rings* trilogy. In the eight years since the release of *I'm Not There,* Blanchett has come to be regarded as one of the greatest performers of her generation; to this viewer, though, her acting style has only become more mannered, cold, and calculating. Yet it is precisely this froideur that is tapped so deftly by both actress and director in *Carol*: Blanchett's older, more experienced seductress comes on to Therese like hot ice.

If Haynes's film reveals a longtime A-lister revitalizing her signature acting style, it also showcases the talents of a still-ascending performer. Playing the woman who breaks up with Jesse Eisenberg's Mark Zuckerberg in *The Social Network* (2010), Mara is on-screen for only a few minutes but is the most memorable presence in David Fincher's Facebook origin story; starring the following year in the title role of that director's take on *The Girl with the Dragon Tattoo,* the actress proved that her allure could not be diminished even by a wholly unnecessary remake. Silent for long stretches of *Carol*, Mara's Therese is often a beholder, a witness to—but by no means a passive participant in—the love affair that is so completely transforming her. The spark ignited in the actress's enormous, watchful eyes when Therese and Carol first spot each other in Frankenberg's indelibly signals curiosity and desire. Throughout the film, as the two women head west on a road trip—eventually consummating their relationship, in a deeply intoxicating love scene, in Waterloo, Iowa ("Isn't that awful?" Carol laughs between cigarette puffs when announcing the town's name to Therese the morning after)—Mara's orbs operate as the film's primary mode of communication.

The ways in which Therese sees the world, in fact, form the very basis of her professional ambitions. In one of the deviations from the source novel, Therese is not an aspiring set designer but a photographer. (*Carol*'s script was written by Phyllis Nagy; known primarily as a playwright, she is the author of a two-act stage adaptation of Highsmith's most famous book, 1955's *The Talented Mr. Ripley*. Significantly, *Carol* is the only Haynes project for which he had no hand in the screenplay.) Therese's black-and-white snaps of her beloved suggest an affinity with Ruth Orkin and Helen Levitt, acknowledged influences on the look of *Carol*. But the photographer whose style, sensibility, and muted color palette most clearly define the film is Saul Leiter, whose oeuvre was also a touchstone for *Mildred Pierce*: characters, Therese especially, often look out of rain-slicked or befogged windows; subdued greens, grays, and yellows—with the occasional shock of red—are the dominant hues.

Carol, like *Mildred Pierce*, was shot on Super 16 by Edward Lachman, the cinematographer on all of Haynes's feature-length projects since *Far from Heaven*. "I wanted 16 because I really wanted that grain ... dancing on the surface of the screen," Haynes told Taubin in 2011. Just as kinetic—and palpable, if not always explicit—are the feelings of two women whose romance deepens even as it goes largely unarticulated.

As always in Haynes's work, exteriors (of Carol's Packard, of the hotels and roadside diners where the besotted women rest and refuel) and reflective surfaces (the vanity-table mirror in which we see Carol stroke Therese's hair) are fundamental in conveying states of interiority. "It would be Carol, in a thousand cities, a thousand houses, in foreign lands where they would go together, in heaven and hell," Highsmith writes. Haynes's film gloriously demonstrates what a much more romantic declaration this is than "I do."

—*Artforum*, September 2015

Curt McDowell and Tom Rubnitz

Gay underground moving-image eminences Curt McDowell and Tom Rubnitz were born in and chronicled different decades, lived on opposite coasts, worked in different formats, and were drawn to dissimilar subjects. Despite their vastly disparate oeuvres, however, their work—which screens at Anthology for a week, presented in conjunction with "THINGS: A Queer Legacy of Art and Play," an exhibition at Participant Inc. that runs through August 21—abounds with anarchic impulses, whether the lawlessness of desire in McDowell's films or the giddy mayhem of doll play and drag dress-up in Rubnitz's videos. (The artists also share a brutal biographical detail: they both died of AIDS-related causes, McDowell in 1987 at age 42, Rubnitz in 1992 at 36.)

"God gave him a calling in life and that was to make pornography," George Kuchar, the creator of such canonical lo-fi camp fantasias as *Hold Me While I'm Naked* (1966), once said of McDowell, who was Kuchar's student at the San Francisco Art Institute (they'd soon become lovers and artistic collaborators). Shot on black-and-white 16mm and made in SF primarily during the 1970s, that storied decade of gay lib and libertinism, several of McDowell's films are organized around hot man-on-man action: asses are plowed, cocks devoured, sluices of cum spurted. But the XXX activities are often part of a larger, more cerebral project, of McDowell trying to make sense of who he is by figuring out who and what turns him on.

One of his earliest films, *Confessions* (1971), showcases his gifts for the carnal memoir. The 11-minute short opens with McDowell, then in his mid-20s, lying in bed and speaking directly to the camera. The mustached, louchely alluring filmmaker recounts, ostensibly for his parents, his sexual exploits ("I cornholed anything that would bend over"). The monologue is less an abject apology than it is a moment of self-reckoning. That inclination toward auto-interrogation continues in *Confessions* as McDowell, heard off-screen, asks members of his circle, "Tell me what's right and what's wrong about me." The query and the variety of responses it prompts are good-natured, never solemn or maudlin—and are intercut with extreme close-ups of an array of coital practices (or what the theorist Linda Williams memorably termed "meat shots").

Other works, like *Loads* (1980), more audaciously delineate and depict McDowell's desires, including his predilection for straight men. Undeniably, sex is seriously scrutinized in McDowell's films. But they are also defined by a ludic sensibility, as the title of *Wieners and Buns Musical* (1972) suggests. This outré songfest, featuring a sailor-suited McDowell in a pansexual love triangle with a married couple played by Ainslie Pryor (a frequent player in the director's films) and Kuchar, anticipates the sexed-up screwball of *Thundercrack!* (1975), a 160-minute opus as awash in bodily fluids as it is in B-movie clichés.

Written by and costarring Kuchar, *Thundercrack!*, which can be loosely described as a dark-and-stormy-night tale involving an octet of horny men and women (including the director's sister, Melinda) and an even more oversexed gorilla, is exceptional in its polymorphous perversity and sidesplitting dialogue. One-liners range from the deliberately corny, lubricious food metaphor ("Just a little longer and we'll have mustard and ketchup and mayonnaise," one fellow says to the woman who's avidly deep-throating him) to the floridly theatrical pronouncement. The latter is the specialty of the incomparable Marion Eaton, who became a cult star largely thanks to her work with McDowell. Here she plays Gert Hammond, a widow who hosts the motley crew of fornicators—and who pleasures herself with a variety of peeled cylindrical vegetables. "A harmless excursion into the steaming tropics in the name of art," Mrs. Hammond says, with excessive rhetorical relish, of an exploit of one of her guests—a summa that could serve as a tagline for this torrid, comic debauch.

Food is treated much more wholesomely, though no less ingeniously, in several of Rubnitz's gleeful, Day-Glo-hued videos, works that distill his singular sunny absurdity. The 90-second *Strawberry Shortcut* (1989) features Rubnitz regular Lady Bunny, the drag demigoddess, in a panic, having forgotten to provide dessert for her ladies' luncheon. A sickening, saccharine concoction of jam, doughnuts, cherry 7UP, Reddi-wip, and the fruit of the title saves the social, the sweet excess wonderfully amplified by the winks and goofy grins of the party hostess and her drag sistren.

Some of those extravagantly bewigged and maquillaged performers would reappear in Rubnitz's best-known work, the YouTube favorite *Pickle Surprise*, also from '89. They also show up in *Wigstock: The Movie* (1987), a 20-minute documentary of the legendary end-of-summer drag be-in held for many years in Tompkins Square Park. Rubnitz was an exuberant ethnographer of the East Village queer scene, capturing Pyramid Club luminaries like the peroxided, snake-hipped John Sex in the buoyant music video *Hustle with My Muscle* (1986) and the spy-spoof trailer *Undercover ... Me!* (1988)—

and the three-fourths human, one-quarter toy Frieda the Disco Doll in *Plastic Rap* from 1983 (sample lyric: "Holly Hobby is in the house"). But grim reality was never far from Rubnitz's ebullient visions. The last line in the credit scroll of *Strawberry Shortcut* reads: "Dedicated to the Hope for a Cure for AIDS."

—*Village Voice*, August 10, 2016

Nighthawks

(Ron Peck, 1978)

By the late 1970s, with disco's dominance, perhaps no place promised more utopian possibility than the dance floor, regardless of where one fell on the Kinsey scale. Implicitly hetero movies capitalized on this belief most successfully with *Saturday Night Fever* (1977), featuring John Travolta's Tony Manero as the grapevining prince of Brooklyn's Bay Ridge. The next year saw the release of *Thank God It's Friday*, set in an elysian boogie emporium in Los Angeles, where the euphoria peaks with Donna Summer's performance of "Last Dance." A landmark in LGBTQ literature, Andrew Holleran's *Dancer from the Dance* (1978) stands as the first great disco novel, vivified with descriptions of gay revelers moving to the rhythm en masse.

Ron Peck's quietly revolutionary debut feature, *Nighthawks*, also from 1978, takes a less sanguine view: here the dance floor becomes a space of both lusty liberation and disheartening ritual. Set in London, the film, which Peck cowrote with Paul Hallam, centers on one of cinema's first fully realized, complex gay protagonists: Jim (Ken Robertson), a semi-out geography instructor at a comprehensive school and a compulsive club-goer. During the day, we follow Jim, unfailingly polite and patient, as he gives his rambunctious tween and teen students lessons on India and acquaints a new substitute teacher, Judy (Rachel Nicholas James), with the school. After sundown, Jim—growing restless in his tidy, tiny Notting Hill apartment—hits the bars, where he cruises, moves to the beat, and keeps up his end of banal conversations ("Crowded, isn't it?").

The camera fully immerses us in Jim's nocturnal rites, frequently assuming his point of view. (*Nighthawks*' cinematographer is Joanna Davis.) In the film's opening scene, Jim, a lager in one hand and a pack of Marlboro Reds tucked into the waist of his snug jeans, scans the bodies on the main floor of a club, as metallic, synthy disco blares. (Short, compact, and handsome, Robertson bears more than a passing resemblance to Al Pacino, who, two years later, would star in *Cruising*, a stygian companion to *Nighthawks*; both movies are crucial artifacts of the pre-AIDS era.) Through Jim's eyes, we observe the intricate choreography of guys both assessing others and being inspected themselves. Making his way through the gazing scrum, Jim chats up Mike (Tony Westrope), a twink in a sleeveless white tee with wispy, middle-parted hair.

Following a hard cut—a transitionless editing technique used throughout the movie, one that sharply underscores the rote patterns in the schoolteacher's life—Jim is now in Mike's cramped flat, kissing him on his bed. Another cut: desultory morning-after conversation. And another: Jim drives Mike to the nearest Tube station, gingerly suggesting a follow-up date. They'll see each other a few more times, then stop. The cycle repeats with other men: Neal, Peter, an unnamed American banker temporarily stationed in the capital city.

"Don't you get anxious about whether or not you're ever going to see these people again?" Judy asks Jim after the two have grown close enough that he casually comes out to her during after-work drinks. (Only two other colleagues of Jim's know that he's gay.) *Nighthawks* boldly wrestles with that question, refusing to dismiss it outright while also refraining from presenting Jim's behavior as aberrant in any way. He candidly discusses the misery he experienced with a recent live-in lover, all the while delicately hinting at the unhappiness that Judy—the mother of two young children and married to a man we never see—endures at home. "I enjoy not having any ties, not knowing who I'm going to meet," Jim declares. That freedom may occasionally be depleting. But it is freedom nonetheless. Each evening out promises excitement—sometimes realized, sometimes not—in public and private spaces where gay men in England were only beginning to feel a modicum of safety. (Homosexuality was partly decriminalized in the country in 1967.)

And there are ecstatic moments that elevate Jim's routine nightclubbing. One energetic dancer is filmed for a full minute or two, his limbs in constant motion as he loses himself to the four-on-the-floor rhythm. To a disco ballad, shirtless couples sway in tender embraces. Recalling his first time at a gay club while a still deeply closeted young man, Jim describes the experience to Judy as a kind of deliverance.

Eventually, Jim reconciles his nocturnal self with his diurnal one. In an electric segment near the end of the film, one of the instructor's pupils—a scrawny, snarling adolescent with a teddy boy quiff—demands to know: "Is it true you're a queer?" Jim calmly replies in the affirmative and then answers a host of ensuing questions from his students, wild with curiosity: "Do you carry a handbag?" "Do you dress in women's clothes?" "What do you do in bed?" "Are you ashamed of it?" "Sir, what does your family think about it?" His responses to these naïve queries evince as much forbearance as that earlier shown to Judy when she voiced her slightly patronizing concern about his dating habits.

Peck was adamant that his nuanced film not be held up as an all-encompassing portrayal of gay codes and customs. As detailed in Vito Russo's *The Celluloid Closet* (1981), Peck wrote the following in a program note accompanying *Nighthawks*: "The film only shows one part of the gay scene. ... Almost any film starts off with the burden of trying to redress an imbalance, to make homosexuality visible in the cinema. We need hundreds of gay films, not half a dozen."

We have surpassed, by at least tenfold, that wished-for milestone in the 40-plus years since Peck composed that statement. A filmmaker who contributed an especially vital body of work to queer cinema can be seen briefly in Peck's movie: Derek Jarman, who would make a feature that serves as an exuberant counterpart to *Nighthawks*. In 1984, Jarman, excitedly experimenting with a new camcorder, chronicled the action at Benjy's, a gay club in London's Mile End district. This ebullient footage, with a small but buoyant crowd shimmying to Frankie Goes to Hollywood, wouldn't be screened until 2014, under the title *Will You Dance with Me?* Recorded deep into the dual catastrophes roiling the UK at the time—Margaret Thatcher's prime ministry and AIDS, the disease that killed Jarman in 1994—the project reminds us that heaven can be found even in hell.

—*4Columns*, June 26, 2020

"The Oscars Made Me Gay"

For the first time in my TV-viewing herstory, I didn't watch the Oscars last year—and thus reclaimed nearly four hours that would otherwise have been spent suffering through the most narcotizing tedium. I plan on liberating myself from the dull, decorous pageantry again this Sunday, even if it means missing out in real time on ceremony host Chris Rock's digs at the roster of blindingly Caucasian nominees. I admit that I'd be pleased if two of those contenders, Rooney Mara and Cate Blanchett, had respective wins in the Best Supporting Actress and Best Actress categories for *Carol*, Todd Haynes's exquisite adaptation of Patricia Highsmith's great 1952 lesbian romance. Their victories (or those of *Carol*'s nominees in four other categories, which conspicuously do not include Best Director or Best Picture) will doubtless be celebrated by some as further proof of how "progressive" Hollywood has become, at least regarding LGBTQ issues. But they will never restore the Oscar telecast to what it once was, when many people still lived in the closet: an overt-ops mission to advance the most outré homosexual agenda, one that turned susceptible American youths into inverts and tribadists.

I say this with firsthand experience: I grew up during the 1970s and '80s, transfixed every year from my childhood through my postadolescence by the televised derangement endorsed by the Academy of Motion Picture Arts and Sciences—viewing that unquestionably led to my becoming a practitioner of the sapphic arts. Oscar ceremonies from 1970 to 1989 were the opposite of conversion therapy; the telecasts from that era served as an ex-straight ministry.

The '70s in particular were the golden years of Oscar outrageousness and homo insurrection, exemplified by the 1974 streaking of Robert Opel, who flashed the peace sign and scurried past David Niven as the English actor was introducing to the stage Elizabeth Taylor, among the biggest of gay icons, then as now (as forever). Opel had gained access to the Dorothy Chandler Pavilion in Los Angeles, where the ceremony was held for many years between 1969 and 1999, thanks to his press credentials with *The Advocate*, the national gay magazine; his nudie infamy helped him establish Fey-Way Studios in San Francisco, a gallery that specialized in homoerotica (and where Opel would be murdered in 1979).

I was a kindergartner at the time of this prank—surely I had been in bed hours before Opel's full-dong assault? But I remember it vividly, even if only a version constructed in my tiny fevered brain from my parents' descriptions of the one-man flash mob. Could Mom and Dad also have told me (already, at age five, completely movie-mad) about Edith Head's win during that same 1974 show for Best Costume Design for *The Sting*, the eighth and final time she took home an Oscar in that category? It must have been the 1982 awards ceremony—which would have included Head, who died in 1981, in its ghastly "In Memoriam" segment—that sparked my longtime obsession with the costuming legend. I'll never forget being completely fascinated with, perhaps even slightly terrified by, the incongruities of Head's signature prim look—bangs, bun, and glasses—with her filthy- and queer-sounding name. Seventeen years after this primal early-'80s encounter with the costumier, I'd face a room of po-faced academics, many unconvinced by my graduate-school paper arguing that Head's designs for the actresses in Alfred Hitchcock's *Vertigo* and *Marnie* were among the lezziest ever created.

Other moments from the 1982 ceremony also served as key episodes in my homosexual indoctrination. The mighty Barbara Stanwyck, previously unknown to me, was awarded the Honorary Oscar for four decades of screen roles, several of which—as a jailbird in *Ladies They Talk About* (1933), a dragoon leader in *Forty Guns* (1957), and a lavender-leaning madam in *Walk on the Wild Side* (1962)—cemented her status as eternal dyke idol. The musical acts featured on that late-March night of '82 also kept the annual AMPAS ritual maximally fruity. Resplendent in sequined, floral-patterned white suit, Liberace performed a medley of the compositions nominated for Best Original Score. Even more outlandish than Mr. Showmanship's ivory-tickling was the production number showcasing the Best Song contender "For Your Eyes Only," from the James Bond film of the same name: Sheena Easton makes her entrance by emerging from an intergalactic vehicle, surrounded by 007 villains—Dr. No, Odd Job, Blofeld (stroking a toy cat), and Jaws—plus a battalion of astro-dancers. A Bond surrogate arrives onstage in a white Lotus Esprit, setting off explosions and green laser beams. Easton, now packing heat, finishes the number before lifting off into outer space with the spy who loves her. Only the Oscars of this era could transform the most dully heterosexual movie genre—Bond films—into the swishiest cabaret act.

This unhinged flamboyance seemed to be everywhere in the culture at the time, not limited to just one long evening at the Dorothy Chandler Pavilion. Even AM radio embraced extreme-camp peacocking, with the Village People charting two top-ten singles in the late '70s. As it happens, *Can't Stop the Music*, the 1980 box office disaster that purported to tell the origin story of that gaudy sextet, was cowritten and coproduced by Allan Carr, the proudly out, rotund, caftan-loving impresario who went on to oversee the 1989 Academy Awards.

The opening number of that show, which I, spellbound, watched on a dinky TV in a college dorm, still endures as the nadir—or apex—of Oscar lunacy. Carr paired a helium-voiced Snow White (played by Eileen Bowman) with a tone-deaf Rob Lowe in a cracked version of "Proud Mary." But that was only part of this deranged Mary's vision: Merv Griffin, singing "I've Got a Lovely Bunch of Coconuts" in a Cockney accent, introduced the Disney character to the Brat Packer on a set made to look like the Cocoanut Grove, where Tinseltown geriatrics (some barely mobile) like Roy Rogers and Dorothy Lamour were trotted out onstage and where the tables soon became animated dancing machines. According to Robert Hofler in *Party Animals*, his 2010 book about Carr, after the broadcast, Hollywood eminences such as Paul Newman, Gregory Peck, and Billy Wilder sent a letter to AMPAS calling the show "an embarrassment to both the Academy and the entire motion picture industry."

And so began the regrettable era of Oscar restraint and respectability. But that '89 show, produced by a man whose "unspoken goal," per Hofler, was "to bring gay into the Hollywood mainstream," succeeded in converting me into a card-carrying daughter of darkness: less than a year after Carr's fiasco, I was fully initiated into same-sexing, my place on the Kinsey scale undoubtedly the result of overexposure to decades of shameless exhibitionism.

—*Village Voice*, February 24, 2016

Portrait of a Lady on Fire

(Céline Sciamma, 2019)

Sapphically swoony but occasionally didactic, Céline Sciamma's *Portrait of a Lady on Fire* weighs down its love story with Linda Nochlin–esque digressions. Although set in 1770, this same-sex romance is deeply informed by the art-herstorical spirit of the 1970s, earnestly recalling Nochlin's famous query: Why have there been no great women artists? If the film lurches at times with schematic dudgeon—devolving into a checklist of coolly outraged points to be made—it also gloriously blooms as a tale of lesbian ardor.

Sciamma's movie, her fourth as writer-director and the winner of the best screenplay award at the Cannes Film Festival in May, opens with Marianne (Noémie Merlant) stiffly posing in a *robe battante* for her life-drawing students. "Take time to look at me," she instructs her dewy distaff charges (and, by extension, the film's spectators). One of her pupils has upset Teacher by bringing out from storage a painting—the title of which Sciamma's film shares—that Marianne created years ago. The canvas prompts a flashback of Marianne, laden with art supplies, in a small vessel keeling in choppy waters as it makes its way to the coast of Brittany. She has been dispatched to a seaside chateau to fulfill an assignment: painting the wedding portrait of Héloïse (Adèle Haenel), betrothed to a Milanese suitor.

Marianne must complete this commission surreptitiously, for Héloïse "refuses this marriage," as the reluctant bride's mother (Valeria Golino)—a countess whose own likeness was painted by Marianne's father—explains. A previous attempt at a portrait (by a male painter) had to be abandoned owing to Héloïse's refusal to cooperate; a shot of that unfinished picture yields the none-too-subtle sight of a headless woman. But now the comtesse has devised a ruse: Marianne will pretend to be Héloïse's companion, joining her on her daily littoral strolls and memorizing every aspect of her visage, to be re-created without her knowledge.

Sciamma wisely prolongs the wait for our first glimpse of the face of Héloïse/Haenel, who enters the film about 20 minutes in. She's initially seen from the back, stridently walking, then breaking into a sprint, halting perilously close to a cliff's edge. When she finally turns around to address Marianne, the moment thrills as a true star entrance, with Haenel's enormous, piercing emerald eyes seemingly filling half the screen.

Marianne may be tasked with scrutinizing Héloïse, but the unhappy aristocrat is just as ravenous for biographical information about her consort. In the best of these episodes, we witness the sheer delight that each woman experiences after being introduced to something novel by the other, as when Marianne plays a snippet of Vivaldi on the harpsichord for Héloïse, a former convent resident who has known only sacred music. In the worst, the interactions have the leaden quality of a Socratic dialogue. "Being free is being alone?" Héloïse asks rhetorically—and insipidly. After Marianne admits the truth about why she's really at the Breton manor—candor that moves Héloïse to actually pose for her—artist and subject engage in a dully sententious Q&A. To Héloïse's inquiry as to why women artists are forbidden from painting nude male models, Marianne responds: "It's mostly to prevent us from doing great art. Without any notion of male anatomy, the major subjects escape us."

Beyond these rehashed second-wave polemics, *Portrait of a Lady on Fire* grows wobbly with its utopian vision of an interclass sisterhood, in which Sophie (Luàna Bajrami), the young, tiny maid of the *grande maison*, enjoys an uncomplicated friendship with Marianne and Héloïse. While this amity occasions one of my favorite minor scenes—Sophie heating cherry pits to insert into a compress to alleviate Marianne's menstrual cramps, a sequence that puts a new spin on the term *period piece*—the triumvirate can sometimes appear as an empty emblem. One facile tableau shows the three women, hidden by tall grass, making themselves visible at the exact same moment; another reveals the trio, silhouetted in vespertine light, trudging in lockstep.

Yet the frustrating results of Sciamma's heavy hand (which also encumbered her previous feature, 2014's *Girlhood*, about female French African teenagers from the banlieues) are offset by the much more pleasing effects of her slow hand. By the time of Marianne and Héloïse's first kiss, deep into the film's second half, Sciamma has skillfully built up our anticipation of this pivotal event. Prior to that sensational smooch—which takes place, with an apt melodramatic flourish, under a sea arch—the director and her two principal performers have vivified the telltale signs of falling for someone. Each glance or pause that lingers a second too long communicates not just erotic longing but cerebral enmeshment. "Do all lovers feel they're inventing something?" Héloïse asks Marianne, in one of the film's best lines, shortly before they fall into bed. Languid and sex-drunk the morning after, they're clearly eager to start reinventing.

Carnal, tender, ignited by boundless curiosity, the love story between Marianne and Héloïse is rooted in a real-life romance: Sciamma wrote the part of Héloïse specifically for Haenel, her ex-girlfriend. The two first collaborated on

Sciamma's debut feature, *Water Lilies* (2007), in which Haenel plays the sexually manipulative captain of a high-school synchronized-swimming team; some years after that film's release, they became a couple. The actress famously came out by acknowledging her relationship with Sciamma during the 2014 ceremony for the Césars, France's equivalent of the Oscars. Concluding her acceptance speech after winning in the Best Supporting Actress category (for playing the more balanced of two sisters in Katell Quillévéré's drama *Suzanne*), Haenel haltingly said, "I wanted to thank Céline ... because ... because I love her, voilà."

Last month, Haenel spoke even more fervently about Sciamma. Their romantic past came up in the middle of a live follow-up interview Haenel did with *Mediapart*, a French investigative news site that published in early November a detailed article supporting the actress's claims that Christophe Ruggia, director of *The Devils* (2002), had sexually harassed her for three years, beginning with the shooting of that film, Haenel's first, made when she was just 12. Meeting Sciamma, Haenel explains, proved transformative: "We had a long and beautiful love affair together, and when I talk about people who saved my life I begin with her. ... She was someone who listened to me ... who listened to my anger." Likewise, Marianne gives Héloïse her undivided attention—without which no beautiful love affair can flourish.

—*4Columns*, December 6, 2019

Stonewall

(Roland Emmerich, 2015)

A campaign is underway, so the *New York Times* reported on Monday, to create a national park recognizing the Stonewall uprising of June 1969. As it happens, I read that article while en route to a screening of another commemoration of the legendary queer insurgency: Roland Emmerich's *Stonewall*, a ghastly project that places a lily-white muscle twink from Indiana as the tour guide for that pivotal event, with various trans characters and street queens of color assuming secondary roles and providing emotional succor to the Aryan beauty. The casting and storyline notoriously ignited another LGBTQ intifada in August—if only on the spleen-soaked battlefields of social media—after outraged viewers of the film's trailer called for a boycott. While insisting on the wholesale condemnation of any cultural product after having seen only a promo spot has never struck me as a savvy tactic, I'll admit that many of the political failings suggested by that roughly two-and-a-half-minute clip are fully borne out in *Stonewall*. What the trailer does not adequately prepare you for, however, are the movie's stupefying mise-en-scène and dialogue crimes.

Emmerich's film is not the first bad docudrama of the rebellion at 53 Christopher Street that ushered in the modern gay-rights movement: 20 years ago, Nigel Finch's *Stonewall* was released to similar complaints about its use of a white hayseed hunk as the main protagonist, ministered to and schooled by a multiracial group of gender nonconformists. Yet *Stonewall* '95, inspired by Martin Duberman's essential

1993 oral history of the lavender revolt, at least achieved some semblance of authenticity by virtue of being shot in the West Village and other Manhattan locations. Emmerich's *Stonewall*, in contrast, was shot in Montreal, its ersatz Sheridan Square seemingly constructed of discarded tubs of Boy Butter. The dominant hue of the film is a sickly yellow, a shade that lies somewhere on the spectrum between that of the cheese curds ladled on poutine and tearoom backsplash.

Best-known as the director of such bloated spectacles as *Independence Day* (1996), *Godzilla* (1998), and *The Day After Tomorrow* (2004), Emmerich clearly struggles when working with a budget of less than $20 million. That's not to say, though, that *Stonewall* is without special effects, namely inadvertent time travel. More than one of the songs—including the Staple Singers' "I'll Take You There," the film's anthem—that Danny (Jeremy Irvine, a vanilla nonentity), our Hoosier hero, and his new friends dance to at the Mob-controlled homo hangout were released several years after 1969. "Let's do this," says Seymour Pine (Matt Craven), the NYPD morals inspector who led the raid on the Stonewall Inn—and a seeming clairvoyant with knowledge of bro catchphrases that wouldn't become popular until decades later.

Stonewall was written by Jon Robin Baitz, who, like Emmerich, is openly gay—a detail that's salient only insofar as it offers further proof, as if any were needed, that same-sexers are sometimes the most egregious trivializers of queer history and the homosexual agenda. "I'm too mad to love anybody right now," cries newly militant, brick-hurling Danny to Ray (Jonny Beauchamp), who exists in the film solely to weep after being spurned by the midwesterner and who appears to be partly inspired by Sylvia Rivera, a real-life habitué of Stonewall and later a cofounder of Street Transvestite Action

Revolutionaries. Too besotted with this corn-fed, bubble-butt cicerone, Emmerich's film can stir only this response: Mary, *please.*

—*Artforum* online, September 23, 2015

The Misandrists

(Bruce LaBruce, 2017)

Combining the righteous zeal of '68 with the carnal fun of 69-ing, several films by the queer punk-porn polemicist Bruce LaBruce hinge on his talent for simultaneously, and hilariously, skewering and celebrating radical chic. *The Raspberry Reich* (2004), for instance, his far-out saga of fellating freedom fighters, centers on the Herbert Marcuse–spouting Gudrun, the leader of a gormless cadre of hunky Red Army Faction aspirants in Berlin. Her call to her followers to ignite "the homosexual intifada" leads to plenty of man-on-man action and more puckish—and, depending on your own political and sexual predilections, unimpeachable—sloganeering: "Heterosexuality is the opiate of the masses!" Inevitably, the Maoist messiah (whose first name is a nod to Gudrun Ensslin, one of the founders of the guerrilla RAF) and her acolytes are revealed to be a bundle of irreconcilable impulses and wild contradictions: with her incorrigible appetite for dong, Gudrun, for one, never practices what she preaches. Just as inexorably, their ultra-leftist platform is repurposed as a niche lifestyle come-on, giving rise to "terrorist nights" at a gay bar. "The revolution," Gudrun is forced to admit, "has been postponed."

More than a decade later, and after a dispiriting detour into gay-zombie movies, LaBruce expands on some of the topics dissected in *The Raspberry Reich* with an oblique sequel, *The Misandrists*. As terrifically titled as its predecessor (though nearly all the homo auteur's films are stamped with catchy names), LaBruce's latest sends up, while also saluting, another extreme doctrine: lesbian separatism. This piquant satire about man-haters evinces a kind of love for their ideology; LaBruce's ribald cine-tracts are often so funny because he has such deep, exacting knowledge of his targets.

Though the sapphically inclined have on occasion figured in LaBruce's work—notably in *Super 8½* (1994), which includes a dyke-porn impresaria among its principals—*The Misandrists* marks a milestone for the director: it's the first of his films to consist almost entirely of women, here a gender encompassing a wide variety of expression. *The Misandrists* is not just an invigorating alternative to the unending cascade of banal queer-themed fare. (My ardor for the film has only increased since enduring *Disobedience*, starring two A-list Rachels, Weisz and McAdams, tediously enacting lez lust.) It's also a stimulant to our impoverished political imaginations. If nothing else, LaBruce's outlandish scenarios activate thought experiments for those pondering a corrective to our present gynophobic kakistocracy.

Those less inclined toward sedition should still have a good time, provided they get a kick out of gender-reassigning linguistic interventions. An opening intertitle, establishing time and place, sets the tone and prompted my first chuckle: "1999, somewhere in Ger(wo)many." (Soon to follow are "womanifest," "womanage," and "womansplain"; I must indulge in the last verb on that list by pointing out that the coinage, a distaff twist on a term not popularized until more than a decade later, is an easily forgiven anachronism.) Frolicking and smooching in a field are Hilde (Olivia Kundisch) and Isolde (Kita Updike), two young comrades in the Female Liberation Army (FLA), a baker's dozen of wimmin supremacists led by Big Mother (Susanne Sachsse, who played Gudrun in

The Raspberry Reich and once again slays with her insurgent brio). Their petting is interrupted by Volker (Til Schindler), a wounded male Marxist on the lam. Taking pity on a fellow dissident, even one who belongs to the unspeakable sex, Isolde convinces Hilde to help her hide the fugitive in the basement of their separatist stronghold.

That plot strand is lifted directly from Don Siegel's *The Beguiled* (1971), a baroque tale of sexual hysteria. (*The Misandrists,* which had its festival premiere in February 2017, preceded Sofia Coppola's decorous, high-profile remake of that swampy Southern gothic by three months.) A key component of LaBruce's lavender agitprop is his unerring, wide-ranging cine-poaching. Just as *The Raspberry Reich* quoted Godard's *La Chinoise* (1967) and Dušan Makavejev's *WR: Mysteries of the Organism* (1971), among other titles, to advance its homosexual agenda, *The Misandrists* pays homage to a variety of films, spanning decades, nations, and traditions, to make the case for a no-man's-land: *Zero for Conduct* (1933), Jean Vigo's tale of boarding-school anarchists; *Therese and Isabelle* (1968), Radley Metzger's soft-core rendition of Violette Leduc's anguished memories of adolescent girl-on-girl action; *In the Realm of the Senses* (1976), Nagisa Oshima's landmark of erotic extremes.

Fun to spot, the citations typify LaBruce's breezy erudition. Arthur Schopenhauer is quoted while two other FLA combatants watch gay-male porn. Mandated—I mean womandated—by Big Mother, the viewing serves two purposes: as an extra-strength dose of aversion therapy and as technical instruction for the all-female XXX movies the separatists plan to make to fund their off-the-grid compound and recruit others to the cause. One of the chief matriarch's lieutenants, Sister Kembra (Kembra Pfahler, shero of the Cinema of Transgression and lead singer of the Voluptuous Horror of Karen Black), lectures the FLA fighters on parthenogenesis, delivering a science lesson on asexual reproduction as important as the Darwinism defended in *Inherit the Wind.*

But the texts that LaBruce seems most fluent in, and thus able to exalt and lampoon with equal precision, are the various idioms that dominated certain strains of second-wave feminism. A great bit features Sister Barbara (Caprice Crawford), another of Big Mother's adjutants, launching into a Gaia-infused, spoken-word-poetry-cadenced discourse on the superior gender's elemental characteristics: "A woman is a fever that never subsides. ... She is luna, and she is lacuna."

The goddess-y jibber-jabber may be giddily burlesqued, but other aspects of the FLA's essentialist praxis are scrutinized more seriously. Specifically, *The Misandrists* excavates the turf of TERFs—trans-exclusionary radical feminists—effectively pointing out the narrowness of a movement that defines *women* solely as those born with vaginas. "I believe that I am a woman as I am," pleads an FLA enlistee on the verge of being exiled for having the "incorrect" anatomy. Her claim broadens closed minds, both those of her sister-warriors and that of the recuperating male captive in the cellar. This time, the revolution isn't postponed but fully achieved. Roughly every other line in LaBruce's riotous, exhilarating movie deserves to be hashtagged in perpetuity, but here's hoping this FLA *cri de guerre* has a life beyond social media: Freedom for female people!

—*4Columns,* May 25, 2018

Tár

(Todd Field, 2022)

Dense with riveting talk and boosted by a mesmerizing performance from Cate Blanchett in the title role, Todd Field's film proves as seductive as the protagonist herself. Haughty, erudite, handsome, supremely accomplished, and regally gay, Lydia Tár, a world-famous composer and conductor, calls to mind both the "suave sappho" and the "lessoning lesbian," two archetypes in the unsurpassable taxonomy devised by Parker Tyler in his essential 1972 compendium, *Screening the Sexes: Homosexuality in the Movies*. These categories—the former exemplified by the soignée, fur-clad Stéphane Audran in *Les Biches* (1968), the latter by Dorothea Wieck's compassionate teacher at a girls' boarding school in *Mädchen in Uniform* (1931)—were not uncommon in pre-Stonewall depictions of lez romance, in which imbalances, whether of status, finances, age, power, or all of the above, served as the erotic engine. A contemporary embodiment of a 20th-century paradigm, Lydia is felled by modern-day methods: a distorted, unflattering video of the titaness that goes viral and a #MeToo scandal.

That *Tár*, for the most part, engages intelligently with highly charged sociopolitical issues that have fueled innumerable idiotic think pieces is just one of its many pleasing surprises. That this wholly original, effortlessly lofty film is by Field—an actor turned writer-director whose previous two features, *Little Children* (2006) and *In the Bedroom* (2001), were muddled literary adaptations of middle-class malaise and anguish in New England—is another. *Tár*'s greatest pleasure, though, may be its casting. Field wrote the film with only one person in mind: Blanchett, whose punctilious performing style I have often found stifling and off-putting. But, much as Blanchett's froideur was tapped so deftly for her portrayal of the eponymous character in Todd Haynes's *Carol* (2015)—his superb interpretation of *The Price of Salt*, Patricia Highsmith's 1952 sapphic romance—her starchy acting finds a perfect outlet in shaping Lydia's imperiousness. (In fact, Carol Aird, an older, more experienced mondaine who beguiles a 19-year-old department-store clerk, might be thought of as a forerunner of the classical-music deity.)

Focusing on just a few tumultuous weeks in the conductor's life, *Tár*, in an early sequence set at the *New Yorker* Festival, briskly establishes the protagonist's high-culture achievements: she graduated Phi Beta Kappa from Harvard; earned a PhD in musicology from the University of Vienna; had appointments at the five major US orchestras; won awards for composing; and, since 2013, has been the principal conductor of the Berlin Philharmonic, the first woman to hold the position. Interviewed onstage by Adam Gopnik (the host magazine's insufferable, long-standing fixture, who plays himself), Lydia's icy self-possession and skill at bewitching an audience are abundantly on display. After casually dismissing gender bias in her field—it's never held her back, at any rate—she eloquently holds forth on the wisdom imparted by Leonard Bernstein (a mentor of Lydia's and the film's lodestar), the marriage of Alma and Gustav Mahler (whose Fifth Symphony she is preparing to record), the epiphanies that emerge during rehearsal, and her upcoming memoir, *Tár on Tár*. (When uttered, those three monosyllables sound ludicrously pompous, as intended; the sly dig is even funnier once we learn more about Lydia's decidedly non-Europhilic background.)

At a reception following this Q&A, an effusive young woman flirts with the conductor, whose too-eager responses are closely monitored by her assistant, Francesa (Noémie Merlant); the adjutant, we gather, has had to intervene in these situations many times before. Next Lydia is off to a lunch meeting with Eliot Kaplan (Mark Strong), a dilettante conductor whose obscene riches as an investment banker have endowed a fellowship that Lydia founded to provide opportunities for young, aspiring female orchestra leaders; its alums include Francesca and a flame-haired woman (seen only fleetingly) named Krista, who was once, we are to infer, a plaything of Lydia's. Since spurned, Krista has been sending Francesca desperate emails and texts, which her increasingly anxious boss orders her to delete.

Often shot in long takes, Lydia's tête-à-têtes—with, among others, Gopnik, Eliot, and her wizened predecessor at the Berlin Phil, Andris (Julian Glover)—are showcases of volubility, absorbing conversations in which names like "Schopenhauer" and "von Karajan" flow effortlessly in the river of words. Her charisma and command grow even more when she is the sole speaker, switching from English to *Deutsch* and back again as she leads rehearsal sessions of the orchestra, whose first violinist, Sharon (the great Nina Hoss, seen too little here), is also Lydia's spouse. Whether the women, who live in a luxe, spectacular home in the German capital with their young daughter, were colleagues or lovers first remains deliberately unclear, just one more example of the conductor's pattern of blurring the boundaries between professional and private life—lines that Lydia seems intent on transgressing again with the newest member of the philharmonic, 20-something cellist Olga (Sophie Kauer).

With her elegantly tailored suits, Lydia brought to mind another sapphist well-known for her bespoke garments: Fran

Lebowitz, who once said, "There's too much democracy in the culture, not enough in the society." The towering virtuosa—long enshrined in an autocratic role, too drunk on her own power—would certainly agree with the first part of that statement. Confronted with Gen Z standards at a Juilliard master class (surreptitiously recorded), Lydia at first tries in good faith to counter the claim of a "BIPOC, pangender" student who professes to despise Bach for his "misogyny." She cautions against "siloing what is acceptable and unacceptable," exhorting this pupil not to "be so eager to be offended." What should have been a dialogue, however, ends up becoming a soliloquy.

When Lydia's inevitable downfall arrives in the final act, the otherwise cool, stately *Tár* spins out of control, and its final line proves too trite for a film so thoroughly committed to precision in ideas and language. The missteps do not ultimately detract, though, from the perverse thrill of witnessing such an intricate portrayal of a suave sappho, a lessoning lesbian, one whose Olympian brilliance and talent are vitiated by the most plebeian of shortcomings: petty vanities, desperate ego needs, pathetic hypocrisies.

—*4Columns*, October 14, 2022

The Wounded Man

(Patrice Chéreau, 1983)

The late French maestro Patrice Chéreau—who directed not only films but also operas and plays, led a highly regarded drama school, and acted occasionally—was drawn to stories of outsize, ungovernable emotions. In *Queen Margot* (1994), his most commercially successful movie, crazed kings sweat blood and royals rut in the street while all of Paris becomes a graveyard, the avenues clogged with butchered bodies in the aftermath of the Saint Bartholomew's Day Massacre. Similarly clamorous and densely populated, *Those Who Love Me Can Take the Train* (1998) also reveals Chéreau's talent for adeptly orchestrating psychic chaos, as a series of tempestuous couples and exes—of multiple sexualities—bicker, reconcile, and fall out once more.

Yet he also excelled at more modestly scaled portraits of people coming undone by their needs, particularly when they can't articulate them. That's especially the case with 1983's *The Wounded Man (L'Homme blessé)*, the new 4K restoration of which is now available on home video from Altered Innocence. Wanting to make a film about "the subproletariat of homosexuality," Chéreau drew inspiration from Jean Genet's highly autobiographical *The Thief's Journal* (1949). Chéreau and his cowriter, the novelist and photographer Hervé Guibert—both openly gay—worked on the script for six years. (Although it was Chéreau's third movie—following *The Flesh of the Orchid*, a baroque thriller from 1975 starring Charlotte Rampling at the peak of her decadent glamour, and

1978's *Judith Therpauve*, with Simone Signoret as a French Resistance vet determined to save a *gauchiste* newspaper—he would waggishly hail *The Wounded Man*, a much more personal project, as his first.) After finding that an adaptation of Genet's novel wasn't quite working, he and Guibert, as Chéreau explained in 1985, "kept only the basic idea: an impossible love story between a young boy and an older guy who disappears all the time."

That "young boy" is 20-year-old Henri (Jean-Hugues Anglade), who still lives at home—a flat so cramped that his parents sleep on a foldout sofa in the living room—in an unnamed town. While a fleetingly glimpsed pile of typewritten pages on his twin bed suggests either an academic pursuit or his own prose efforts, Henri appears to have nothing better to do with his time than accompany the family to the train station (an uncredited Gare du Nord), from which his younger sister is leaving for a program in Frankfurt.

But in one of the waiting rooms of the rail station, something feral awakens in this guileless youth, sporting a shawl-collar cable cardigan that further underscores his innocence. He locks eyes with Bosmans (Roland Bertin), a nattily attired, portly, middle-aged gent, who's long treated the transportation hub as a cruising ground. Henri seems at once attracted to and repelled by this man, aimlessly racing through the station—but is he hoping to escape or meet up with the fop? Descending into the bowels of the depot, Henri encounters a butch beauty named Jean (Vittorio Mezzogiorno, an Italian actor dubbed by Gérard Depardieu), who enlists the stripling to help him rough up an elderly john. The initiation rite complete, Jean rewards the tyro with a kiss.

So begins a frenzied, compulsive circuit for Henri, his manic actions punctuated by avant-jazz godhead Albert

Ayler's explosive saxophone on the soundtrack. He cannot stay away from the station for more than a few hours, where he pursues or is pursued by Bosmans, used by Henri in the hopes of being reunited with the elusive Jean, with whom he is besotted. Reedy and twitchy, Anglade appears here in his first lead role; he would become a star later in the '80s thanks to his work in the films of Luc Besson and Jean-Jacques Beineix, pioneers of the *cinéma du look*, a movement distinguished by its gossamer artifice and striking color palette. Although a few vibrant hues speckle Chéreau's film—the pink neons of the run-down carnival where Henri doggedly trails Jean; the red-and-white glow of a Coke machine (its exhortation, SERVEZ-VOUS, "Serve yourself," an apt tagline) next to a scrum of young hustlers huddled by a depot staircase—grim slate grays and other muted, muddied tones dominate.

Another of the basic senses prevails: *The Wounded Man* might be thought of as an exemplar of *cinéma du smell*. Effluvia seem to drift off the screen directly into our nostrils, whether Henri's BO (his mother remarks that he hasn't taken a shower in a while); the stench of the railway lavatory bustling with tearoom trade; the pungent scent of Jean's soiled uniform of blazer, T-shirt, and faded jeans—duds that, left behind in the apartment the brute stud shares with an infinitely forbearing girlfriend (Lisa Kreuzer), the much smaller Henri will don as yet another display of his deranging infatuation.

Shot in 1982—the same year the CDC first used the term *AIDS* to name the burgeoning health crisis that was only just beginning to be understood—*The Wounded Man* stands as one of the last films alighting on gay life that, although not technically produced during the pre-AIDS era, would not feel an obligation to address the disease. (Diagnosed with the illness in 1988, Guibert would candidly document the ravages of AIDS on his body in books and in a video, which aired on French television after his death in 1991.) Like *Cruising* and the German *Taxi zum Klo* (Taxi to the Toilet), both of which premiered in 1980, Chéreau's movie—the potency of its unsanitized eros diminished slightly by the too-predictable final-act *Liebestod*—blithely renounced the "positive images" then being demanded by gay activists. (That demand hasn't entirely faded away, of course, and is only one aspect of the larger, reductive debates surrounding the "politics of representation.")

Although gay characters appear in later Chéreau films—as in the abovementioned *Those Who Love Me Can Take the Train* and *Son Frère* (2003), which traces the rapprochement between two estranged siblings, one hetero, the other homo—he "never wanted to specialize in gay stories," as he told *The Guardian* in 2011, two years before his death at age 68. "Everywhere love stories are exactly the same. The game of desire, and how you live with desire, are the same," he added. *The Wounded Man* demonstrates the sordid transcendence, the ennobling ludicrousness of that game.

—*4Columns* May 19, 2023

Candy Darling: Dreamer, Icon, Superstar

(Cynthia Carr, 2024)

To travel from Massapequa Park, a small town on Long Island, to Penn Station on the LIRR takes about an hour. It was a commute that Candy Darling made countless times between 1962, the year she turned 18, and 1974, the year she died, at age 29. The return trip from Manhattan—where she would first meet Jackie Curtis, Andy Warhol, Paul Morrissey, Jane Fonda, Werner Schroeter, and so many other important collaborators and friends—often required Candy to travel under the cover of dark and to take a cab from the station directly to the Cape Cod house where her mom, Terry Slattery, lived, the same home that parent and child had moved to in 1957 following Terry's divorce from Candy's violent, alcoholic father. A loving mother, though never entirely without shame about her trans daughter, Terry did not want her glamorous child to be visible to gossiping neighbors. Candy, who never had a permanent home as an adult, whose underground cachet never translated to a living wage, had no choice but to endure the ignominious treatment whenever she had nowhere else to go. On those 60-minute LIRR sojourns, she had time to think. She would often write in her journal. Some of her entries are exceptionally profound, like this one, seemingly anticipating Judith Butler's ideas by decades: "I am not a genuine woman, but I am not interested in genuineness. I'm interested in the product of being a woman and how qualified I am. The product of the system is what is important. If the product fails, then the system is not good. What can I do to help me live in this life?".

How she answered that question during her too-abbreviated time on earth—she died of lymphoma, perhaps caused by the potentially carcinogenic female hormones she'd been taking on and off since 1965—is the subject of Cynthia Carr's compassionate and richly detailed *Candy Darling: Dreamer, Icon, Superstar,* the first full-fledged biography of a performer and personality who had a particular genius for interpreting and refracting the blonde goddesses of golden-age Hollywood. Carr's is also the first major remembrance that discusses Candy using an evolved discourse about trans lives. Nearly all the prior notable Candy commemorations, in various media, contain language or choices that today would be considered archaic at best.

The two Lou Reed–written songs that name-check her, for example, are putative homages laced with derision. "Candy Says" from 1969 begins: "Candy says, 'I've come to hate my body / And all that it requires in this world.'" Reed's most successful single, 1972's "Walk on the Wild Side," says this about Candy: "In the back room she was everybody's darlin' / But she never lost her head / Even when she was giving head." The selection of Stephen Dorff to play Candy in Mary Harron's Valerie Solanas biopic, *I Shot Andy Warhol* (1996), would be an unthinkable transgression in this decade, though the fact of the actor's cis manhood may be less vexing than his terrible portrayal. The year after Harron's movie saw the publication of *My Face for the World to See: The Diaries, Letters, and Drawings of Candy Darling, Andy Warhol Superstar,* a pale-pink volume styled as a clasped diary abounding with indelible first-person reminiscences, a few of which reappear in Carr's book. Some of the terms and phrases used in the otherwise loving prefatory material for *My Face*—inconsistent personal pronouns, "drag queen," "she was born a he"—now scan as injurious. Even a tribute from as late as 2010—the melancholic documentary *Beautiful Darling,* produced by and prominently featuring Jeremiah Newton, one of Candy's closest friends and the executor of her estate, and a key resource for Carr—includes comments from talking heads that rattle with their impolitic declarations about the subject's gender. (Casting here is also a problem: though never seen, Chloë Sevigny provides the "voice" of Candy when excerpts from her journals are read. Would a cis woman's ventriloquism for a legendary trans woman's innermost thoughts ever be tolerated in 2024?)

Deftly, without a trace of sanctimony, Carr, who dedicates her book "to the trans community," recounts Candy's life in a way that most honors and respects who she was, without erasing the terminology of a more benighted era. On reconciling the name Candy was given in 1944—James Lawrence Slattery—with the name she chose for herself, Carr writes in her introduction: "The terms 'dead-naming' and 'misgendering' did not exist during Candy's lifetime. ... She began her life as a tortured effeminate boy because she wasn't really a boy. She was always she, and I will be using she/her pronouns for her throughout." Carr always refers to her subject as Candy. But she lets stand the references to Candy as "Jimmy," "son," and "he" from her family and childhood friends. As Carr astutely explains, to do so otherwise would risk an ahistorical, less complex analysis: "To change their words is to deny the context that surrounded her—the disorienting childhood she had to negotiate while living in a homophobic, transphobic world with a boy's name and a boy's body. I have not sanitized that context."

Born in Queens, Candy spent most of her miserable childhood on Long Island. She noted in a 1970 journal entry that she "was a recluse at seven," shutting herself away after being tormented so often by other kids. She hated going to school—avoiding it "became the focus of her life"—and dropped out at 16. Her greatest salve and a foundational influence was the *Million Dollar Movie*, a kind of precursor to TCM, in which starry productions from the '30s, '40s, and '50s were broadcast on television. Rapt in front of the TV set, she was besotted with one studio-era blonde in particular: Kim Novak, whose oeuvre, especially *Picnic* (1955), *Jeanne Eagels* (1957), and *Bell Book and Candle* (1958), would greatly inform Candy's sardonic salute to highly stylized Tinseltown acting.

At 16, 17, her world began to expand, as did her ideas about herself and who she could be. (Carr notes that the first reference to "Candy" appears in '62, though monikers like "Hope" were also used; she settled on "Candy Darling" in '65.) A job at a beauty parlor in nearby Baldwin, Long Island, gave her a stage, a showcase for her blonde-bombshell imitations, and a very sympathetic female boss and confidante. In Baldwin, Candy also went to her first gay bar, the Hayloft. She began to wear makeup and women's clothes, changes she tried to keep hidden from her mother. When a meddling neighbor tipped Terry off, she confronted her child. Candy simply asked her mom to wait at the kitchen table; she returned "in a dress, looking gorgeous." As Terry explained to Newton years later, she had an immediate realization: "I couldn't hold my son back."

Manhattan beckoned. She gravitated to Washington Square Park, then a major queer hangout. The Bleecker Street apartment of an unsavory character named Seymour Levy—

Newton calls him a "chicken queen"—served as Candy's crash pad for several years. She did occasional sex work. She "had entered the demimonde ... and that was a comfortable spot for someone who was reinventing herself," Carr writes. "She'd become an outlaw the moment she put on a dress," Carr continues, owing to ancient city laws still on the books that criminalized cross-dressing. It was in this milieu that Candy would meet two other trans titanesses: Holly Woodlawn and Jackie Curtis. The latter, as movie-mad as Candy, wrote a tart spoof of Hollywood titled *Glamour, Glory and Gold,* in which Candy made her Off-Off-Broadway debut, in '67.

Friends, rivals, costars, these three would all become the last Warhol Superstars. Andy, who met Candy in '67, always had a soft spot for her; as Carr bluntly states, "He admired the way [she] could pass." Her entrée into the Factory led to two Paul Morrissey–directed films: 1968's *Flesh,* her screen debut, and 1971's *Women in Revolt* (more on these movies in a moment). Candy was often Warhol's plus-one at parties and openings; Carr notes that "she was beautiful, polite, witty, poised—the perfect date." She now sat with Warhol's crowd at Max's Kansas City, where she likely met Roger Vadim (who would become one of Candy's many short-term lovers) and his then-wife, Jane Fonda (with whom she would share a scene in the 1971 neo-noir *Klute*). It may have been at the Factory that she met Werner Schroeter, the German auteur who cast Candy in a supporting role in *The Death of Maria Malibran* (1972), a feverish tribute to the 19th-century opera singer of the title. Candy's work onstage continued apace: Jackie gave her the lead in the smash downtown production *Vain Victory: The Vicissitudes of the Damned* in '71; the next year, Candy graduated from Off-Off- to Off-Broadway, with the role of Violet, a waifish seductress, in Tennessee Williams's *Small Craft Warnings.*

Many of these career milestones, though, were accompanied by indignities and humiliations. She was paid $25 a day for her work in *Women in Revolt.* When Candy walked into the women's dressing room for *Small Craft Warnings,* the lead actress screamed, "Get it out of here!" Candy was assigned the broom closet, onto which she affixed a star. Her most crushing disappointment was not being cast in the role she considered herself the most eminently qualified to play: the lead in the 1970 film adaptation of Gore Vidal's *Myra Breckinridge,* his best-selling ribald satire about a trans woman with an encyclopedic knowledge of '40s movies (Raquel Welch was given the part; Candy never even got an audition).

Carr seamlessly incorporates these professional triumphs and setbacks within the larger context of Candy's "inchoate" and "paradoxical" life. The adjectives are apt, reflecting the era in which she lived. It was a time when the term *transgender* would not be widely used until at least two decades after her death (*transsexual* would have been the politest word, though Candy rejected it, identifying simply as a woman with a "flaw": her penis); when the concept of gender fluidity was all but nonexistent; when an immutable binary reigned supreme. "Candy would never be a sixties person," Carr writes, explaining one of her subject's many contradictions. "As the culture went through its sea change, into something rich and strange and occasionally violent, Candy wasn't really in sync. Issues that preoccupied so many of her generation ... didn't interest her. Nor did she ever assess her own situation as political. ... Yet her very existence was radical." Her own vision of femininity was conservative—"If I am going to be a woman, I want the whole thing: a home in the suburbs, a husband, and strange as it may sound, children," she wrote in her notebook. At the same time, she keenly sensed how *constructed* that ideal was, as the journal entry cited above indicates, a presaging précis of gender studies. Likewise, her attention to the superficial had its own kind of depth. "Candy knew that she was beautiful—but was it the right kind of beautiful? Her obsession with appearance was not rooted in narcissism," Carr observes. "It was how she affirmed her female identity in a world where there was very little support for even the idea of gender fluidity. Beauty was also useful to her as armor. She preferred that people focus on the surface."

Beyond Carr's discerning overview of Candy's life and epoch, she vivifies her biography with piquant details, the result of her thorough reporting. Lily Tomlin, then at the height of her *Laugh-In* fame, was so impressed by Candy that she arranged for her to have an audition at the renowned midtown cabaret Upstairs at the Downstairs. (The tryout went nowhere, but a year before her death, Candy landed the most lucrative gig of her career: being the opening act at the hot new nightclub Le Jardin, a forerunner of Studio 54.) Tomlin's partner in love and work, Jane Wagner, paid for Candy's badly needed dental care. Lauren Hutton, nearing her zenith as a top model, was immediately enchanted with the Superstar on their first meeting, a chance encounter at Halston's atelier. The most bizarre detail of their friendship: Hutton showed Candy how to tame a tarantula. The most touching: Hutton accompanied a terrified Candy to Cabrini Medical Center, the hospital where she would later die, insisting that she have a private room and giving her sick friend some of her own negligees.

So many of Candy's performances, the truest index of her genius, were never documented or are difficult to access. There isn't even a reliable description of her Le Jardin show; Carr notes, "There were no reviews, and the few remaining accounts do not quite correspond." Fortunately, *Flesh* and *Women in Revolt*, featuring two of her greatest star turns in her slim filmography, are available on the Internet Archive. They demonstrate her sublime gift for conjuring a specific kind of acting magic, in which her loving, studied replications of silver-screen luminaries are spiked with wry shrewdness. The mimicker is transformed into an original.

Candy Darling is the second of Carr's comprehensive studies devoted to a New York City legend who died much too young, following her superb 2012 biography of artist David Wojnarowicz, *Fire in the Belly*. That book never privileged the life over the work; paying assiduous, passionate attention to Wojnarowicz's polymathic output, Carr demonstrated her subject's brilliance and originality over and over again. Oddly, when it comes to writing about Candy's acting—*her* work—Carr often seems indifferent or obtuse. When discussing *Flesh*, in which Candy and Jackie are seated on a couch and read aloud from old movie magazines while Joe Dallesandro gets a blow job from Geri Miller, Carr merely recapitulates what happens in this segment and transcribes the dialogue. There is no analysis: no mention of how funny the incongruity is between Candy and Jackie's actions and Joe and Geri's or of the ways that Candy's supercilious, prudish delivery delights as a meticulously rendered takeoff on the affected, remote sex symbol that someone like Kim Novak epitomized in the 1950s. (Why Carr included this synopsis without offering any commentary is all the more puzzling in light of the fact that, during her 1984–2003 tenure at the *Village Voice*, she ranked among the preeminent critics of avant-garde performance.)

Carr's assessment of *Women in Revolt*—a riotous spoof of feminism, in which Candy stars with Jackie and Holly as members of PIG (Politically Involved Girls)—proves even more dispiriting. She complains of "scenes that go on way too long" and the film's "implausible notions" and incoherence: all hallmarks of the *entire* Warhol/Morrissey corpus, movies that were made to showcase personalities and cared nothing about plot or realism. Carr dismisses Candy—portraying a Park Avenue debutante who briefly has her consciousness raised only to abandon women's liberation to make it big in Hollywood—as "seem[ing] wooden in some of her scenes, playing the rich-girl as high-toned and snooty. It's a poor person's idea of a rich person." But Candy isn't after class verisimilitude; her acting is informed by her movie fandom, her idols cannily saluted *and* razzed at the same time.

Carr holds in higher regard a performance by Candy in a still, not moving, image: Peter Hujar's *Candy Darling on Her Deathbed,* taken in September '73, shortly after she was admitted at Cabrini Medical Center and the day before exploratory surgery revealed an enormous tumor that her doctor described as being "like a tree root growing." In full maquillage, lying on her side, cocooned in her hospital-bed duvet, a long-stemmed rose next to her, Candy masks her fear by assuming a pose she must have seen countless times before—when, as a lonely, bullied child, she studied the *Million Dollar Movie* with exacting scrutiny, dreaming of the woman she would become.

—*Bookforum,* Spring 2024

III.

Cinema, Industrial-Size and Smaller (with a focus on heterosexual depravity)

The Beguiled

(Sofia Coppola, 2017)

Ever since her feature debut, *The Virgin Suicides* (1999), a dreamy, diaphanous tale about the mysteries of girlhood, Sofia Coppola has ranked among cinema's finest distillers of mood (especially languor) and milieu. Those qualities abound in *The Beguiled*, her sixth film, an adaptation of Thomas Cullinan's Civil War–set novel of the same name (published in 1966), which was first transferred to the screen by Don Siegel in 1971. Coppola's version of Cullinan's Southern gothic (which I haven't read) differs wildly from Siegel's in tone: where his film is florid, frenzied, and swampy, hers is more restrained, composed, clement. This is not always a compliment.

Its action confined primarily to a Greek Revival mansion that houses a girls' school in the Deep South—where repressed desire hangs heavy in the air—*The Beguiled* opens with one of the few scenes to take place outdoors. (Coppola's film was shot at Louisiana's Madewood Plantation House, where Beyoncé set part of *Lemonade*'s "Sorry.") On a solo expedition, pigtailed peewee naturalist Amy (Oona Laurence), one of the institution's charges, encounters the unexpected while picking mushrooms: a wounded Union soldier, Corporal John McBurney (Colin Farrell), bleeding heavily under an oak tree that drips with Spanish moss. She aids the enemy combatant by leading him, their arms around each other, back to her academy, presided over by Miss Martha Farnsworth (Nicole Kidman), a hard-praying Christian who reluctantly agrees to take in the blue-belly.

Siegel's film, which stars Clint Eastwood at the height of his vulpine allure, just before his *Dirty Harry* incarnation, punctuates this rescue mission by having the grime-caked soldier give his young savior, no older than 12, a kiss on the mouth; the scene in Coppola's movie is smooch-free. That kiss—so predatory, so wrong—immediately establishes McBurney's sexual menace, a threat that Coppola chooses to reveal more gradually, more coolly. The drop in temperature largely results from the different affects of the performers playing the Union man. Eastwood's low, slow delivery is that of a seducer wholly confident in his ability to ensnare. Farrell, speaking in his native Hibernian brogue—his McBurney is an Irish mercenary—plays the character with more Old World courtliness and affability.

But the soldier is still a peerless flirt and manipulator. After stitching up McBurney's suppurating wound, Miss Martha installs him in the music room, where he soon becomes the object of fascination for all seven of the school's inhabitants. The headmistress continues to minister to her newest resident, her wet sponge shown in close-up as she inches it closer to his groin. The recuperating soldier's other frequent visitors include the dispirited instructor Edwina (Kirsten Dunst, in her third film with Coppola), first seen glumly going over the conjugation of *être* with three of her students, and Alicia (Elle Fanning, reteaming with the director for the first time since 2010's *Somewhere*), the eldest of the pupils and the most carnally curious and assured. Each bedside chat reveals the immobile man making promises that can only be broken and instigating rivalries among his helpmates—his cooing and cajoling leading to a gruesome payback.

Here, too, Coppola favors temperance, or at least a more controlled emotional turmoil, a sharp contrast to Siegel's baroque, bizarre ambience and backstory. The Marthas in both versions are fragile martinets. But in the '71 film, the school leader—played by Geraldine Page, who, as a veteran of Tennessee Williams productions, inhabited the part of the ultimately vengeful she-savage more nimbly than Kidman does—is tantalized by memories of the dead brother who was also her lover. Freaky flashbacks illustrate these incestuous reminiscences in Siegel's film, rife with other outlandish formal elements—like the superimposition of a swirling chandelier when McBurney is deep in a lip lock with one of his de facto harem.

The Beguiled '71 gluts; Coppola's film tamps down and reduces. Coppola and her cinematographer, Philippe Le Sourd, forgo ornate, unhinged visuals for simpler beauty: shafts of sunlight pouring through windows or through tree branches, candles illuminating a celebratory feast. Some of this stripping away includes excising a character: Hallie, the enslaved woman at the Farnsworth house so shrewdly portrayed by Mae Mercer in Siegel's movie, appears nowhere in Coppola's. "I didn't want to have [an enslaved] character in *The Beguiled* because that subject is a very important one, and I didn't want to brush over it lightly," Coppola says in the press notes. "This movie is about this one group of women left behind during the war." Intended as some kind of brave admission, the comment instead scans as evasion—as an unwillingness to grapple with vile truths, a reluctance to stray from decorousness.

For some, the sexual hysteria in Siegel's movie is ugly, an unrepentant expression of woman-terror. But I've always been fascinated by the sheer excess of '71's *Beguiled*, by the ways that its surfeit of lust and scheming somehow lays bare—and, in a perverse way, honors—the fury of the Farnsworth females. Coppola's *Beguiled*, like nearly every film she's made, teems with rich, period-exact surfaces. McBurney may suffer grievous bodily harm in *The Beguiled*, but Coppola's movie never breaks the skin.

—*Village Voice*, June 21, 2017

A Star Is Born

(Bradley Cooper, 2018)

A Star Is Born, a melodrama about the invincible love between a once-great talent sinking deeper into addiction and his rapidly ascending protégée, stands as one of moviedom's most enduring meta–fairy tales. And, like all fairy tales, it presents a set of symptoms for the amateur psychoanalyst, also known as the spectator, to decipher. The latest iteration of *A Star Is Born*—directed by Bradley Cooper, who acts opposite Lady Gaga—marks the fifth time the tale has been told. (George Cukor's *What Price Hollywood?*, from 1932, is the progenitor of the four films with the title *A Star Is Born* that have been made, beginning with William Wellman's 1937 version.) Is it more accurate to call this cherished property a franchise—or a manifestation of obsessive-compulsive disorder?

A star is born: the declaration chimes syntactically with "A Child Is Being Beaten," Freud's 1919 essay on fantasies, sadism, and masochism, all prevalent themes in Cooper's movie and its predecessors. Every interpretation of *A Star Is Born* is a hall of mirrors, featuring long-established A-list performers whose characters constantly reflect and refract the career trajectory of the real person playing them. The constellation of *Star*s is dense with ego-ideals, especially Cukor's 1954 rendition, a comeback vehicle for Judy Garland, who portrays a gifted singing and dancing hopeful devoid of the prodigious self-destructive urges that plagued the actress off-screen. Cooper's remake, the first *Star* of the 21st century (and the first since the 1976 redo, starring Barbra Streisand and Kris Kristofferson), is engorged with ambition. The project announces not only Cooper's directorial debut but also Lady Gaga's first leading role in a movie. But the stars here aren't reborn so much as they are rebranded.

I mean this less dismissively than it sounds. There's often tremendous satisfaction in witnessing the sheer level of commitment evinced by the film's two leads, especially by Cooper, who also cowrote the script (with Eric Roth and Will Fetters) and served as a producer. Cooper—who became a celebrity as one of the debauchees in *The Hangover* (2009) but soon thereafter established himself as a regular in the far more exalted films of David O. Russell—immediately, overwhelmingly proves the vastness of his goals for *Star* 5.0. In the film's opening seconds, we hear an arena crowd screaming—sound that reaches a deafening roar as we are introduced to Cooper's Jackson Maine, a roots rocker who washes down some pills with booze before tearing into the country-fried scorcher "Black Eyes."

As he does throughout the film, Cooper sings the number, which he cowrote, live; the guitar-wailing is also his own, not the product of an ax-dubber. Marveling at this scene, losing myself in its engulfing spectacle, I felt "little jabs of pleasure"—that memorable expression delivered in *Star* '54 by James Mason's Norman Maine to Garland's Vicki Lester, describing the elation of watching her sing. Those spiky thrills aren't limited to Cooper. Playing the mononymed Ally, the powerhouse-piped, bighearted aspirant whose gifts Jackson nurtures and whose success eventually surpasses his, Lady Gaga embraces her role in a vise grip—her dedication to Cooper's vision unwavering, her determination to prove herself in a new medium touching. (Like her costar, the duchess of dance pop also sings live in the film and cowrote and coproduced several tracks.)

And yet soon those little jabs of pleasure give way to something less tingly, safer: nods of admiration. Torquing Susan Sontag's definition of camp as "seriousness that fails," I think of Cooper's movie as seriousness that succeeds, but perhaps too well or too cleanly. A showcase for Cooper and Lady Gaga to demonstrate their proficiency in untested fields, the film becomes manicured and risk-averse. What's missing is a sense of the *brutality* of performing, singing especially—its demands on both the performer and the audience—that Sam Wasson, in his biography *Fosse* (2013), elucidates so indelibly when describing a young, pre-*Cabaret* Liza Minnelli: "Liza had a big voice, one that conveyed the punishing truth about making entertainment: It was mean. It was messy. It was a C-section and she was both mother and baby." A star is born, cut out of the womb: blood is on the floor and flesh must be stitched back together.

The analogy—gruesome and unimpeachable—also applies to the star who birthed Liza: Judy Garland, particularly in Cukor's *Star*, a film that can leave a viewer reeling from not only the actress-singer-dancer's titanic talent but her equally enormous vulnerability and tremulousness. Lady Gaga, in contrast, shows grit yet never exposes herself too much. As Ally—who sports a Yes T-shirt and shuns makeup in several of her initial scenes—develops her own musical style, branching off from Jackson's unalloyed turbo-blues, she begins to dress and sound more and more like ... Lady Gaga: neo-glam maquillage and costumes, tinny synth-R&B anthems.

Cooper follows a different tack, sounding nothing like himself. He trained for months to lower his voice an octave, a raspy rumble thickened with a southwestern drawl (Jackson hails from Arizona). He sounds, in other words, just like Sam Elliott. That impressively mustached screen vet, a frequent portrayer of cowboys and other exemplars of laconic masculinity, here plays Bobby, Jackson's much older brother and fed-up manager. The aping is acknowledged; the siblings nearly come to blows over the fact that Jackson "took" Bobby's voice. But it's an odd gambit. Cooper reveals his prowess at reconstructing his voice, seeming to dare us to check the basso timbre against the original model—and to heartily, quickly concur that the pupil should be awarded an A-plus.

A bigger problem is what those voices are saying. Advising and quickly falling in love with Ally, Jackson utters hokey homilies that we are meant to receive as profoundest insight: "Talent comes from everywhere, but having something to say and a way to say it so that people listen to it, that's a whole other bag." Ally, during a visit with Jackson in rehab—his destination after he humiliates her with his drunken bumbling at the Grammys, where she has just been crowned Best New Artist—grants him a hollow, anodyne dispensation: "It's okay. It's not your fault. It's a disease." Or is the fault in our stars?

—*4Columns*, October 5, 2018

Ad Astra

(James Gray, 2019)

We are in the midst of a zero-gravity craze. In the past year, a crop of movies about outer-space travel, both fiction and fact (or fact-based), have been released. Not all have been successful launches. Some—like the glum Neil Armstrong biopic *First Man*, directed by Damien Chazelle and featuring Ryan Gosling in the lead role, and the archival-footage-bonanza *Apollo 11*, a documentary assembled by Todd Douglas Miller—were clear tie-ins to the 50th anniversary of the moon landing. Others, such as Claire Denis's outré *High Life*, find, in their interstellar milieu, a vast canvas on which to explore psychosexual fantasias. Set in "the near future," James Gray's *Ad Astra*, the latest entry in this mini-movement, is a galactic fable devoted to dismantling certain myths: about the folly of ambition, about sclerotic codes of masculinity. The film's Latin title means "to the stars." But the satisfactions of Gray's project lie in a special branch of astronomy—the study not of planets, etc., but of the supernova at the center of *Ad Astra*: Brad Pitt.

Pitt plays Roy McBride, a rocket man who, in the movie's opening minutes, assures us via voice-over, a device used throughout *Ad Astra*, which Gray cowrote with Ethan Gross, that he loves his work: "I always wanted to become an astronaut." Yet just the slightest hint of doubt can be heard in this putatively unequivocal declaration. Roy—renowned at SpaceCom, his employer, for his imperturbability, evidenced in a heart rate that never rises above 80 beats per minute—

seems to be straining to convince himself as much as the audience of his ardor for his profession.

Roy's apprehension increases over the course of the film, as he embarks on a mission to Neptune to discover what happened to his father, Clifford (Tommy Lee Jones). McBride père, "the most decorated astronaut in the history of" SpaceCom, disappeared near the eighth planet more than a decade ago; he may be responsible for setting off the cosmic activity that's been killing earthlings by the thousands.

During his nearly three-billion-mile voyage, Roy makes stops at the moon and Mars, responds to a mayday call, and grapples with discomfiting truths about his dad—and himself. Roy's voice-over grows more self-castigating: "I've let so many people down." Flashbacks reveal the disappointed face of Eve (Liv Tyler), Roy's wife, from whom he's now separated.

I will confess that I found much of Roy's first-person narration corny, especially in *Ad Astra*'s final third, when the introspective celestial voyager determines to break free of the poisonous patriarchal ideology that Clifford has spent his life propagating. I will also admit that any annoyance I experienced over this soliloquizing did little to diminish the pleasure I took in gazing at Pitt, who's often filmed in extreme close-up. To explain this apparent contradiction, I must cite the cine-sage Boyd McDonald, who wrote about films in the '80s for gay publications like *Christopher Street* and who, as this excerpt from his appreciation of the actor Richard Widmark shows, clearly had his priorities in order: "He demonstrates the importance of the movie star over the movie and thus the importance of star reviews over mere movie reviews, with their constant complaints about plot. A movie is the last place in the world to look for literary distinction. But there are hundreds of players, men and women, whose work I find worth watching in any picture they make."

Born in 1963, Pitt, to my mind, is the only A-list male performer over the age of 50 who has been unfailingly charismatic throughout the long arc of his career, magnetism that has only deepened as he has aged. That allure was abundantly displayed this summer in Quentin Tarantino's *Once Upon a Time ... in Hollywood*: as Cliff Booth, the underemployed stuntman Pitt portrays, the actor poignantly combines rakish charm and middle-aged vulnerability. (His antithesis is George Clooney—two years Pitt's senior and his costar in *Ocean's Eleven*, from 2001, and its two sequels—whose debonair detachment has curdled into sour smugness over the decades.)

While Roy's off-screen narration in *Ad Astra* can at times verge on the garrulous, he is a man of few words during the on-screen action. His silence shouldn't be confused with stoicism, though. On his solo mission, tears fill his eyes. Overwhelmed by painful memories—of his father, of his own failings—he crumples in anguish. These unguarded moments are made all the more touching by the shades of sorrow that sweep across Pitt's face: a beautiful vista of still-boyish handsomeness that bears the signs of senescence—the wrinkles, the pouches under the eyes, the no-longer-drum-taut cheeks—with grace rather than terror.

Ad Astra may be a work of science fiction. But it is also a male weepie, a genre to which Gray, who favors emotional extravagance—manifest in his earlier films like the romantic tragedy *Two Lovers* (2008) and the 1920s period piece *The Immigrant* (2013)—is especially well-suited. Gray is an unabashed melodramatist, drawn to affective excess, prone to recycling the hoariest of clichés in his scripts; *Ad Astra*'s voice-over reaches its nadir when Roy muses, "In the end, the son suffers the sins of the father." Yet crucially Gray is not a shameless sentimentalist, a fitting descriptor for a filmmaker like Alfonso Cuarón, whose space opera *Gravity* (2013) revolves around a protagonist larded with a backstory involving a dead daughter; Roy and Eve are, thankfully, childless.

Although *Ad Astra* is occasionally vexing to listen to, it is always astonishing to look at. Gray and his cinematographer Hoyte van Hoytema have created a work of dazzling spectacle; indelible tableaux include Roy descending (and later falling from) a ladder of unfathomable height and a hypnotic walk he takes down a corridor while on a base at Mars—a slo-mo amble seemingly light-directed by James Turrell. The dread-drenched, inconceivable enormity of the galaxy recalls that found in Stanley Kubrick's *2001*, a masterwork of anti-psychology to which Gray's movie serves as temperamental opposite. And yet for all of *Ad Astra*'s visual acumen, the technical virtuosity remains subordinate to the movie's greatest special effect: the maturing, tear-dampened visage of an actor who emits a force field more powerful than earth-destroying cosmic rays.

—*4Columns*, September 20, 2019

Django Unchained

(Quentin Tarantino, 2012)

As irritating, if not quite as inflammatory, as a hemorrhoid, Quentin Tarantino's *Django Unchained* makes a queasy Oscar-season obverse not to Steven Spielberg's *Lincoln*, as some have suggested, but to Kathryn Bigelow's *Zero Dark Thirty*. Though operating in vastly different genres—*ZDT* is a fact-based thriller about events of the past 11 years, *Django Unchained* an antebellum revenger deeply in thrall to spaghetti westerns and blaxploitation movies—both are responses to eras in which the torture and subjugation of other human beings was part of US policy. One film unequivocally presents the horror of legally sanctioned physical abuse; the other is a little turned on by it.

Django Unchained, Tarantino's eighth film (or seventh, if you count the bisected *Kill Bill* as one entity), operates in the same avenging-angel vein as his previous movie, the World War II–set *Inglourious Basterds* (2009), in which Nazis are scalped and set aflame. In both films, the writer-director imbues his florid cinephilia, the engine of all his productions, with the power to wield divine retribution, to turn history's most vile abusers into its most cowering victims. This cartoonish fantasy works quite well in *Inglourious Basterds*: there is indeed something deeply, perversely satisfying about watching SS officers beg for their lives or the instantaneous combustion of the higher-ups of the Third Reich, gathered to attend a screening of a Nazi propaganda film.

Yet the cathartic thrills of witnessing that righteous, murderous revenge are gravely compromised in *Django*

Unchained by Tarantino's obsession with the ghastly torments inflicted on those who were considered chattel. The film opens in 1858 in Texas, where Teuton bounty hunter King Schultz (Christoph Waltz), posing as a dentist, buys Django (Jamie Foxx) from his enslavers. In exchange for the now-freed man's assistance in a contracted kill, the good German promises to reunite Django with his wife, Broomhilda (Kerry Washington, her character's improbable name explained in a signature Tarantino digression), and rescue her from the sociopathic plantation owner Calvin Candie (Leonardo DiCaprio) in deepest Mississippi.

A whole mess of nasty peckerwoods and slavers will get their due, either from bullets pumped into them or from sticks of dynamite detonated. These are high-volume, generic deaths, filling the screen with so much red or orange. Where Tarantino really likes to pull the camera in close is during those moments that further objectify the already abject. Punished for trying to run away, an enslaved man is torn to pieces by dogs (a scene returned to in flashback); two shirtless, perspiration-soaked Black men bare-knuckle battle for Candie's pleasure (the victor of this "Mandingo fight" being the one who doesn't die). Most egregiously, a slow pan down the body of a naked Django, strung up by his feet and only seconds away from castration by a Candie henchman, captures every taut muscle, every bead of sweat.

About the one white man who isn't a blue-eyed devil: Schultz is unmistakably a benevolent force, but Waltz is essentially reprising the role he played in *Inglourious Basterds*, in which he dominated the screen as the suave Nazi colonel Hans Landa. Both Landa and Schultz are exceptionally eloquent polyglots whose perorations seem to punctuate every scene. So much screen time, in fact, is devoted to Schultz's orotund speeches that taciturn Django ("I don't know what 'positive' mean") is frequently overshadowed. In this, Tarantino's film, for which he has coined a new genre, the "southern," resembles not so much his beloved spaghetti westerns or Richard Fleischer's notorious, similarly themed 1975 melodrama, *Mandingo* (which the late, great critic Robin Wood passionately, if not altogether convincingly, once hailed as "the greatest film about race ever made in Hollywood"), but *The Blind Side*.

—*Artforum* online, December 24, 2012

Fifty Shades of Grey

(Sam Taylor-Johnson, 2015)

The staggering popularity of E. L. James's 2011 erotic novel and BDSM primer, *Fifty Shades of Grey*, particularly among a certain female demographic, gave rise to the condescending genre tag "mommy porn." However disdainful the label might be, my own anecdotal experience on various modes of transportation suggests that the book's most conspicuous readers—those who preferred actual paper products, with emblazoned covers, to anonymity-ensuring Kindles or Nooks—were indeed mothers: on the subway I've spotted several moms, their kids next to them and absorbed in their own distractions, lost in James's prose; on a Paris-bound Eurostar two years ago, I looked up to see a woman, whose husband and two young children were playing cards, turning the pages of *Cinquante nuances de Grey*.

The brazen spirit of those readers is entirely absent in Sam Taylor-Johnson's adaptation of James's bestseller, whose central couple is 21-year-old virgin Anastasia Steele (played by Dakota Johnson, charming and sleepy-eyed) and a dom six years her senior, Christian Grey (Jamie Dornan, an Irishman whose strenuous attempt to effect a flat American voice seems to have left him too tired to wield the flogger with much authority). Yet through her largely sanitized retelling of Anastasia's deepening thralldom to a billionaire telecommunications entrepreneur with an extensively kitted-out playroom, Taylor-Johnson spares viewers from the source material's greatest liability: James's own voice and writing tics, which suggest nothing so much as a nonlubed and nonconsensual fist fuck of the English language. Told from Anastasia's first-person point of view, the novel bafflingly anthropomorphizes its heroine's psyche, split into her "inner goddess" ("My inner goddess has her pom-poms in hand—she's in cheerleading mode") and "subconscious" ("My subconscious has found her Nikes, and she's on the starting blocks"). Equally appalling are James's similes ("Anticipation hangs heavy and portentous over my head like a dark tropical storm cloud").

Taylor-Johnson, the former YBA whose only feature prior to this one is the wan John Lennon biopic *Nowhere Boy* (2009), and screenwriter Kelly Marcel do, however, retain much of the dialogue from the original, such as Christian's avowal "I don't make love. I fuck ... hard"—the repeated demonstration of which in James's novel is what made it a publishing phenomenon in the first place. In the film, though, the tech magnate's boast largely has to be taken on faith: rapid edits during the sex scenes—whether vanilla or involving spanking, blindfolds, restraints, etc.—fragment the body, Johnson's curled toes or agape mouth serving as semaphore for carnal abandon. Further lulled by the movie's redundant soundtrack ("I Put a Spell on You," "Beast of Burden," and so on), I remained alert by comparing *Fifty Shades of Grey* with some of its predecessors, R-rated movies that also prominently feature role-playing and/or their virginal protagonists tied spread-eagle to a bed like, to name just two titles from the same decade, Paul Schrader's *Cat People* (1982) and Adrian Lyne's *9½ Weeks* (1986). If *Fifty Shades of Grey* the movie has anything to teach us, it's that today's MPAA appears to be reverting not just to the Hays Code but to the Old Covenant.

Then again, heterosexual, "transgressively" erotic entertainments from 30 years ago weren't subject to the demands of brand management and corporate synergy. A visit to fiftyshadesmovie.com invites potential ticket buyers to "share your girls night out plans" (coupled, Valentine's Day–celebrating spectators have a separate slide on the site); the *New York Times* recently noted that Target has been selling an official movie tie-in "vibrating love ring." And so, in the interest of consumer reporting, I'll say this: the book isn't better than the movie, and the film isn't better than the book. Both are inferior to the tableaux I imagined playing out in the heads of my fellow rail passengers as they took in—willingly and avidly, with no safewords needed—James's more successful sentences.

—*Artforum* online, February 11, 2015

Moonlight

(Barry Jenkins, 2016)

A question is posed to the main character of Barry Jenkins's wondrous, superbly acted new film, *Moonlight*: "Who is you, man?" The beauty of Jenkins's second feature, which follows *Medicine for Melancholy* (2008), a romance centered on Black bohemians in San Francisco, radiates from the way that query is explored and answered: with specifics and expansiveness, not with foregone conclusions. It is asked by a Black man of another Black man—men to whom so much poisonous meaning and deranged mythology have long been ascribed, men too often not deemed worthy to be given a chance to respond to this most fundamental of inquiries.

Divided into three chapters, *Moonlight* tracks its protagonist, Chiron, in as many stages, each titled with his name or nickname: at ages nine ("Little," played by Alex Hibbert), 16 ("Chiron," Ashton Sanders), and approximately 26 ("Black," Trevante Rhodes). The film takes place primarily in Liberty City, a housing project in Miami where Jenkins grew up, as did the playwright Tarell Alvin McCraney, whose unproduced drama *In Moonlight Black Boys Look Blue* the filmmaker adapted for the screen. Like Jenkins and McCraney were, Chiron is being raised by a drug-addicted mother, Paula (Naomie Harris).

Crucially, in the movie's first section, Little is also being cared for and guided by Juan (Mahershala Ali), a local drug kingpin who provides the crack that is ravaging Paula; Juan's house—which the trafficker shares with his even more doting girlfriend, Teresa (Janelle Monáe, fantastic in her big-screen debut)—is where the boy runs to when life with Mama proves too much. This is one of the many painful contradictions in the film, which are highlighted without being ceaselessly underscored: an empty dope hole, in fact, will serve as a sanctuary for Little, first seen rushing past Juan as the child tries to outrun three tormentors, followed by cinematographer James Laxton's sinuous, pirouetting camera. The boy finds refuge in the boarded-up house and holds an empty crack vial to the light, a stretch of silence that Hibbert, among the most watchful young performers I've ever seen, makes spellbinding.

Extricated from the drug den by Juan, Little, in this and in most of his interactions with his surrogate father, will remain wordless. He is too consumed with absorbing all of Juan's communication, whether verbal or non-. Juan teaches the boy to swim, cradling him, pietà-like, in the ocean. His counsel to his charge is just as loving: "At some point you gotta decide who you gonna be. Can't let nobody make that decision for you."

But others, like those kids chasing him, have already made up their minds about who and what Little is: "soft," "a faggot." (McCraney is gay; Jenkins is not.) The taunting and abuse become worse in *Moonlight*'s middle section, all while teenage Chiron, whose beanpole build only exacerbates his vulnerability, struggles to make sense of his own desire. He is able to express it near the same patch of beach where he had that earlier swimming lesson. The encounter is initiated by a friend named Kevin (played as a teenager by Jharrel Jerome), a boastful, nominally straight lothario who shares—and is turned on by—his quiet pal's inchoate yearning "to do a lot of things that don't make sense." *Moonlight* was shot in widescreen, to fully capture both Miami's languorous, sunstroked beauty and that of extremely intimate moments like this one between Kevin and Chiron, their surfeit of feeling expanding out to the farthest reaches of the screen.

A betrayal in the second section leads to more than one reconciliation in the third and to an even swoonier kind of romance. In his mid-20s and now living in Atlanta, Black (the sobriquet was bestowed on Chiron by Kevin in high school) has entered his onetime mentor's profession and has built up a carapace of muscle. A phone call from Kevin (played as an adult by André Holland), the first time Black has heard from him in a decade, prompts a drive back to Florida and a reunion that—filled with so much pain, regret, omission, tenderness, and love—is almost too much to bear. Here, again, the film calls attention subtly yet sharply, in a few lines of dialogue, to appalling realities of warehoused Black male bodies, of the prison-industrial complex. "I got sent up for some stupid shit," Kevin, grinning, tells his old friend as they're catching up in the diner where he now does double duty as a waiter and cook. "Same stupid shit they always put us away for."

After the restaurant clears out, Kevin plays a song on the jukebox for Black—I won't name the title for fear of ruining the surprise; the track, like all the others heard in *Moonlight*, beautifully distills a mood. The lyrics serve as an apology and maybe even a seduction. Both times that I've watched *Moonlight*, I've been reminded of a work that precedes it by almost 30 years and that was made in an entirely different idiom: Marlon Riggs's *Tongues Untied* (1989), a personal video essay full of spoken-word poetry and monologues about desire, shame, and racism that declares, "Black men loving Black men is the revolutionary act." In Jenkins's film, that love—whether carnal, paternal, or something else—has many permutations. It also need not extend to another person. "I'm *me*, man," Black replies when Kevin asks him that key question mentioned above, a declaration of ever-endangered pride and self-worth.

—*Village Voice*, October 19, 2016

Red Sparrow

(Francis Lawrence, 2018)

Jennifer Lawrence is the emblematic performer of current screen dystopias. She became one of the highest-paid actresses in the world owing to her recurring role as Katniss Everdeen, the flinty teen heroine of *The Hunger Games* tetralogy (2012–15), set in an unspecified, postapocalyptic future in which the citizens of Panem, a nation formed from the ruins of North America, are mandated to watch televised kid-on-kid savagery. The A-lister reteams with Francis Lawrence, who directed all but the first film of that franchise, for *Red Sparrow*, a dour, disagreeable spy thriller that takes place in actual countries—the former Eastern Bloc—in a time that's just about now. Rooted in some version of reality, *Red Sparrow* nonetheless suggests a bleaker hellscape than anything found in imaginary Panem.

The movie opens with its heroine, Dominika Egorova, played by Lawrence, enjoying a moment of tranquility—one of the few instances in this nearly two-and-a-half-hour film when her body isn't imperiled or brutalized. She sits on her bed in a meditation pose, listening to music before rushing to tend to her disabled mother, with whom she shares her spartan Moscow flat. Lawrence's delivery of her perfunctory first line—"You're awake, Mama"—signals, in just five syllables, not only the lazy, low-camp Russian-accented English spoken by most of the international (though largely Anglophone) cast but also the overall leadenness of the film.

After we watch Dominika carry out various tasks that further underscore her filial devotion, we learn that she is more than just a dutiful daughter. Dominika races off to the Bolshoi, to perform in what will be her final ballet: her partner drops her and her leg is irreparably damaged. But the career-destroying error was no accident, as the prima ballerina's uncle Vanya (Matthias Schoenaerts)—a high-ranking official in Russia's intelligence agency and the much younger brother of Dominika's dead dad—proves to his niece with grainy black-and-white photos that reveal plotting by two of her corps members. (Though his character's name evokes Chekhov and czarist Russia, Schoenaerts bears more than a passing physical resemblance here to Vladimir Putin.) The evidence will lead her to commit the first of two bludgeonings in a steam-filled locker room.

That is not the sole example of repetition. *Red Sparrow* abounds in quasi-profundities uttered more than once. "Every human being is a puzzle of need" lingers afterward as one of the more successful of these maxims; it is initially articulated by a character known only as Matron (a role that Charlotte Rampling, in the movie's lone instance of felicitous casting, vivifies with droll flourishes). Matron oversees the training at State School Four, or "Sparrow School," where Dominika, now desperate for funding for herself and *matushka* since her Bolshoi sponsorship has ended, has been dispatched by Vanya to learn how to seduce—and compromise—the enemy. (Before shipping her off to sex-as-a-weapon finishing academy, Vanya had sent his niece on a test run of honey-trapping, an incident that sordidly plays out like a Harvey Weinstein–at–the–Peninsula tableau.)

"The Cold War did not end. It shattered into one thousand pieces," Matron lectures her charges—making explicit the nominal political argument of the film, axiomatic to any spectator who has been sentient since 1991. (*Red Sparrow* is based on the 2013 novel of the same name, which I haven't read, by Jason Matthews, who turned to fiction writing after a 33-year career with the CIA; the screenplay is by Justin Haythe.) "Only Russia is willing to make the sacrifices to be invincible," she continues, as the comely young trainees, mostly women, "learn to love on command," exercises played out primarily with the opposite sex. A hand job Dominika administers is recorded and projected on an IMAX-size screen for her classmates to analyze. Forced to succumb, at Matron's insistence, to a fellow recruit who, a day earlier, tried to rape her, the spy apprentice reveals that she may have smuggled in some samizdat Susan Brownmiller: "Power. That's what he wants," Dominika declares, an assessment that detumesces her assailant.

But despite her familiarity with the tenets of intro-level gender studies, Dominika is not a feminist of any kind—the decrees of the female-led espionage thriller demand that the heroine adhere only to the politics of pummelings, as last summer's graphic-novel-based *Atomic Blonde*, starring Charlize Theron, also made clear. The earlier film, though, set in Berlin just before and after the toppling of the Wall, benefited from kicky synth-pop energy and a riveting central performance. Theron brought an appealing aloofness to her role as an MI6 agent, a sly froideur that still generated heat. Lawrence, in contrast, plays her part as a complete blank: she's a void made even more robotic by her silly pseudo-Slavic intonation.

However distinct, *Atomic Blonde* and *Red Sparrow* each have an increasingly labyrinthine storyline. Yet only the latter was accompanied by a comma-deficient plea from the director to journalists, in a bit of PR dark arts that has become all too common, to "keep all major plot points including the ending secret." It would be impossible for me to "spoil" anything I couldn't coherently recapitulate, but I hope Francis Lawrence won't be too upset if I mention that Dominika's first assignment after "whore school" (her words) takes her to Budapest, where she is to get friendly with Nate Nash (Joel Edgerton), a CIA operative who serves as the point of contact for a Russian mole.

With Dominika's relo to Hungary, *Red Sparrow*'s violence grows more baroque: one character, subject to a whirring skin grafter, has strips of his epidermis brandished by his attacker as if the thug were showing off a prize Fruit Roll-Up. Against this barbaric backdrop, Dominika and Nate, enemy spies, fall in love. Or do they? Watching the two engage in some countertop rutting, I thought of another of Matron's directives: "You must inure yourself to what you find repellent." *Red Sparrow*, a joyless genre exercise, inadvertently advances the premise that most, maybe all male-female mating could be thought of as a ruse, the basest kind of transaction, the bleakest form of pleasure. And thanks to that unwitting thesis, *Red Sparrow*, a film putatively about the further immiseration of the post-Soviet world, allowed this restless viewer to engage in an outlandish thought experiment: imagining the post-heterosexual era.

—*4Columns*, March 2, 2018

Song to Song

(Terrence Malick, 2017)

Each new film that Terrence Malick, the once notoriously unhurried director, has made in the rash of projects since *The Tree of Life* (2011) evinces a further regression, an increasingly witless sacralizing of male-female coupledom. The title of Malick's latest, *Song to Song*, set in Austin against the backdrop of that city's South by Southwest music festival, is just a preposition and an *s* removed from Song of Songs, the Old Testament celebration of sexual love (which, unlike this movie, is genuinely lusty); the biblical evocation signals the vaporous quasi-spirituality to follow from the feeble philosopher of man-woman relations. The auteurist affectations and tics that have come to define the various labile dyads—always rupturing and reconciling beneath crepuscular skies—in *Song to Song* and its immediate predecessors, *To the Wonder* (2012) and *Knight of Cups* (2015), have produced in this viewer a condition that I can only diagnose as heterophobia.

As with most Malick movies released during this century, there is only the barest frame of plot in *Song to Song*, the particulars of which are often incoherent or vague; even character names seem to be superfluous, prosaic details that can only interfere with the director's lofty vision. The one protagonist whose name I did catch (the others I learned from scanning the press materials afterward) is Faye, played by Rooney Mara. She is an endeavoring musician (evidenced by the electric guitar she half-heartedly strums once or twice) in a relationship, achronologically charted, with Ryan Gosling's BV, a songwriter and associate of Cook (Michael Fassbender), an Armani-clad rock 'n' roll executive and debauchee who once employed Faye. The boss and former underling betray BV, the ramifications of which are haphazardly parceled out; in the aftermath of this tryst, Cook will seem to be on a more righteous path when he marries Rhonda (Natalie Portman), a bottle blonde whose choice of profession—she's a kindergarten teacher supplementing her income with hash-slinging—telegraphs an innate goodness soon to be ludicrously corrupted.

Of this central quartet, Faye emerges as the most prominent figure, her dominance sealed by the reams of voice-over—that most fatiguing of Malick trademarks—that Mara solemnly intones. For the first 15 minutes of *Song to Song*, I held out hope that Malick's prime positioning of Mara, an actress whose tremendous powers of observation give *Carol* (2015) so much of its erotic pull, indicated a return to the pleasingly odd, fully fleshed-out heroines of his first two movies: Sissy Spacek's Holly in *Badlands* (1973) and Linda Manz's Linda in *Days of Heaven* (1978). But despite the screen time she's allotted, Mara's Faye often scans as ornamental—as much so as the models and strippers who clutter *Knight of Cups*, Malick's obtuse peek into the spiritual void of Hollywood.

In fact, so enervated, so physically insubstantial is Rooney's character that we rarely see Faye engage in the kinetic activity most often performed by Malick's women: twirling. The aspiring rocker barely seems to have the strength to stand erect. BV often holds his lover aloft in the countless games of airplane they play while lolling in bed; out in the world, he carries her in his arms as if she were a tuckered-out toddler. Tasked with having to move from point A to point B, Faye leans against a brick wall as she advances forward, often stopping to touch every crevice in the surface. The action is common enough in Malick's oeuvre, an instance of the magical mystery tour promised by even the briefest period spent outside (all part of "life's journey," to use the absurd subtitle of his previous movie, the 2016 documentary *Voyage of Time*). But this putative moment of transcendence—to the wonder!—plays like a horribly directed rehearsal for *The Miracle Worker*, or like *Christina's World* rendered as a live-action cartoon.

When prone, however, the blank guitarist gets up to all kinds of mischief. "I took sex, a gift. I played with it. I played with the flame of life," Faye says, off-screen, in *Song to Song*'s final quarter. Her transgressions include not only those romps in chic, sterile rooms with Cook but also a lavender interlude with a Parisian (given a dog but no occupation or reason for being in Texas) played by Bérénice Marlohe. This listless episode of sapphistry, which, at its most lubricious, reveals a hand burrowing below a waistband, follows an earlier incident meant to suggest same-sexing as the utmost in depravity: terror darkens the faces of Rhonda and Faye after they've kissed, their intimacy the bidding of Cook.

The moment, underscored by the bugged-out peepers of Mara and Portman, is too laughable to provoke outrage. But I remain baffled by what Malick holds up to be the most exalted order of human closeness: heterosexual coupling that seems perversely sexless. BV and Faye nuzzle and cuddle, he teases her with a caterpillar, she propels herself ever skyward on a swing. "You wanna go back to a simple life. I want the same," she addresses her lover in voice-over before a final embrace on a rock during the magic hour. It is the simple life of children, playmates unsullied by carnal desires.

—*Village Voice*, March 15, 2017

Spencer

(Pablo Larraín, 2021)

Of all pop-culture pathologies, none has metastasized quite like the fascination with the British monarchy. There is especially no slaking the appetite for details on those within the immediate circle of the woman who has been sovereign since 1952—her coronation ushering in "the Betty Windsor show," per the satisfyingly acidulous words of Liverpudlian filmmaker Terence Davies in his 2008 documentary-memoir, *Of Time and the City*. To limit the scope of this obsession solely to dramatic feature films, the past 15 years have given us high-profile biopics about Betty herself (Stephen Frears's *The Queen*, from 2006), Betty's dad (Tom Hooper's *The King's Speech*, 2010), and now, inevitably, Betty's former daughter-in-law—alias "the people's princess," who became a corpse at 36, her premature demise the subject of the worst song ever recorded by Elton John (or anyone) and other maudlin displays of necromania.

When it was first announced last year, I could not imagine a project less appealing than Pablo Larraín's *Spencer*, which loftily bills itself in early on-screen text as "a fable from a true tragedy," and narrows its focus to a despairing three days—December 24–26, 1991—in the life of Diana, Princess of Wales (née Diana Frances Spencer, hence the movie's title). And yet I couldn't wait to see it, if only because of my enduring, insatiable enthrallment with the star who was cast, incongruously, to play England's Rose: Kristen Stewart. The very discordance between performer and role, though, turns out to be one of the more invigorating aspects of a film that spends nearly two hours advancing already axiomatic notions—obscene opulence does not equal freedom; protocol is a prison—with easy ironies, weighty symbols, and portentous phrases.

Scripted by Steven Knight, *Spencer* is Larraín's third feature to center on a towering 20th-century figure. In the first, *Neruda* (2016), the Chilean filmmaker took an oblique approach to one of his country's most exalted heroes, the poet and politician of the title. (That sidelong strategy also animated Larraín's great trilogy about the trauma of the Pinochet regime: *Tony Manero*, 2008; *Post Mortem*, 2010; and *No*, 2012). At once a fact-based chronicle, a detective story, and a metafiction, *Neruda* is devoid of fastidious re-creation—the kind of mimesis that overwhelmed *Jackie*, also from 2016, and Larraín's first film in English. It was also his first to star an American A-lister, Natalie Portman, whose baffling portrayal of Mrs. John Kennedy in the wake of the president's assassination confused narcosis with grief.

Spencer forms a diptych with *Jackie*: two female secular saints, both clad in and/or accessorized with Chanel, and each a crucial player in propping up the myths of majesty, with one key difference. Camelot, a term the First Lady deployed to describe her husband's truncated term in office, was a chimerical metaphor; the royal residences where Diana lived, on the other hand, were all-too-real immurements. Or so *Spencer*—which takes place at Sandringham House, in Norfolk, where yuletide has long been celebrated by Betty Windsor, here played by Stella Gonet and reduced to a fleeting presence who stares with blank disdain when not summoning her corgis—is at great pains to remind us. The camera lingers just a little too long on the tags affixed to Diana's garments, a new outfit required for every repast of her 72-hour stay: P.O.W., in which the initialism for "Princess of Wales" could just as easily scan as "prisoner of war."

The belligerent power holding her captive is, of course, Prince Charles (Jack Farthing), to whom Diana had then been married for ten mostly miserable years (they'd separate in 1992 and divorce in '96). "Yes, everyone here hears everything," the heir apparent sniffs to his wife—an ominous avowal that becomes a catchphrase in *Spencer*, a film that fervently believes that anything worth saying is worth uttering twice or thrice.

And what is everyone hearing in the echoey corridors of Sandringham House? For starters, the nonverbal noises emitted when the princess is in the throes of her well-documented mental-health disorders, which a project as unsubtle as *Spencer*—its broadness punctuated by Jonny Greenwood's agitated score and cinematographer Claire Mathon's frenzied camera movements—is all too eager to dramatize: Diana regurgitating, in one of several episodes depicting her heaving into a toilet bowl, her Christmas Eve dinner, a purge followed by a late-night binge of lobster and three-tiered cakes; Diana harming herself with a pair of wire cutters. When Her Royal Highness does use her words to communicate her distress, Larraín and Knight stray further from the public record. But their fanciful notions of their unhinged heroine suggest less a 30-year-old woman (and mother of two adored and adoring young sons) in crisis than a highly melodramatic teenager—one who talks to the ghost of Anne Boleyn, says "fuck," and imperiously shoos away a royal staffer with this declaration: "Now leave me. I wish to masturbate." We know why the caged bird wanks.

And what do these indecorous commands *sound* like? To my not especially sophisticated ear, Stewart re-creates the princess's distinct elocution—Received Pronunciation tinged with Estuary English—without too much strain. Yet sometimes the indelible mannerisms of the actress, a native Southern Californian, leak out. That's especially the case with Stewart's throaty laugh, heard in a late scene when Maggie, Diana's most cherished dresser (played by Sally Hawkins), makes a surprising announcement. (Maggie's proclamation won't seem all that startling, though, to those viewers convinced that the character's awful bowl cut must be an auguring signal.)

There's something undeniably absurd about watching this quintessentially American performer share scenes with two UK actors—Hawkins and Timothy Spall, as an equerry to the Queen Mother—famous for their work with Mike Leigh, whose droll, intensely observed portraits of the British working class are the antithesis of a gewgaw like *Spencer*. But these oddities also have their own unexpected pathos, lending dignity to a film bloated with tawdry psychologizing. Five years ago I wrote that Stewart "is one of her generation's most quicksilver performers," an assessment I still stand by. Tasked with inhabiting a martyr, one whose prolonged woes were largely caused by the masks she was forced to wear, Stewart refuses to let the masquerade swallow her whole.

—*4Columns*, November 12, 2021

Suspiria

(Luca Guadagnino, 2018)

A triumph of riotous style and a lot of fun, Dario Argento's *Suspiria*, released in 1977, plays like a Henry James plot drowning in pools of crimson and gore and glutted with witchy jibber-jabber (aka Latin). In the film—the paragon of the *giallo*, the genre of visually voluptuous Italian horror movies that peaked in the 1970s—a young American dancer named Suzy Bannion (Jessica Harper) arrives at a *tanz* academy in Freiburg, Germany, and discovers that the school is a front for necromancers conspiring to sacrifice the students to the coven queen. Embracing *Suspiria*'s loopy storyline, J. Hoberman, in a 2009 appreciation of Argento's film, called it "a movie that makes sense only to the eye." In contrast, Luca Guadagnino's remake, the color palette of which resembles the inside of a baby's diaper, proves unintelligible and vexing at every level. *Suspiria* 2018 assaults the eye, distresses the ear, and maligns the mind.

Running at a distended 152 minutes, nearly an hour longer than the original, Guadagnino's version instantly signals the leaden solemnity that will be its doom. An intertitle announces, as if we were at the Bayreuth Festival: "Six acts and an epilogue, set in a divided Berlin." Guadagnino and the screenwriter David Kajganich have cynically chosen the year that Argento's film was released—and specifically the German Autumn, those deranging weeks in 1977 when the Red Army Faction mounted a full-on revolution against Deutschland—as the backdrop for *Suspiria* 2.0. Previously known for the sunny

Euro-sybaritism of his movies, like that in last year's *Call Me by Your Name,* Guadagnino here has repurposed traumas of the 20th century—invariably, the Holocaust will be evoked—as garlands for a thriller about grueling barre exercises and Black Mass in the basement. "Free Baader!" "Free Meinhof!" goes an off-screen call-and-response in the opening sequence: a game of Marco Polo designed to flatter the dilettantish.

Those rebel yells are heard as Patricia (Chloë Grace Moretz)—an escapee from the terpsichorean academy founded by sorceress Helena Markos and maybe an RAF recruit—approaches, in a state of extreme agitation, the office of her wizened psychotherapist, Dr. Josef Klemperer (Lutz Ebersdorf, alias Tilda Swinton; more on this in a moment). "They'll hollow me out and eat my cunt on a plate," the dancer tells her shrink of her diabolical distaff teachers—in German. It's the first of many wearying instances when the English that is the film's lingua franca halts for the dialogue to be gussied up with verbal bursts in Continental tongues.

Dull-witted ostentation—as opposed to the lurid, lysergic embellishments, the retina-tickling blasts of color that give Argento's film such kicky energy—abounds in Guadagnino's *Suspiria.* Madame Blanc (Swinton, a frequent star in the director's films), the choreographer at the occult dance company, for example, is a welter of referents: in one scene, wearing a floor-scraping black dress, she is meant to summon Martha Graham; in another, with a cigarette burning between two fingers, Pina Bausch. In yet another, she exhibits the soigné bearing of Lucinda Childs. The American newcomer to the troupe (Dakota Johnson), now known as Susie Bannion (not Suzy), is larded with a backstory, doled out in time-toggling fragments, involving a Mennonite upbringing and a dying ma.

For a project that Guadagnino, who is 47, was determined for decades to reshape as his own (as a teenager, he would aspirationally write "*Suspiria* by Luca Guadagnino" in his notebooks), this reimagining rarely includes a set piece in which he rises above epigone. As we watch the limbs of Olga (Elena Fokina), one of Susie's classmates, being torqued by the invisible hands of she-demons in a danse macabre of flails, grunts, bile, and piss, a better, similar scene in another movie also set in (then extant) West Berlin immediately comes to mind: that of Isabelle Adjani twitching and moaning like an animal in a U-Bahn passageway in Andrzej Zulawski's *Possession* (1981).

The one element of *Suspiria* that is wholly Guadagnino's own is also, unsurprisingly, the movie's dopiest conceit. Though I knew instantly that the actor playing Dr. Josef Klemperer, a major character, was a latex-distorted Tilda Swinton (whose filmography includes more than one hammy, prosthetically enhanced performance), Guadagnino, his cast, and his crew have insisted otherwise (at least until press time). They claim the doctor is portrayed by one Lutz Ebersdorf—who, per his florid bio in the media kit (Hermann Nitsch is name-checked), is an 80-year-old Kleinian analyst here making his acting debut. "I believe that people can organize themselves to perpetrate crimes and call it magic," Dr. Josef K. says at one point. Likewise, people can throw a lot of turgid nonsense into a script and call it a movie.

—*Artforum*, November 2018

Wonder Woman

(Patty Jenkins, 2017)

Perhaps Wonder Woman's greatest superpower is enduring for the past 75 years as a wildly unstable signifier. Patty Jenkins's *Wonder Woman*, starring Gal Gadot in the title role, further adds to this complicated, contradictory cluster of signs and symbols.

Forged from deeply feminist sympathies, the character debuted in All Star Comics, a predecessor of DC Comics, in 1941 (three years after Superman and two after Batman). She was the creation of William Moulton Marston, who, as Jill Lepore details in her spirited book *The Secret History of Wonder Woman* (2014), proudly claimed that the Amazonian princess was meant to be "psychological propaganda for the new type of woman who ... should rule the world." After Marston's death, in 1947, the superhero was forced to retreat into domesticity; the comic now featured supplements called "Marriage a la Mode." The editors of *Ms.* restored her sisterly derring-do in the early 1970s, putting her on the cover of the first issue of the magazine under the banner WONDER WOMAN FOR PRESIDENT. Her second-wave revival continued, however diluted, in the Lynda Carter–headlining TV series that ran from 1975 to '79. The plastic pop of that show was fabulously detourned in Dara Birnbaum's great contemporaneous video piece *Technology/Transformation: Wonder Woman* (1978–79).

The icon has been greeted more warily in this century. Jenkins's movie (her first since *Monster*, 2003's ripe Aileen Wuornos biopic) arrives six months after the comic-book character was dropped as an ambassador for a U.N. campaign seeking to achieve gender equality; the decision was a response to petitioners who objected to the superhero's "impossible proportions" and scanty, jingoistic costuming. It follows a year after Gadot's Wonder Woman made a fleeting appearance in Zach Snyder's *Batman v Superman: Dawn of Justice*, the intro mandated by the imperatives of franchise-building and continuing the sprawl of the Warner Bros. DC Extended Universe series. In Jenkins's *Wonder Woman*, the battles that structure the movie aren't those taking place on the screen but those behind it, a struggle more salient here than in any other superhero movie: it's the conflict between the demands of the marketplace ("I think what the studio realized was that they had an asset to exploit, to pull in a larger section of the populace that would ordinarily not be our demographic for that kind of film," Charles Roven, one of *Wonder Woman*'s producers, told the *New York Times* earlier this month) and the aims of ideology ("Wonder Woman is so hard to put on film because the fight for women's rights has gone so badly," Lepore wrote in the *New Yorker* in 2014).

The fight's fixed, of course, but there are moments in *Wonder Woman* (the screenplay for which is credited to Allan Heinberg, who's written comics for both Marvel and DC) that even Shulamith Firestone might have approved of. That's especially true in the opening scenes, following a present-day prologue in which Diana Prince, Wonder Woman's alter ego, opens a package delivered by a Wayne Enterprises truck to her office at the Louvre. Inside is a tintype photo, from a century earlier, of Wonder Woman and Steve Trevor (Chris Pine), an American soldier, standing on the Western Front (Marston's superhero premiered the year that the US entered World War II; Jenkins's fights in World War I).

That memento sends the narrative back further in time, to young Diana's upbringing in the all-female enclave on Themyscira, aka Paradise Island, a piece of land that could form an archipelago with the Isle of Lesbos and Cherry Grove. Led by Queen Hippolyta (Connie Nielsen), Diana's mother, and the regent's sister, Antiope (Robin Wright), the Amazons in Jenkins's movie are not only of different races but also various forms of gender expression, from stone butch to soft femme—a welcome, near-subversive display of body types and builds.

But when the separatist compound must accommodate an interloper—Steve Trevor, fished out of the sea by Diana after his plane goes down—any hopes that *Wonder Woman* will sustain its appealing misandry are soon dashed. "Be careful in the world of men, Diana. They do not deserve you," Hippolyta warns her daughter, who insists on sailing off with the Yankee soldier/spy to fulfill her tribe's noble duty of protecting the defenseless from German mustard gas and other horrors. (That line is one of several uttered on Themyscira that could have been the title of a tract published in *Off Our Backs*, their potency watered down by the fact that Nielsen, like many actors in *Wonder Woman*, both on and off the island, delivers them in an inscrutable accent.)

Ma's prophecy was right. Gadot must spend the rest of the movie performing as a kind of idiot savant: Diana may be able to translate Sumerian (one of the "hundreds of languages" Amazons can speak) and, when suited up, deflect bullets with her magic bracelets, but she has never seen snow, ice cream, or Edwardian-era attire before, all of which must be deciphered for her by Steve. In short, the world must be, yes, mansplained to the superhero by a character played by an actor who exudes all the charm of a hedge-fund analyst at last call. That tedious parsing includes Steve's defining of "no-man's-land" as he and

Diana survey the trenches in Belgium. During this scene and many others, especially the final one, when the warrior princess formulates her cuddly bellicose philosophy ("Only love can save the world"), I wished only for Diana to return to the literal no-man's-land where she was reared.

—*Village Voice*, May 31, 2017

Babylon

(Damien Chazelle, 2022)

A distended saga about Hollywood from 1926 to 1932 (with a coda set in 1952), *Babylon* begins with a deluge of elephant shit and ends with a tearstained face. The film is awash in other (human) bodily fluids, too: piss, blood, vomit, phlegm. It is the most incontinent film of the year.

This leaky vessel is also the latest entry in a recent boomlet of features, all released since September, devoted to cinema's past. These include Andrew Dominik's sordid Marilyn Monroe quasi-biography, *Blonde*; Steven Spielberg's mawkishly autobiographical *The Fabelmans*; and Sam Mendes's ineptly sociological *Empire of Light*. Centering on six main characters, many of whom are transparently based on real-life figures, during the era when movies made the transition from silents to talkies and adopted a puritanical production code, *Babylon* belongs to a genre we might call the hysterical historical. Clamorous and benumbing, Chazelle's film is a three-hour cartoon with expletives, dildos, and excreta.

The title of this bumptious epic unimaginatively lops off a word from Kenneth Anger's two *Hollywood Babylon* books, which have endured for years as queasy compendiums of the Dream Factory's seamier side (the first volume was published in the US in 1965, the second in 1984). These chronicles, strewn with a fair share of myths, are rife with vile scandals and myriad degradations. Chazelle repurposes and contorts some of them, starting with the notorious 1921 death of an aspiring actress who had attended a blowout hosted by the silent-film star Roscoe “Fatty” Arbuckle. (His analogue in the film answers to “Piggy”; the ultimate fate of the surrogate for that unfortunate partygoer is unclear.)

It would seem, in fact, that Chazelle has used Anger’s books as a template for his project. Or is it just a coincidence that *Hollywood Babylon* also opens with a pachyderm tableau (specifically, the eight enormous white plaster elephants that D. W. Griffith insisted on for 1916’s *Intolerance*)? Chazelle unquestionably set out to dramatize, to increasingly diminishing returns, these lines from the first few pages of Anger’s tome: “The Twenties is sometimes referred to as ‘Hollywood’s Golden Age,’ and golden it was, in sheer exuberant movie-making creativity as well as in financial returns. Film folk of the period are depicted as engaging in madcap, nonstop off-screen capers.” What Chazelle disregards is the sentence that follows: “The legend overlooks one fact—fear. That ever present thrilling-erotic fear that the bottom could drop out of their gilded dreams at any time.”

Fear is precisely what is missing from *Babylon*, which staggers from one manic set piece to the next. For as excitable (and apocryphal) as Anger’s prose can be, he nonetheless captures the despair and desperation that have been an inextricable part of Hollywood since the storied ’20s—and that have been the backdrop of scores of books and movies about the psychic cruelties of the moviemaking industry, ranging from Nathanael West’s corrosive 1939 novel, *The Day of the Locust* (and its 1975 film adaptation), to David Lynch’s destabilizing *Mulholland Drive* (2001) to Jean Stein’s haunting oral history from 2016, *West of Eden*. Any tragedy in *Babylon*—an off-screen suicide of a minor character, for example—is quickly followed by a sight gag or effluvia.

Only at the very end, when it slides into sentimentality, does *Babylon* ease up on the fratty energy. Its first big scene, a bacchanal held at the hangar-size mansion of studio macher Don Wallach (Jeff Garlin), introduces the film's core sextet. Manny Torres (Diego Calva), who starts out as Wallach's gofer but rises to become a movie executive, immediately falls in love with party-crasher Nellie LaRoy (Margot Robbie), a bawdy starlet-hopeful whose career trajectory resembles that of Clara Bow. Looking for the powder room amid all the lusting, thrusting bodies is Elinor St. John (Jean Smart), a gossip columnist whose surname nearly matches that of an actual Hollywood journalist of the time, Adela Rogers St. Johns. Stumbling into the orgy is Jack Conrad (Brad Pitt), a leading man who evokes real-life idols Douglas Fairbanks Jr. and John Gilbert. The carnal revelry slows down for a moment to make way for a slinky number ("My Girl's Pussy") by Lady Fay Zhu (Li Jun Li)—clearly a stand-in for the Chinese American luminary Anna May Wong—whose attire (top hat and tuxedo) and action (smooching a woman spectator on the mouth) are feeble homages to Marlene Dietrich in *Morocco* (1930). Ace Black trumpeter and bandleader Sidney Palmer (Jovan Adepo) sets the tempo at the Wallach rager, his bombastic jazz composed by Justin Hurwitz, who has scored all of Chazelle's five features to date. (The least fleshed-out of this principal group, Sidney will confoundingly be used to illustrate one of Hollywood's most grotesque practices, blackface.)

Much of *Babylon* plays like a parlor game designed to flatter the TCM devotee: guessing who's who or which movie or scandal is being referenced affords the same empty pleasure as figuring out which Vincente Minnelli, Jacques Demy, or Stanley Donen film Chazelle was saluting in *La La Land*, his wan 2016 musical. When Nellie, now a huge star hailed as "the Firecracker from New Jersey" (one of Clara Bow's sobriquets was "the Brooklyn Bonfire"), steps on a soundstage in 1928 to make her first talkie, it's evident that Chazelle is summoning *The Wild Party,* Bow's debut sound film from 1929. To demonstrate the snafus and glitches still being worked out as actors, directors, and technicians made the adjustment to this new dimension, Chazelle subjects us to eight takes of the same scene—at least five too many—yet another instance of his predilection for deadening excess.

However stupefying, Chazelle's decision to end the film with a flagrant redundancy is at least of a piece with his pleonastic tendencies. Throughout, *Babylon* quotes segments from *Singin' in the Rain*—the best, most beloved meta-movie to depict cinema's shift from silence to sound. Yet when Manny, now two decades removed from his Hollywood escapades, takes a seat in an empyreal movie house where that 1952 musical is being shown, Chazelle focuses on the exact moments in the original that his film pinched from. Why? The comparison can only be unflattering. Or perhaps Chazelle thinks his flaccid project will one day assume its place among the exalted ranks of *Singin' in the Rain* or one of the other great works—*The Passion of Joan of Arc, Psycho, 2001*—excerpted in a montage in *Babylon*'s closing minutes. Those clips are meant to remind us of the "magic of cinema," to assure us of the imperiled art form's immortality. *Babylon* can only hasten its demise.

—*4Columns,* December 23, 2022

Trenque Lauquen

(Laura Citarella, 2022)

In 2006, shortly before David Lynch's *Inland Empire* was released, I interviewed Laura Dern, the film's star, on the phone. I was eager to know how she approached the several different personae she inhabits in this oneiric, labyrinthine movie. "There was clearly a mystery, as there always is—there's a mystery to solve as the actor in the story," she explained. Her answer has stayed with me ever since, reminding me that the best cinema—or, at least, the kind of cinema I respond to most ardently—immerses us in enigmas that are open-ended, that defy pat resolution.

Mysteries exhilaratingly multiply—for the actors, for the characters they play, for the audience—in *Trenque Lauquen*, a film created by two other Lauras: Citarella, the director, and Paredes, who plays the protagonist, also named Laura, and who cowrote the script with Citarella. Made over six years, *Trenque Lauquen* shares some cast and crew with *La flor*, Mariano Llinás's protean magnum opus from 2018; both are from the Argentine producing group El Pampero Cine, which counts Citarella and Llinás as two of its four members. Both films boast expansive running times—*La flor* clocks in at almost 13 and a half hours; *Trenque Lauquen* at nearly four and a half—that elapse fleetingly, leaving us transfixed by their densely detailed fictions.

While *La flor* features a quartet of actresses in multiple, disjointed scenarios and genres, *Trenque Lauquen* keeps its focus on one woman and, despite its achronological structure and copious digressions, follows a more or less cohesive arc. Citarella's latest also continues the themes of her earlier work, in which a woman is either drawn to mystery or remains a mystery herself. (Both scenarios describe Laura in *Trenque Lauquen.*) In *Ostende* (2011), Citarella's first feature and her inaugural collaboration with Paredes, here also playing a character named Laura, the protagonist, while spending a few desultory days at a hotel in the eponymous seaside town, becomes obsessed with the odd activities of a possible throuple consisting of an older man and two women. The mostly wordless *La mujer de los perros* (or *Dog Lady*, 2015)—codirected and cowritten with Verónica Llinás (sister of Mariano), who also plays the title character—tracks, over the course of a year, the nomadic peregrinations of a middle-aged woman living off the grid with an ever-growing circle of canine companions. What led to this extreme situation is never specified. (In a much smaller part in *Trenque Lauquen*, Verónica Llinás plays another character living in isolation, though not as dire.)

I find myself reluctant to give even a perfunctory synopsis of *Trenque Lauquen*, since many of the film's delights emerge from the deliriously original plots and subplots that Citarella and Paredes have concocted. (Two days after seeing the film, I came across this passage from Elizabeth Hardwick's 1969 essay "Reflections on Fiction," which aptly applies to the narrative thrills of Citarella's movie: "The parts bear a mysterious and clouded relation to the whole. The pages turn, one after another, and it is a distinguishing aspect of the novel that, around the next corner, almost anything can happen. We hardly know which to treasure most: expectation confounded or satisfied.") If I am circumspect or parsimonious in my description, I intend it not as dereliction of duty but rather as a gesture of deference to you, the potential viewer, who should buy a ticket to *Trenque Lauquen* knowing as little about it as possible.

The puzzles begin with the title. *Trenque Lauquen*, like *Ostende*, takes its name from a town in the province of Buenos Aires; translated from the Indigenous Mapuche language, it means "round lagoon" or "round lake." The name has an almost incantatory power, much like the text of the terse note that Laura, a biologist from the Argentine capital who was on an assignment classifying various flora in Trenque Lauquen, has left behind: "*Adiós, adiós, me voy, me voy*"—"Farewell, farewell, I'm leaving, I'm leaving."

Trenque Lauquen begins in medias res. Two men—Rafael (Rafael Spregelburd), Laura's older, lordly boyfriend from the capital city, and Ezequiel (Ezequiel Pierri; all the principal characters share the first names of the performers playing them), a ginger-headed, teddy-bearish local who drove the botanist to outlying fields—have teamed up, if only temporarily, to search for the vanished woman and, more to the point, try to piece together why she disappeared in the first place. Both in the film's first 20 minutes—before the randomly ordered flashbacks of Laura's activities in *Trenque Lauquen* begin—and during any segment in which she does not appear on-screen, she is always the structuring absence, much like two other legendary Lauras: Laura Hunt, the beautiful, murdered (though not as deceased as we are first led to believe) ad executive in Otto Preminger's 1944 film-noir paradigm *Laura*, and Laura Palmer, the slain high-school homecoming queen of *Twin Peaks*, the cult TV series Lynch created with Mark Frost that first aired in the early '90s and was revived for a third season in 2017.

The Laura of *Trenque Lauquen* joins the exalted ranks of her namesakes. Assiduous and unassuming, she is hungry for adventure, for sleuthing—a predilection that leads her to falling in love at least twice. (In the town named after a round lake, pointed romantic triangles proliferate.) Of one of her darlings, she says, "I lost the fear of getting lost, of dying." It is an exceptionally romantic line in a movie that, throughout its numerous detours, stands as one of the greatest romances I've seen since (Lynch again) *Mulholland Drive.*

But Laura's romances don't always require another human to be the object of her enthrallment; she senses untold mysteries not only in people but also objects, the natural world. More broadly, *Trenque Lauquen* (like *La flor* before it) reaffirms what we are too perilously close to forgetting: that going to a cinema, especially to succumb to a movie that makes a not-insignificant demand on your time, is itself a commitment to adventure—a folly, perhaps, but what memorable romance isn't?

—*4Columns*, April 14, 2023

Blonde

(Andrew Dominik, 2022)

No corpse has been picked over more than Marilyn Monroe's. In the 60 years since her death, in 1962—at age 36, an apparent suicide—the screen legend has been the subject of not just scores of books and movies but also plays and operas. "Monroe was an infinity of character and mystery that was impossible for me, or anyone else, to explore, because it was so vast. There is always more and more and more," in the words of Maurice Zolotow, the first of her legions of biographers (who also include Norman Mailer and Gloria Steinem).

More and more and more. Ushering Monroe studies into the new millennium, Joyce Carol Oates's immoderate, turbid, lurid novel *Blonde,* published in 2000, is a fictionalized psychobiography of the actress. Several real events and people, both major and minor, in the icon's difficult, abbreviated life provide the scaffolding for this thick tome, though Oates condenses and invents many others. Points of view shift frequently; excitable typefaces (italics, all caps, small caps) and punctuation marks (exclamation points, scare quotes) abound. All undergird the book's unwavering high-gothic tone, typified by passages such as "The secret place between her legs had been rent and bloodied and claimed by the Dark Prince." That is just one of an infinite number of degradations, whether actual or embellished or wholly imagined by Oates, that constitute the bulk of her book, the central tragedy of which is the irreconcilable schism between the protagonist's two selves: the woman who entered the world, in abject circumstances, as Norma Jeane Mortensen in 1926 and the actress / erotic fantasy rechristened Marilyn Monroe by Twentieth-Century Fox in 1946.

Yet no matter how feverish and frenzied, Oates's book often surprises with astute maxims: "Genius has no need of technique"; "There's a curse on the actor, always you are seeking an audience. And when the audience sees your hunger it's like smelling blood. Their cruelty begins." Undeniably, her heroine suffers. But she also struggles, fights back, attempts to understand herself and ameliorate her misery. Andrew Dominik's long-gestating adaptation of Oates's novel closely adheres to (and sometimes amplifies) its Grand Guignol tone but largely elides its protagonist's intricacies. His film, agitatedly switching from black-and-white to color and back again and constantly changing aspect ratios, is a sordid passion play garlanded with formal frippery, a florid, necrophilic epic that suggests Monroe was born for only one reason: to die.

While a movie version (even one with an ample running time of almost three hours) of a book that's more than 700 pages will obviously demand excisions, it's telling that Dominik's *Blonde* chops many of Oates's chapters devoted to her subject's childhood, adolescence, and early adulthood: the years when Norma Jeane, beset by tremendous difficulties but not yet encumbered by her screen name, endeavors mightily to figure out how not only to survive but to thrive. In the movie, however, one trauma quickly follows another. It opens with seven-year-old Norma Jeane (portrayed at this age by Lily Fisher) nearly killed by her mentally ill mother (Julianne Nicholson), who blames the child for driving away the man who fathered her. Following a brief montage of the magazine covers that featured the cheesecake poses of Norma Jeane, who began modeling in 1944, we follow the peroxided actress-hopeful—

now incarnated by Ana de Armas—as she glides, the camera tight on her wiggling ass, into the office of a studio executive, who immediately rapes her.

This reptilian movie mogul, played by David Warshofsky, is known as "Mr Z" in both the book and the film and is transparently a stand-in for Darryl F. Zanuck, the predatory head of Fox at the time. He is not the only man to victimize her. Her second husband, "the Ex-Athlete," aka Joe DiMaggio (Bobby Cannavale), beats her and demands that she quit acting. Her third, "the Playwright," alias Arthur Miller (Adrien Brody), lifts lines from their intimate conversations for his latest opus without telling her. Two Hollywood failsons (played by Xavier Samuel and Evan Williams) with whom Norma Jeane formed a prestardom throuple carry out a ruse of savage psychological cruelty.

Tasked with the formidable challenges of not only enacting nonstop suffering but also inhabiting one of pop culture's most enduring idols, de Armas, best known for the 2019 whodunit *Knives Out* and last year's James Bond installment *No Time to Die*, eerily recalls Monroe (even if her Cuban accent hasn't been entirely filed down and her slender frame doesn't quite summon Monroe's voluptuous proportions). And yet there's something animatronic (Anamatronic?) about her performance, just one part of the hollow verisimilitude of *Blonde*, which fastidiously re-creates trailers for various Monroe vehicles (like 1953's *Niagara*) and snippets of her most indelible scenes, like the "Diamonds Are a Girl's Best Friend" number from the '53 musical *Gentlemen Prefer Blondes*—technically accomplished moments that remain emotionally inert.

The uncanny valley wrought by *Blonde*'s painstaking, futile replications, though, never matches the revulsion provoked by Dominik's own interventions to quite literally get inside his subject. *Blonde* is ghoulishly obsessed with Monroe's pregnancies and reproductive organs. Shots of floating fetuses fill the screen so often that I wondered whether Operation Rescue had invested in the film. As a physician adjusts a speculum before performing an abortion, we peer down Monroe's vaginal walls.

Only once does *Blonde* attempt to show Monroe's genius as a performer, the magic she created when the cameras were rolling. At a screen test for the 1952 noir *Don't Bother to Knock*, she stupefies the assembled movie men by burrowing deep into her character's fractured psyche. The segment calls to mind Betty Elms's stunning audition sequence in David Lynch's *Mulholland Drive* (2001). Coincidentally, in the late 1980s, Lynch, whose oeuvre is defined by totemic blondes, had tried to make a film about Monroe. That feature was ultimately abandoned, but the legend lived on in his work. "You could say that Laura Palmer"—the tragic heroine of *Twin Peaks*—"is Marilyn Monroe, and that *Mulholland Drive* is about Marilyn Monroe, too. Everything is about Marilyn Monroe," Lynch notes in the 2018 book *Room to Dream*. Even when approaching her obliquely, Lynch's movies and TV shows have done more to grapple with the complexities and contradictions of Monroe than nearly any other project devoted to her. Certainly more than Dominik's film, in which everything is actually about Marilyn Monroe—an everything that amounts to nothing.

—*4Columns*, September 30, 2022

The Substance

(Coralie Fargeat, 2024)

Among the most piercing aperçus in a book full of them is this sentence from Hilton Als's 2013 essay collection, *White Girls*: "She was as conscious of her body as she was fearful of it; in short, she was a woman." That fear—that hatred—of the corporeal self so particular to women reflects, in large part, the terror and rage of being reduced to nothing but a body, one subjected to countless harms by millennia of misogynist fiats. Heightening the lucidity of Als's observation is its equable tone. In contrast to that calmness, a string of recent high-profile productions, made for screens big and small and all falling within the body-horror genre, attempt to dramatize his insight as clamorously as possible. Alexia, for instance, the serial-killer protagonist of Julia Ducournau's *Titane*, which won the Palme d'Or at Cannes in 2021, undergoes extravagant physical transformation, not least by becoming pregnant via sexual congress with a car. Last year brought us both the gender-swapped, Rachel Weisz–headlining *Dead Ringers*, a blood-soaked limited series for Prime Video that didactically demonstrates the infernal history of gynecology, and Yorgos Lanthimos's *Poor Things*, a Frankenstein-inspired tale in which the insatiable carnal needs of the stitched-together heroine—played by Emma Stone, who won the Oscar for Best Actress for her performance—are upheld as proof of her unimpeachable, virtuous sex positivity. (Coincidentally, all three have been crisply demolished in *4Columns*.) The latest entry in this ignominious canon is Coralie Fargeat's *The Substance*, another

Cannes prizewinner, for Best Screenplay. It is by far the most inane, repetitive, and benumbing of this cluster, so much so that its predecessors seem like *Jeanne Dielman* in comparison.

The premise, which is also the lone idea, of *The Substance*, the French filmmaker's second feature (following 2017's *Revenge*), could fit on a grain of rice. Fearing complete obsolescence, a middle-aged, once-feted actress, Elisabeth Sparkle (Demi Moore), begins injecting herself with a black-market elixir that allows her to become a "better," younger version of herself. This springtime state lasts strictly for seven days, after which the fading star reverts back to her over-the-hill misery for another week; the on-off sequence repeats. Complications—and set pieces flagrantly cribbed from immensely superior movies—arise when Sue (Margaret Qualley), Elisabeth's 20-something avatar, drunk with fame and adulation, begins to disregard the inviolable deadline. The longer Sue extends her stay, the more decrepit Elisabeth becomes.

Taking strident, impotent aim at the pitilessness of Hollywood, the boorishness of male entertainment machers, impossible beauty standards, and female self-hatred, *The Substance* is an orchard of worm-filled, low-hanging fruit. Fargeat's attempts at savage satire are undermined by her oddly generic, anachronistic vision of celebrity and the Dream Factory itself. After an opening montage of the physical decay and desecration—cracks, a dropped ketchup-slathered burger—of Elisabeth's star on the Walk of Fame, we are introduced to the past-her-prime performer taping a TV exercise show given the Pynchonian name *Sparkle Your Life with Elisabeth*. This segment inescapably summons Jane Fonda's workout tapes, a phenomenal success ... of the 1980s (and merely one cycle in Fonda's long career, not its terminus). Even though Sue is an ascendant supernova and thus a logical candidate to headline, say, a hotly anticipated film or prestige streaming series, she, too, hosts a television aerobics program with a lusterless title: *Pump It Up with Sue*. (The antecedent of *It*: Sue's taut butt, endlessly filmed bobbing in extreme close-up.) Bewilderingly, as a sign of her A-lister status, Sue is asked by the vulgar network head, Harvey (Dennis Quaid)—his villainous name typical of the film's thudding obviousness—to host *The New Year's Eve Show*, the kind of ancient variety spectacular hospitable to has-beens.

This nonsensical framework typifies Fargeat's inability to skewer the cultural ills that so aggravate her. In lieu of precisely parodying her targets, she relies on superfluous repetition, leading to *The Substance*'s distended 140-minute running time. Any incident meant to stoke our dudgeon, its "cruelty" immediately apparent, must be shown at least twice, as with a card affixed to a bouquet of consolation roses given to Elisabeth after the network sacks her. The note, amply lingered on and filling a large part of the screen, reads: "Thank you for all the years with us. You were amazing!" Worried that the audience may not understand the significance of the past tense, Fargeat found it necessary to include, a few seconds later, a tight close-up on "were." Incessantly we hear, thanks to Elisabeth's calls to Substance HQ to complain whenever Sue has exceeded her time limit, this bit of Goop-derived philosophy: "Remember, there is no 'she' and 'you.' You are one. Respect the balance."

The Solomonic directive invariably ignored, we must endure the wearying repetition of the Elisabeth-to-Sue-and-back-again metamorphosis, each with more dire consequences for the former. The first instance of this transformation demonstrates, if only fleetingly, some striking visual power, a keen sense of the physical and psychic violence wrought by outlandish youth-restoring techniques: as naked Elisabeth writhes on her blindingly white bathroom floor, Sue emerges from her dorsally, via the older woman's split spinal column. But Fargeat quickly blunts the force of this scene by larding it with a gratuitous reference to the "Stargate" sequence in *2001*.

That is not the only Stanley Kubrick film quoted. *The Shining* is copiously cited, as is Brian De Palma's *Carrie*, at least three movies by David Lynch, and essentially the entire corpus of David Cronenberg. (Even the score of Alfred Hitchcock's *Vertigo* is repurposed.) As with all epigones, Fargeat succeeds in replicating only the superficial aspects of what she's referencing—the geysers of blood and mass destruction unleashed by Sissy Spacek's telekinetic teen during the climax of *Carrie*, for example—while evincing no capacity to imbue these special effects with any original meaning. The incarnadine mayhem in De Palma's movie indelibly captures the fathomless ire of its tormented heroine, if not all female adolescents. The sluices of gore that inundate the final act of *The Substance*, on the other hand, make us conscious not of Elisabeth's body but of our own, and its most urgent need—to flee this movie, which evaporates from the mind instantly.

—*4Columns*, September 13, 2024

IV.

Star Studies

Adèle Haenel

Those who saw last year's *BPM (Beats per Minute)*, Robin Campillo's pulsating drama about the Paris branch of ACT UP in the early 1990s, will never forget Adèle Haenel. She plays Sophie, the headstrong dyke member of the activist group. Fury burns in her gleaming green eyes. Her whistle at the ready, Sophie—tall, toned, physically solid—leads her comrades as they storm the headquarters of a drug company and shout, "Melton Pharm, *assassin*!" At one of the coalition's weekly meetings, fake blood still staining her T-shirt, she vents her frustration with the improvised tactics of some of her confreres at an action carried out earlier that day. At another of those assemblies, she demonstrates how to jam a fax machine. She lustily smooches a cute brunette with a Caesar cut. She's one of the best gyrators of her mostly gay-male cohort on the dance floor, transported by house-music beats.

Haenel rivets without ever upstaging any of her castmates in this electric ensemble production. *BPM*, which was voted the best foreign-language film of 2017 by both the New York Film Critics Circle and the Los Angeles Film Critics Association, is likely her best-known movie in the US to date. But the actress, born in Paris in 1989 and now 17 years into her career, is easily the most renowned in France among her *BPM* costars, several of whom made their screen debut in the film. Whether veteran or novice, though, most of *BPM*'s actors share one trait: they are out. Campillo, whose movie reflects his own biography—he joined ACT UP–Paris in 1992—has said of his troupe, "It seemed quite logical to me that in a film about a group that makes visibility one of its weapons, the majority of the actors should be gay themselves, and openly so."

The occasion for Haenel's coming out couldn't have been more high profile. At the ceremony for the Césars—France's equivalent of the Academy Awards—in February 2014, Haenel, who had just won in the Best Supporting Actress category for her performance as the more stable of two sisters in Katell Quillévéré's *Suzanne* (2013), concluded her brief acceptance speech with this: "And above all I wanted to thank, ehm ... I wanted to thank Céline ... because ... because I love her, voilà." Céline is writer-director Céline Sciamma, with whom Haenel had made *Water Lilies* (2007), and who, some years after that film's release, became the actress's romantic partner. The declaration is halting—and all the more touching for being so. However nervous or overcome with emotion Haenel appears while making her proclamation, her words evince the boldness that defines her work. We may have our share of openly queer actresses of Haenel's generation on this side of the Atlantic, but it's hard to imagine any of them first announcing their lavender affiliation from the stage of the Dolby Theatre on Oscar night.

Haenel's on-screen intensity recalls that of Isabelle Adjani in her greatest roles from the 1970s and '80s. (The affinity between the two is underscored by the title of a 2015 monograph on the younger actress, *Histoires d'Adèle H.*, a play on the title of Adjani's breakthrough film from 1975, François Truffaut's *L'Histoire d'Adèle H.*) Haenel's fervor is apparent from the first moment we see her in Christophe Ruggia's *Les Diables* (*The Devils*, 2002), her debut, shot when she was 12 years old. She plays Chloé, a speechless, severely autistic girl, one of two siblings abandoned by their parents; she and her doting brother, Joseph (Vincent Rottiers), also of pubescent age, are continually sentenced to and breaking out of children's homes. *The Devils* made almost inconceivable demands of its neophyte colead. Not only must Haenel embody an animal-like ferocity—Patty Duke in *The Miracle Worker* comes to mind—but she is often nude, her breast buds the focus of uncomfortable attention. She performs a primitive, amorphous sexuality; in the film's second half, Chloé constantly touches, hugs, and licks Joseph, contact that leads to incestuous heavy petting.

It is unsettling, at times unbearable, to watch someone so young be so wholly committed to such a feral role. In one of the interviews compiled in *Histoires d'Adèle H.*, Sciamma says of Haenel's performance in *The Devils*, "It's as if she were possessed by something else, in a total and intimidating incarnation"—an assessment I can't dispute. During the five-year gap between *The Devils* and Sciamma's *Water Lilies*, Haenel did not act, focusing instead on her schooling—and maybe on recovering from that total and intimidating incarnation.

While much less outrageous than Ruggia's movie, *Water Lilies* has its own provocations. The film, Sciamma's first feature, revolves around the erupting desires of a group of 15-year-old girls—and specifically the strong libidinal power that Haenel's Floriane, the vixenish captain of a synchronized-swimming team, has over tiny, awkward Marie (Pauline Acquart). In that *Histoires* Q&A, Sciamma notes that Haenel's *Water Lilies* character was constructed as "a vamp, with the idea of the Hollywood bitch, but also of what she was behind the scenes: a vamp invents herself, she always plays at being a vamp, she has to be up to the level of her beauty, her status, her physical appearance." Haenel firmly grasps the intricacies of the part, one that requires high levels of dissimulation: Floriane, desperate to maintain her baseless reputation for (heterosexual) promiscuity, cruelly leads Marie on, eventually asking her besotted friend to deflower her, in a byzantine scheme to deceive Floriane's boyfriend. That scene, like much of *Water Lilies*, is cold and clinical; Haenel, reveling in the role of lycée femme fatale, provides the lone source of heat.

No matter how much her projects vary in tone, style, and subject matter, Haenel always adjusts the temperature. Languorous and narcotic, Bertrand Bonello's *House of Tolerance* (2011)—which traces the final months at an upscale Parisian brothel at the dawn of the 20th century—is, like *BPM*, a superb ensemble period piece enhanced by Haenel. As Léa, she stands out as the most unflappable among her sex-worker sistren, the one least concerned with sweet-talking the clientele. When one belle epoque john complains, "No one knows what you're thinking," she dismisses him with a curt "I don't think anything." Playing someone for whom acquiescence is the foremost professional requirement, Haenel burrows deep to find Léa's impervious sense of self. That extreme self-possession is also manifest in her knockout cameo in Bonello's *Nocturama* (2016), about a massive attack on the French capital carried out by a cadre of millennial and Gen Z terrorists. In the aftermath of the bombings, Haenel, whose character is credited only as the "young woman on a bicycle," dispassionately remarks, "It was bound to happen."

In Thomas Cailley's offbeat romantic comedy from 2014, *Love at First Fight* (the original title, *Les Combattants*, is free of dopey puns), Haenel's Madeleine, a grad-school dropout and doomsday prepper, is similarly convinced of our inevitable annihilation. There's immense pleasure in watching this anhedonic, monomaniacal survivalist inure herself to the worst—an afternoon snack consists of a whole herring puréed into a blood-entrails-and-scales smoothie—and dedicate herself to developing warrior strength. Just as satisfying is witnessing the undeniable and yet confounding chemistry between Haenel and Kévin Azaïs, who plays Arnaud, a mild-mannered woodworker so intrigued by Madeleine that he enrolls in the same elite army training course that she signed up for months ago. The two seem drawn together by both raw lust and a sibling-like camaraderie—ambiguous cathectic energy that gives the duo, and Haenel especially, greater erotic mystery.

Even when Haenel portrays characters with no overt sexual appetite, as she does in the Dardenne brothers' *The Unknown Girl* (2016), she radiates a corporeal vitality. Playing physician Jenny Davin, the latest of the Belgian filmmakers' secular saints, she's driven to uncover the circumstances surrounding the death of a young African woman whose body has been found near a construction site, and whose demise Jenny feels partially responsible for. Like many of the Dardennes' recent films, *The Unknown Girl* creaks with melodramatic plot devices to arrive at its moment of uplift. But Haenel, who appears in nearly every frame, always keeps us watching. She's constantly on the move: when not auscultating patients at her clinic or making house calls at all hours, Jenny, as amateur PI, is running down leads. Her gait is resolute, typifying the doctor's casual grace. Her eyes pierce with laser focus.

The Unknown Girl, like all the Haenel films mentioned here except *The Devils* and *Suzanne*, received theatrical distribution in the US, if only in a very limited release. The actress does not seem to care, though, whether the US will ever receive *her*. In an interview with Haenel for *The Guardian* tied to the UK release of the Dardennes' movie, journalist Jonathan Romney notes that she, unlike many of her European coevals, has shown no interest in making a Hollywood film. "It's not my thing," she answers. "People say: 'Oh, you've got to reach the maximum number of people …' What's the difference if I reach three million people, or 20 people, or three?" Her response—candid, refreshing, even a little daring—constitutes another kind of coming out.

—*Artforum*, Summer 2018

David Bowie

Pop music's premier Proteus, David Bowie told *Rolling Stone* in 1972, "I feel like an actor when I'm onstage, rather than a rock artist." The remarks were made during the first US leg of his "Ziggy Stardust" tour, during which the singer summed up his flamboyant multitudes with these lines from "Moonage Daydream": "I'm an alligator, I'm a mama-papa comin' for you / I'm the space invader, I'll be a rock 'n' rollin' bitch for you." Reptile, androgynous life force, alien, dissolute strumpet: The Film Society of Lincoln Center's weeklong celebration of Bowie's magnetic big-screen performances reveals how much his scripted roles grew from the alter egos he created for his recording career.

Even before his breakthrough 1969 single, "Space Oddity," Bowie, born 66 years ago in Brixton, had shed multiple musical personae. He had also intensely studied mime—theatrical movement that was crucial in the creation of Ziggy Stardust. The singer dramatically runs into an invisible wall during his performance of "The Width of a Circle," one of 16 numbers captured in D. A. Pennebaker's concert doc *Ziggy Stardust and the Spiders from Mars* (1973), a record of that tour's terminus at London's Hammersmith Odeon on July 3, 1973. It was also, unknown to the enraptured teen fans, the final appearance of the epicene, eyebrow-less, pomegranate-mulleted messiah from outer space: "Not only is it the last show of the tour, but it's the last show that we'll ever do," Bowie announces, a fitting prelude to the evening's final song, "Rock 'n' Roll Suicide."

A master of rebirth, Bowie is also death-obsessed. In Alan Yentob's *Cracked Actor* (1975), an installment of the BBC arts-documentary series *Omnibus,* the singer softly admits to an off-screen interviewer who presses him on the destructive forces of his most notorious creation, "Yes, I had a kind of psychosomatic death wish, I think. But that's because I was so lost in Ziggy." Filmed during Bowie's North American "Diamond Dogs" tour in 1974, *Cracked Actor* suggests those self-annihilating impulses shouldn't have been relegated to the past tense: the singer, in the nascence of his "plastic-soul" phase, which culminated with the release of 1975's *Young Americans,* appears at his most cadaverous, his emaciation partly the result of cocaine abuse.

And yet that otherworldly, skeletal frame, accentuated onstage in '74 by Bowie's disco-dandy look—red suspenders, high-waisted trousers, broad-brimmed fedoras atop a strawberry-blond pompadour—unleashed all kinds of erotic urges in his fans. "I like people who are AC/DC, you know what I mean?" one concertgoer tells the BBC crew in *Cracked Actor.* This bulky, coquettish kid, his face slathered in red and blue makeup, is but one of many Me Decade youths—hetero, homo, or other—lured into sexual liberation and experimentation by Bowie's directive (and reassurance) in "Rock 'n' Roll Suicide": "Just turn on with me / And you're not alone." (The lyric could serve as a tagline for Todd Haynes's 1998 glam-rock ode, *Velvet Goldmine,* which centers around a thinly veiled Bowie figure.)

Bowie's outré pop-star appeal is deftly exploited in his first major screen role, as Thomas Jerome Newton, the extraterrestrial in search of water for his sere planet in Nicolas Roeg's *The Man Who Fell to Earth* (1976). Capitalizing on the trajectory of Major Tom, the hero of "Space Oddity," though actually based on a 1963 novel, Roeg's film pivots around his lead's gender-tweaking fragility, a delicate decadence that proves irresistible both to the hotel maid who shares his bed and the all-male brain trust working for Newton's World Enterprises.

The performer's mastery of combining aberrant desires with death also made him the perfect choice to play John Blaylock, the cello-playing, club-hopping vampire in *The Hunger* (1983), Tony Scott's Euro-chic, thrillingly ridiculous ode to bicuriosity. After snacking on some new-wave cuties he and his vampire bride, played by Catherine Deneuve, pick up in a Bauhaus-headlining nightclub, John discovers his undead self is aging rapidly. As the nattily attired bloodsucker waits to speak to Susan Sarandon's progeria expert in an Upper East Side clinic, we watch in horror as the actor transforms from beguiling 30-something to Truman Capote–like creature to Strom Thurmond doppelgänger.

As Bowie has aged and all but left behind extreme reinvention, he has not lost the power to surprise. Though many were convinced the performer had retired from music, earlier this year he released *The Next Day*, his first album in ten years, the cover of which features the iconic black-and-white photo of the singer that graced 1977's "*Heroes*", obscured by a white square. This penchant for playful, but never sentimental, nods to the past also deepens the texture of Bowie's memorable bit part as Nikola Tesla in Christopher Nolan's late-19th-century–set magician caper, *The Prestige* (2006). As the Croatian-born inventor emerges, godlike, from a swarm of electrical reactions, we remember where we've seen those lightning bolts before: adorning the stage at the Hammersmith Odeon, later boldly slashed across the face of Aladdin Sane himself.

—*Village Voice*, July 31, 2013

Ida Lupino

Early in her career, the husky-voiced Ida Lupino, one of film noir's greatest, most versatile actresses, was known by a few different sobriquets. Born in 1918 in London to a well-known family of thespians, she was dubbed "the English Jean Harlow" when she arrived in Los Angeles in 1933. By the early '40s, having acted opposite Humphrey Bogart in Raoul Walsh's *They Drive by Night* (1940) and *High Sierra* (1941)—acclaimed performances that nevertheless failed to elevate her to screen-legend status—she joked that she was "the poor man's Bette Davis." But by the end of that decade, when Lupino began directing films, the only woman then doing so in Hollywood, she gave herself her most enduring nickname: Mother. "I love being called Mother," Lupino said of her helmer's persona in 1967, 17 years after she became the second woman (after Dorothy Arzner) to be admitted to the Directors Guild. "I would never shout orders at anyone. I hate women who order men around, professionally or personally. I wouldn't dare do that with my old man ... and I don't do it with guys on the set. I say, 'Darlings, Mother has a problem. I'd love to do this. Can you do it? It sounds kooky but I want to do it.' And they do it."

Adopting the cognomen, which mixes authority (but not autocracy) with warmth (not to be confused with meekness) and chases it with high camp, served as a canny strategy for Lupino, who would direct seven movies from 1949 to 1966—all of which will screen at Film Forum as part of a series, running November 9–22, celebrating her centennial. (From 1956 to 1968, she also directed scores of television episodes, for shows including *The Fugitive*, *The Twilight Zone*, and

Gilligan's Island; on a hiatus from movie acting from 1956 to 1969, Lupino appeared in numerous TV series during those years as well. She retired in 1978 and died in 1995.)

In addition to the films she directed, "Ida Lupino 100" also features her greatest screen roles. Two of my favorites: as tavern entertainer Lily Stevens in Jean Negulesco's *Road House* (1948), Lupino rests a still-smoldering cigarette on top of the piano she plays while giving a near spoken-word rendition of the down-tempo "One for My Baby (And One More for the Road)," her voice a seductive rasp deepened by tobacco and world-weariness ("She reminds me of the first woman that ever slapped my face," an admiring male patron remarks before Lily begins her number). And as Mary—a blind woman determined to protect her kid brother, who's wanted for murder—in Nicholas Ray's *On Dangerous Ground* (1951), Lupino anneals her trusting, vulnerable character with unyielding mettle.

The highlight of the retrospective, though, is the film in which Lupino appeared on both sides of the camera, becoming the first woman in the post-silent era to direct herself: *The Bigamist* (1953). The movie was Lupino's final directorial effort for the Filmakers, the idiosyncratically spelled production company she formed with Malvin Wald and her second husband, Collier Young, shortly after the release of *Not Wanted* (1949). That project, about the highly taboo subject of unwed mothers, marked the unofficial directing debut of Lupino (who cowrote the screenplay); she took over helming duties from Elmer Clifton, who had a heart attack shortly before filming began—and who retained sole director's credit.

The movies Lupino directed for Filmakers included socially conscious melodramas such as *Outrage* (1950), an unblinking account of rape and the cruelties of the legal system, and lean noirs like *The Hitch-Hiker* (1953), about two buddies headed to a fishing trip in Mexico who unknowingly offer a lift to a psychopath. *The Bigamist,* remarkably complex and deeply sympathetic to all three of its protagonists, is a hybrid of both genres—call it a melo-noir.

The film opens in San Francisco, the home base of married couple and business partners Harry (Edmond O'Brien, one of the stars of *The Hitch-Hiker*) and Eve (Joan Fontaine). They are discussing their hopes to adopt in the office of an agency employee, Mr. Jordan (Edmund Gwenn, whose career-defining role as Kris Kringle in George Seaton's *Miracle on 34th Street* from 1947 is a running in-joke here). Though the spouses, wed for eight years, seem happy and appear to be fine candidates for parenthood, Jordan has suspicions about Harry. That mistrust is borne out early in the film when the agent tracks down the aspiring father in Los Angeles, where Harry often travels for work—and where he's now sharing a bungalow with another wife and their infant son.

Confronted by Jordan, Harry recounts the circumstances that led to his "insane double life," setting in motion a flashback as sinuous as those found in the paradigmatic noirs *Double Indemnity* (1944) and *Mildred Pierce* (1945). Feeling lonely and alienated from Eve while on yet another company trip to LA—a city brought vividly to life via the film's on-location shots of Bunker Hill and MacArthur Park—Harry meets Phyllis (Lupino) on a homes-of-the-stars bus tour. He chats her up; she at first rebuffs him with this retort, delivered with Lupino's signature tough-broad hauteur, to his solicitous query about why she's on the touristy excursion: "I'm just crazy about bus rides. Gives me a chance to get off my feet."

But Phyllis soon softens, inviting Harry to the Chinese restaurant—"Early American Chinese. You're gonna love it!"—where she's a waitress and notably the only Caucasian employee. She shares an easy camaraderie with her Asian coworkers, who are presented with none of the baleful stereotypes too common in Hollywood then—and still deployed now. (Another salient detail about Phyllis's workplace: one of the patrons at the mostly empty eatery is a cameoing Collier Young, who wrote *The Bigamist*'s screenplay. In a bit of marital intrigue that further heightens that on-screen, Collier was, as of 1951, divorced from Lupino and, as of '52, married to Fontaine.)

As Harry and Phyllis fall in love, she never fully sheds her carapace, insisting that he never tell her anything about his past. He feels needed by her, especially after she learns she's pregnant—a dependency he fears that Eve, a confident executive, no longer exhibits toward him. *The Bigamist* may be told through Harry's point of view, but he is by no means the movie's hero. Harry, like Eve and Phyllis, is something more profound than that: a person undone by desolation. The film ends in a courtroom, but judgment is suspended.

As for my own judgment, I wish that Lupino's film-directing career had ended with *The Bigamist*. Sadly, her last movie, the manic, exhausting Catholic-schoolgirl romp *The Trouble with Angels* (1966), is also her worst. Despite this blunder, I'd still like to propose this programming suggestion to movie houses around the globe for the remainder of 2018: Make every day Mother's day.

—*4Columns*, November 9, 2018

Jane Fonda

What is a star, and how does one function? Richard Dyer, the British cinema scholar who established star studies nearly 40 years ago, helped pin down the slippery concept with this maxim, found in his 1986 book, *Heavenly Bodies*: "Stars matter because they act out aspects of life that matter to us; and performers get to be stars when what they act out matters to enough people."

The expression *act out* takes on a double meaning when considering the career of Jane Fonda in the 1970s. In that decade, the performer, born in 1937, established herself as "the most politically outspoken star in Hollywood history," as the critic J. Hoberman wrote in a 2001 reappraisal of Fonda. On-screen in the '70s, she acted out the parts for which she would win her two Best Actress Oscars: the haute-boho sex worker Bree Daniels in Alan J. Pakula's neo-noir *Klute* (1971) and the initially meek military wife Sally Hyde in Hal Ashby's 1968-set drama *Coming Home* (1978). Off-screen during this decade, her political activism, particularly her steadfast opposition to the Vietnam War, led her detractors to accuse her of another kind of acting out: misbehaving. The Fonda of this era remains the paradigm of how—if, in fact, it's even possible—to reconcile the committed citizen with the celebrity.

Fonda's attackers in the '70s included Richard Nixon, who placed her on his "enemies list." More insidiously, they also included Jean-Luc Godard, who banked on the actress's engagée persona only to exploit it in a project he codirected with Jean-Pierre Gorin: *Tout va bien* (1972), an ideologically dense film about the fracturing of post-'68 France that's anchored by a squabbling couple played by Fonda and Yves Montand. Far-leftist confreres, Godard and Gorin also collaborated on *Tout va bien*'s acid addendum, *Letter to Jane.* In this 52-minute essay film, both men volubly analyze a photo—showing a stern-faced Fonda meeting with North Vietnamese citizens in Hanoi—that ran in a 1972 issue of the French newsweekly *L'Express.* Near the end of their semiotic scrutiny, Gorin delivers this icy indictment: "One must realize that stars are not allowed to think."

What is a star, and what is one permitted to do? A decade before *Letter to Jane,* Fonda was the subject of another, more sympathetic nonfiction film: *Jane* (1962), overseen by the American Direct Cinema innovator Robert Drew. The nearly hour-long portrait follows the actress, then only two years into her career and not yet 25, in the weeks leading up to a top-billed theater performance. "Jane Fonda, daughter of a famous actor, preparing for her first opening night as a star on the Broadway stage," the narrator announces at the beginning of *Jane,* as we see her at a fitting. The appositive in this intro underscores how much being the child of Henry Fonda burdened the actress in the first decade of her profession, when she was defined not by her politics but by her patrilineage. Fonda *fille* articulates that anxiety in *Jane* when she notes the resentment she's felt from colleagues, who are certain that any part she's landed up to that point resulted not from her talent and dedication but from the sheer dumb luck of the family she was born into. Even in the nascence of her stardom, she was regarded warily—skepticism that her actor brother, Peter, two years her junior, largely escaped.

She was also regarded—as most actresses have been since the birth, nearly a century ago, of the cinema star system—as raw, imperfect material to be reshaped. Fonda lucidly reflects back on the indignities she faced in the first years of her career in Delphine Seyrig's little-seen documentary *Sois belle et tais-toi* (*Be Pretty and Shut Up*, 1981), a survey shot in the mid-'70s of 23 American and European actresses, who share their experiences of the film industry's entrenched sexism. Clearly at ease with Seyrig—a fellow actress-activist of the era, and Fonda's castmate in Joseph Losey's 1973 adaptation of Henrik Ibsen's proto-feminist stage landmark *A Doll's House*—she recalls her humiliating, but far from atypical, makeup test for Warner Bros. That studio released Fonda's first film, Joshua Logan's *Tall Story* (1960), a college-campus romp in which she plays a husband-hunting cheerleader. "It was like I was coming off an assembly line," Fonda says, discussing the maquillage experts who insisted that she dye her hair blonde and encouraged her to have her jaw broken, to give her more sunken cheeks. (She agreed to the former but said no to the latter.) Logan, who was also Fonda's godfather, suggested she'd need even further facial alteration. She recalls his assessment: "'You'll never play in a tragedy because a nose like that cannot be taken seriously.'" Her nose remained intact; her conception of herself did not. "I, Jane Fonda, was here and this image was there, and there was this alienation between the two," she tells Seyrig.

What is a star, and what is one allowed to say—and how? Fonda relays those anecdotes to Seyrig in French, which is the same language she speaks in *Tout va bien* and in two films she made with Roger Vadim, the first of her three husbands: *La Ronde* (1964) and *La Curée* (1966, aka *The Game Is Over*). In this pair of movies, as with nearly all of her work from the '60s, in any tongue, Fonda performs some variation on the soubrette or the sex kitten—types that could fall under the category "ridiculous woman," as the actress bluntly describes her *Tall Story* character to Seyrig. The most outlandish of these ridiculous women—and the last one she would play, not just in the '60s but ever again—was the title character in *Barbarella* (1968), her final film with Vadim.

Fonda ended that decade with the movie that proved her dexterity in a serious part: Sydney Pollack's Depression-set *They Shoot Horses, Don't They?* (1969), in which she stars as one of several scores of contestants in a grueling dance marathon vying for a $1,500 prize. By 1970, she was filming *Klute* and had embarked on her most politically radical period, which would last for the next four years (and for which she would become a target of COINTELPRO, the FBI's covert, frequently illegal program of surveilling and discrediting "subversives"). "What I did was talk—all the time, everywhere, on and on and on in a frantic voice tinged with the Ivy League," Fonda writes in her autobiography, *My Life So Far* (2005), of this epoch, one marked by not only her antiwar activism but also her commitment to the Black Panthers, feminism, economic justice, and American Indian rights.

Yes, she talked, but she also knew the power of reticence. Seconds before her name was announced at the Academy Awards ceremony on April 10, 1972, as the Best Actress winner for *Klute*, Fonda whispers something to Donald Sutherland, her date that night and her costar in the film. Sutherland had also helped her organize the FTA show—as in "Fuck the Army"—an antiwar revue that he, Fonda, and others performed in '71 for US service members, both at home and in the Pacific Rim. (Francine Parker captured the overseas leg of the tour in her 1972 documentary, *F.T.A.*, which features many soldiers speaking on camera about their disgust with the military. The growing antiwar sentiment inside all branches of the US Armed Forces led to the GI movement, with which Fonda's activism was most closely aligned.)

Were the attendees of the Oscar gala, who clap politely, almost tepidly, as Fonda walks up to collect her gold statue, bracing themselves for a harangue? Onstage, she bows and smiles. She thanks the members of the Academy and those who applauded. Then, after a dramatic pause, a slight exhale of breath, and another smile, she concludes: "There's a great deal to say and I'm not going to say it tonight. I would just like to really thank you very much." She quickly exits.

Fonda's '72 acceptance speech is one of the shortest and most potent ever delivered at the Academy Awards, an event that has often served as a showcase for overweening sanctimony and toothless political peroration. In a pleasing irony, Fonda's taciturn remarks were made at a ceremony lauding her portrayal of a character who, among other things, is undergoing the talking cure. Three crucial, spellbinding segments in *Klute* feature Bree Daniels in her matronly analyst's office, sorting through her irreconcilable feelings: about sex work, about the profession she aspires to (acting), about the man she's growing emotionally attached to (Sutherland's eponymous private detective, who's protecting Bree from a sociopathic killer).

At Fonda's request, these episodes in *Klute* were shot last and were entirely improvised. Her therapist is played by Vivian Nathan, one of the original members of the Actors Studio. (With its emphasis on Method acting, the organization had revolutionized performing in the US by the mid-20th century; Fonda studied there early in her career. "It was nothing like what I'd known at the Actors Studio," Fonda says in *Sois belle* of her *Tall Story* role.) Fonda is electric in every moment of *Klute*, but watching her in these scenes with Nathan is like witnessing the sparks of a Tesla coil. Operating on alternating currents, Bree is a dynamic study in contradictions—an imperfect yet indelible symbol of second-wave feminism, the cresting of which nearly coincided with *Klute*'s release. According to Patricia Bosworth's *Jane Fonda: The Private Life of a Public Woman* (2011), Fonda credited her off-screen activities for improving her performances: "On breaks Jane would tell Nathan she was sure her politics were nurturing her acting. Politics had made her more aware, more open."

What is a star, and how does one change? A month after Fonda won her Academy Award for *Klute*, she received an invitation from a North Vietnamese delegation to visit Hanoi and the surrounding area, to witness firsthand the destruction of the country wrought by the US. She arrived in the capital city, alone, on July 8, 1972, and stayed for two weeks. While there, she met with American POWs and recorded broadcasts for Voice of Vietnam radio, to relay to US pilots the damage she saw on the ground and to implore them to stop bombing (an excerpt: "The people beneath your planes have done us no harm. They want to live in peace. They want to rebuild their country").

It was during this trip that the photo of her so disapprovingly dissected in *Letter to Jane* was taken—as was the most notorious snapshot of Fonda, the one for which she would be lambasted as "Hanoi Jane," an epithet still deployed today. The photo, from her last full day in North Vietnam, shows her, with a helmet on and an incongruously gleeful expression on her face (she's singing a Vietnamese song she had memorized to her soldier hosts), sitting on an antiaircraft gun. Admitting later to horrible misjudgment, Fonda writes of the incident in her memoir, "If I was used, I allowed it to happen. ... I realize that it is not just a US citizen laughing and clapping on a [North] Vietnamese antiaircraft gun: I am Henry Fonda's privileged daughter who appears to be thumbing my nose at the country that has provided me these privileges."

Ever since the publication of that photo—a still image that has threatened to eclipse any moving-image work she has ever done—Fonda has repeatedly apologized for her lapse, careful to separate it from her antiwar activism as a whole, for which she, rightly, has no regrets. Upon her return to the US in late July '72, the State Department assailed her, and the Veterans of Foreign Wars passed a resolution insisting that she be prosecuted as a traitor. The overwhelming antipathy from the government (and civilians) did not dissuade her from her cause: that September, she embarked on the Indochina Peace Campaign, a cross-country antiwar speaking tour that she organized with Tom Hayden, soon to be her second husband. In 1974, the penultimate year of the war, Fonda made her second visit to North Vietnam, this time with Hayden and their infant son. The trip served as the basis for the documentary *Introduction to the Enemy* (1974); shot and directed by Haskell Wexler, the film, as Fonda recalls in her book, was "aimed at showing a human side of Vietnam, a view of the people's lives and stories very few Americans would otherwise ever see or hear." The chronicle, an affecting work of diplomacy, succeeds in its mission.

Later in the '70s, Fonda would be the main attraction in another kind of fence-mending vehicle. *Introduction to the Enemy* was the first release of her production company, IPC Films, which repurposed the initials of the Indochina Peace Campaign and was formed in 1973. That year she also conceived of the project that would eventually morph into *Coming Home*, a film partially inspired by Ron Kovic, the paralyzed Vietnam vet with whom Fonda had recently shared a platform at an antiwar rally. Kovic's analogue in Ashby's 1978 movie, set during the Vietnam War but debuting three years after it ended, is Jon Voight's Luke, a paraplegic former marine recovering in a chaotic, understaffed VA hospital.

It is with Luke—emotional, tender, a superior lover—that Fonda's Sally, the dutiful spouse of a tyrannical marine corps captain, played by Bruce Dern, transforms. While her husband is overseeing more carnage in Southeast Asia, Sally volunteers at the hospital and begins an affair with Luke, with whom she has her first orgasm. She changes her hair. She becomes somewhat politicized, outraged by the treatment the vets are receiving. I don't mean to diminish Fonda's acting in *Coming Home*, which is characteristically sensitive, nuanced, and alert. But the film, an absorbing marital melodrama, for which she won her second Best Actress Academy Award, may be too gentle. The conciliatory tone is reflected in the closing of Fonda's acceptance speech at the Oscar ceremony on April 9, 1979: she thanks Hayden for helping her "believe that besides being entertaining, movies can inspire and teach and even be healing."

Who is Jane Fonda, and what have I said about her? As an actress and an activist, Fonda did her most significant, and bravest, work in the 1970s. She has remained dedicated to both pursuits (in the latter category, she's been particularly devoted to adolescent sexual health). Over the following decades, she has reinvented herself more times than any star of her stature: fitness sage, wife of Ted Turner, temporary retiree (she took a 15-year break from films after 1990's *Stanley & Iris*), to name just a few of her incarnations. She has been, often by her own admission, a jumble of generative, sometimes confounding contradictions. To summarize further would be foolish. All I can do is paraphrase her legendarily brief remarks on that 1972 Oscar night: there's—still—a great deal to say.

—*4Columns*, June 1, 2018

Kristen Stewart

She's still big; it's the pictures that are getting smaller. Kristen Stewart, who became one of the most recognizable humans in the world for playing Bella Swan, the tender, tremulous teenage vampire-lover in the massively successful *Twilight* franchise, has lately been showing off her talents in a string of more modest productions. In the almost four years since the fifth and final installment of the *Twilight* saga was released, the actress has scrupulously avoided blockbusters, instead headlining and taking supporting roles in auteurist films made on either side of the Atlantic. Her range post-Bella was demonstrated last month at Cannes, where two disparate projects premiered within days of each other: Woody Allen's 1930s-set *Café Society*, in which she plays a bobby-socked movie studio secretary caught in a love triangle, and Olivier Assayas's resolutely of-this-moment *Personal Shopper*, a shape-shifting ghost story that features the actress in nearly every frame.

They are just two Stewart films scheduled for release this year: *Café Society* opens July 15, the same day as Drake Doremus's sci-fi romance *Equals*; *Personal Shopper* bows in theaters later in 2016, along with Kelly Reichardt's ensemble drama *Certain Women*. Even those (critics and civilian moviegoers alike) who dismissed the actress's work in the bloodsucker juggernaut would have to be impressed by this latest career efflorescence. For those of us who were immediately taken with her portrayal of Bella—as I was on a miserable Saturday afternoon in late November 2008 at a Chelsea multiplex, where I saw the inaugural *Twilight* movie—

Stewart's recent roles confirm what's been evident all along: that she is one of her generation's most quicksilver performers. Crucially, this electrifying mutability is rooted in her genius at communicating, both on-screen and off-, a sexuality that is itself ever-changing: from extremely heteronormative to explicitly sapphic and all libidinal leanings in between.

Stewart's gifts were apparent several years before *Twilight*'s first gleaming. Born in 1990 in Los Angeles to parents who work behind the scenes in the entertainment industry—her father is a stage manager, her mother a script supervisor and producer—Stewart had her breakthrough role in David Fincher's *Panic Room* (2002), released shortly before her 12th birthday. In this Upper West Side home invasion thriller, she plays Sarah, a scooter-riding, Sid Vicious–adoring tomboy and the only child of Jodie Foster's Meg, recently divorced from a 1 percenter husband. Stewart's resemblance to Foster is uncanny: not only does she have the same wide, light-colored eyes and heart-shaped face as her elder, but Stewart is also a dead ringer for Foster during the mid-'70s height of *her* kid-performer years (the era of *Alice Doesn't Live Here Anymore*, *Taxi Driver*, etc.). The preteen toughie Stewart so confidently portrays in *Panic Room* isn't entirely invulnerable—she's diabetic. But, no matter how low her blood sugar, Sarah still has the smarts to use one of her insulin syringes to attack the worst of the guys who've been terrorizing her and her ma. Stewart's mien and mettle in Fincher's movie recall Foster's from three decades earlier—a soft-butch atavism that's the first of many queer signifiers in Stewart's career, more on which in a moment.

Among her 14 other ante-Bella features, *Into the Wild* (2007), directed by Sean Penn, best showcases the skill that the actress would repeatedly demonstrate in the *Twilight* pentalogy: a superb understanding of how to remind viewers of all ages of the chaotic churn of adolescent emotion and desire. In only a handful of scenes in Penn's movie, Stewart—as Tracy Tatro, a peewee Joni Mitchell living in a trailer park in dusty Imperial Valley, California—slinks with burgeoning sexual confidence. "That poor girl is about ready to vault herself onto a fence post," one character says while Tracy stares hungrily at the 20-something adventurer played by Emile Hirsch. Splayed provocatively on her bed in a white tee and panties, the 16-year-old boldly invites him to join her. Undeniably, Tracy enjoys a carnal freedom that Bella doesn't in the *Twilight* films, which, despite their floridly supernatural elements, push a retrograde purity-ring philosophy. Still, the depths of uncontainable yearning Stewart conveys in these movies (at least the first four) is all the more impressive considering the lesser skills of her costars Robert Pattinson, as the pallid vampire she weds and procreates with, and Taylor Lautner, the teen wolf Bella loves ... like a brother.

The *Twilight* franchise's advancement of a conservative agenda of one (undead) man, one woman might have been boosted by the fact that Stewart and Pattinson were dating for much of the series' 2008–12 run. But throughout these years, the actress, refusing to be pigeonholed, signed up for projects that complicated the swoony, boy-crazy, high-femme virgin character that was bringing in box office billions. As Joan Jett in *The Runaways* (2010), Floria Sigismondi's lush recounting of the rise and fall of the jailbait '70s rock group, Stewart no longer slinks—she swaggers, strutting not for guys but for girls. She plays the teenage guitarist like a heat-seeking missile, one aimed at Cherie Currie (Dakota Fanning), the bandmate she's besotted with. Bathed in cherry-bomb-red light, these two share a sultry kiss, the lip-lock initiated by Jett. Stewart's brilliant baby-dyke bravado in *The Runaways*, her unabashed lustfulness, reveals an appetite that *Twilight* tamped down (if not outright forbade). Since that franchise concluded, her characters' desires, sometimes unconventional, have often been expressed in more oblique, though no less stirring, ways.

"Dare I kiss you?" big-shot Hollywood talent agent Phil Stern (Steve Carell) asks his employee and mistress, the felicitously named Veronica "Vonnie" Sibyl (Stewart), in Allen's *Café Society*. "Dare you not?" is her reply, Stewart's intoxicating delivery suggesting both raw need and cool self-assurance.

The film may be another of Allen's creaky nostalgia vehicles, but once again, Stewart's incandescence cannot be dimmed by inferior material. She quite literally glows when we first see her character: Vonnie is enhaloed by sunlight after stepping into Phil's office, where she is introduced to her boss's nephew, New York transplant Bobby (Jesse Eisenberg, in his third film with Stewart), who will soon become her boyfriend. Stewart's steno-pool sophisticate is the luminous orb around which these men revolve, and the sole source of fire in the film. Who else, by the sheer power of sexual magnetism, could make Eisenberg's twitchy worrywart character, a clear stand-in for Allen, seem like a viable love interest? "I can't imagine what it would be like to be larger than life," Bobby tells his beloved after they take in a Joan Crawford movie. "I think I'd be happier being life-sized," Vonnie says, a response made all the richer by the fact that it's spoken by an actress who regularly appeared on IMAX screens not long ago.

But the filmmaker with whom Stewart has most ingeniously refracted her real-life career is Olivier Assayas. In *Clouds of Sils Maria* (2014), the first of her two collaborations to date with the Paris-based auteur, she plays Valentine, the bespectacled personal assistant to Maria Enders (Juliette Binoche), an internationally renowned 40-year-old star of stage and screen. There's a perverse thrill in watching Stewart, long an A-lister, so astutely inhabit the role of helpmate. Though deferential, Valentine doesn't hesitate to challenge Maria, delivering an eloquent defense of blockbusters to her employer when she slams industrial cinema—the very kind of moviemaking that made Stewart a star.

Despite being boss and underling, Maria and Valentine have a relationship that is constantly in flux, the lines between the personal and the professional often blurred. That's especially the case when the two move into a secluded house in Sils Maria, a village in the Swiss Alps, where Maria begins to prepare for a particularly fraught stage revival. Their psychic enmeshment deepens during the weeks that Valentine runs lines with her employer, erotic suspense rising from Stewart's intricately calibrated push-pull with her costar, a battle of wills mixed with affection in which top/bottom, sub/dom are positions that are never quite fixed. While their intimacy never extends to the physical, one scene strongly hints at the possibility before fading to black.

There's even less stability in Assayas's forthcoming *Personal Shopper*, an outré yet unexpectedly touching tale of luxury brands and ectoplasm. Here, Stewart's character, Maureen, in the title profession, is demoted to an even lowlier celebrity adjutant. A studiously disheveled American temporarily in Paris (one whose sartorial style matches Stewart's boho-butch rags in several paparazzi shots over the past few years), Maureen hopes to make contact with her recently deceased twin brother, who possessed the same paranormal gifts she has. When not receiving signals from the dead, she dashes from one high-end shop to the next for the fashion-fascist boss she says she despises, Kyra (Nora von Waldstätten). But does she really? Dropping off some Cartier at Kyra's empty luxe dwelling, the assistant tries on one of her employer's haute-couture frocks (not unlike the ones Stewart has been modeling in a recent Chanel print campaign). This charged, forbidden act is made even more lubricious when Maureen begins to masturbate in Kyra's bed. The actress loses herself in the scene's lurid hall of mirrors, succumbing to the irony of playing a character who gets turned on by pretending to be, however briefly, someone she's not—that is, by acting. The frisson is multiplied as we watch Stewart—who, in real life, must always be on guard against stalkers and other predators—portray someone who thrills at violating the rules and sanctum of her VIP boss.

The smallest role Stewart has in a film in this annus mirabilis is the most evocative. In Kelly Reichardt's *Certain Women*, which the writer-director adapted from short stories in Maile Meloy's 2009 collection *Both Ways Is the Only Way I Want It*, she plays fledgling Montana lawyer Beth Travis in one of the movie's three main vignettes. Anxious about her student loans, Beth has taken a part-time job teaching an adult education evening class on law—a twice-a-week gig that's an eight-hour round-trip commute. Bedecked in ill-fitting cotton/poly-blend cardigans and skirts, Stewart's attorney exudes crippling self-doubt. But one student—ranch hand Jamie (Lily Gladstone)—is immediately smitten with her new teacher, suggesting they go to a diner afterward simply so she can sit across from Beth and hang on her every word. Significantly, Reichardt has switched the genders of the crushed-out pupil; in Meloy's book, the enamored cowpoke is a man named Chet.

Is this reversal a sly acknowledgment of Stewart's own strange avowal/disavowal of her recently reported same-sex relationships? In the September 2015 issue of *Nylon*, the actress said, "If you feel like you really want to define yourself, and you have the ability to articulate those parameters and that in itself defines you, then do it. But I am an actress, man. I live in the fucking ambiguity of this life and I love it. I don't feel like it would be true for me to be like, 'I'm coming out!' No, I do a job. Until I decide that I'm starting a foundation or that I have some perspective or opinion that other people should be receiving ... I don't. I'm just a kid making movies." Her response may be evasive, yet it does nothing to diminish her incontrovertible allure on screen. She's not a kid (she turned 26 in April), but she is still making movies—a dizzying assortment of them, each one further proof of her fearlessness and infinite talent, and each unleashing all kinds of fantasies from spectators of all genders and sexualities. *All* ways is the only way we want it.

—*Village Voice*, June 29, 2016

Lily Tomlin

When Lily Tomlin's first film, Robert Altman's *Nashville,* was released in June 1975, the actress and comedian had been a star for at least five years, celebrated for her array of voluble characters. Some of these personae—Ernestine, the floridly passive-aggressive telephone operator; Edith Ann, an uninhibited five-year-old emotional savant—made their debut during her 1969–73 tenure on NBC's *Laugh-In.* Others, like Bobbi-Jeanine, a bromide-dispensing lounge-circuit organist, premiered on *The Lily Tomlin Show* (1973), the first of her four eponymous TV specials from the '70s. These personalities illustrate Tomlin's tremendous gifts with voice. But in one of the best scenes from Altman's superb ensemble movie, itself dense with talk and song, she mesmerizes with her silence.

In the final hour of *Nashville,* Tomlin's Linnea Reese—dutiful wife to a self-involved attorney, devoted mother of two deaf pubescent children, and a part-time gospel singer—takes a seat at the back of a club where Keith Carradine's Tom, a philandering country-rock heartthrob, is gigging. The Jesus-haired libertine, who met the upstanding housewife at a music studio two months prior, has been calling Linnea at home, pleading to see her again and inviting her to this intimate show. Also in the audience are three of Tom's latest bedmates, each convinced that she is the "someone special" for whom he's written a recent number, "I'm Easy," and completely unaware that the true dedicatee is Linnea, who is calmly sipping apple cider from a wineglass.

As Carradine croons this ballad, Tomlin gives a sublime performance of being seduced, transforming a putatively passive act into an agile display of tiny, potent gestures. With her lips slightly parted, she places her left hand under her modest white blouse and rests it on her clavicle. Near the end of the song, Linnea inhales deeply, closes her eyes for a second or two, and leans gently into the side of a wooden banquette, as if unmoored by her besottedness.

This segment from *Nashville* endures for me as one of the most moving depictions of desire, my pleasure in watching it heightened by the fact that the woman who offers such a compelling interpretation of heterosexual cathexis is gay. At the time of *Nashville*'s production, Tomlin was already a few years into a romantic relationship—which continues to this day—with the writer Jane Wagner, who has also been one of her most vital collaborators. Their partnership is the focus of "Two Free Women: Lily Tomlin & Jane Wagner," a retrospective running this month at Film at Lincoln Center in New York. Organized by Hilton Als and Thomas Beard, the series isn't limited to the pair's joint efforts; projects that Tomlin, the far more prolific of the pair, has made without Wagner's involvement, such as *Nashville*, dominate the program. But by showcasing the rarely revived titles from the Tomlin-Wagner corpus—from the most lauded (the 1991 movie adaptation of their 1985 Broadway hit *The Search for Signs of Intelligent Life in the Universe*) to the most reviled (*Moment by Moment*, a 1978 *film maudit*)—"Two Free Women" salutes a lesbian couple without equal in entertainment history.

Work brought the two together. Tomlin had been impressed by *J.T.* (1969), a CBS after-school special (included in the Lincoln Center series) written by Wagner about a lonely African American boy in Harlem who nurtures a stray cat. Tomlin, preparing to record an Edith Ann album in 1971 and looking to enrich the kindergarten-age character, reached out to Wagner, who eventually joined the comedian in California to help her produce the LP. In a 2006 interview, Tomlin recalled of their initial face-to-face meeting, "I was pretty taken with her as soon as I saw her. We just sort of clicked. We became a couple right away."

Wagner was on the writing staff of all seven of Tomlin's TV specials (the last one aired in 1982), contributing such pensive sketches as "Juke and Opal," the final piece in *Lily* (1973), the second of these one-off shows. This roughly nine-minute segment, which will play as part of the retrospective, features Tomlin and her friend Richard Pryor as a café proprietress and a down-and-outer who's one of her regulars. They banter, bicker, and flirt like lovers or exes, the tenderness between them ineradicable—never more so than when two uptight white social workers enter Opal's eatery and begin asking Juke questions as part of their "community research." The skit, which Als, in an essay on Pryor included in *White Girls* (2013), hailed as "the most profound meditation on race and class that I have ever seen on a major network," may freak out contemporary audiences; Tomlin is coded as Black via costuming and speech—but, crucially, not through makeup. ("Tomlin plays Opal in whiteface, as it were," Als writes.) However discomfiting today, the earnest sequence at its most fundamental level shows two comedy eminences fully in sync, their admiration for each other abundant.

"The work of the brilliant performer is to make a habit of disjunction," Als continues in that essay; his laudatory declaration is directed as much to Tomlin as to Pryor. "Disjunction" aptly sums up *Moment by Moment*, the only film Wagner has ever directed (she also wrote the screenplay), one defined by a fascinating, perverse lack of correspondence. (Just before press time, Tomlin and Wagner asked that the movie be removed from the retrospective.) Centering on the age- and class-discordant relationship between Tomlin's Trisha, a wealthy woman nearing middle age whose marriage is unraveling, and John Travolta's ludicrously nicknamed Strip (as in Sunset), a 20-ish stud, *Moment by Moment* appeals despite its failures. Although Tomlin and Travolta kindle zero erotic heat, they exhibit an intriguing amity that buoys the film, a gentleness and generosity that might have been rooted in a shared vulnerability. Wagner's movie, a serious romantic drama, was a significant departure from the previous work of its stars, then at the height of their popularity. Travolta had become the signal Carter-era male idol thanks to *Saturday Night Fever* (1977) and *Grease*, released six months before *Moment by Moment*; Tomlin had been anointed the "New Queen of Comedy" on the cover of *Time* in 1977, having recently starred in both Robert Benton's offbeat sunshine noir *The Late Show* (charmingly playing a SoCal weirdo turned accidental gumshoe) and her first one-woman Broadway show, *Appearing Nitely*, which she cowrote and codirected with Wagner.

Gutted by the critical savaging of *Moment by Moment*, the actress thereafter stuck to comedies with wider appeal, most famously Colin Higgins's *Nine to Five* (1980), a support-staff revenger hamstrung by too many dopey gags but boasting a felicitously cast lead trio, with Tomlin's Violet Newstead the most revolutionary-minded of the film's pink-collar intifadists, who also include Dolly Parton and Jane Fonda. (Tomlin and Fonda have remained active in the streaming age as the stars of Netflix's *Grace and Frankie*.) Following two other crowd-pleasers—Joel Schumacher's *The Incredible Shrinking Woman* (1981), a cheery spoof of consumerism scripted by Wagner, and Carl Reiner's *All of Me* (1984), a burlesque involving a metempsychosis mishap—Tomlin began touring small venues with embryonic incarnations of *The Search for Signs of Intelligent Life in the Universe*; the play's evolution is tracked in Nick Broomfield and Joan Churchill's documentary *Lily Tomlin* (1986).

An absorbing chronicle, *Lily Tomlin* is structured as a countdown to September 26, 1985, the triumphant Broadway opening night of *Search*, an opus at once exuberant and mournful that reflects on the dashed hopes of second-wave feminism and the raging contradictions of trying "to be politically conscious and upwardly mobile at the same time." Written and directed solely by Wagner, the play—a feat of precise, supple sociocultural analysis—features Tomlin flawlessly embodying a dozen or so different characters, with no props or costume changes. (The '91 film adaptation dispenses with the original's minimalism.)

As they trace the development of *Search* from a work in progress toward its official debut, Broomfield and Churchill incorporate candid backstage incidents: Tomlin inviting Wagner and other members of the crew (all distaff—and maybe all dyke?) to huddle up and sing the chorus of "We Are Family"; Tomlin, distraught over the still-rudimentary show's imperfect sound, announcing the enormous challenges she faces in conveying so many different personae on such a spartan set: "All I have is my voice and my body ... to make it believable."

But the most revealing moment occurs during an iteration of *Search* performed in San Diego in 1984. During the second act, whose characters include a lesbian couple and a sapphic Casanova, Tomlin, not yet off-book, directly addresses the audience, which on this night seems to feature a sizable gaylez contingent: "I didn't write this material. My partner, Jane Wagner, writes my material. And ... I hate to fail her material.

I mean, it's so much better than I am. You know, it's kept me going for years."

At the time of *Search*, Tomlin wasn't "officially" out—very few celebrities of her stature were in the mid-'80s—but her relationship with Wagner had never been hidden, either. In the years since 2000, when Tomlin's sexuality became a matter of public record, her more noteworthy films have included Paul Weitz's *Grandma* (2015), a project written specifically for her, in which she plays a recently widowed, acerbic lesbian poet—a role that nicely, if too programmatically, underscores her status as lavender legend. I'd argue that the greater homage to Tomlin, and to her love-work partnership with Wagner, is to be found in David O. Russell's metaphysically motored screwball comedy *I Heart Huckabees* (2004). Tomlin portrays Vivian Jaffe, an "existential detective" who divides sleuthing duties with her adored spouse, Bernard, played by Dustin Hoffman. Quasi-transcendentalists, the Jaffes champion omnipresent "interconnectivity"—always searching for signs of intelligent life in the universe.

—*Artforum*, September 2019

Maggie Cheung

Maggie Cheung, like all screen sublimities, inhabits multiple temporalities: she is past, present, and future. The filmmaker Olivier Assayas once described the actress as "an up-to-date version of an old-fashioned movie star." He elaborated when I spoke to him a decade ago about *Clean* (2004), the second of two projects he made with Cheung, following *Irma Vep* (1996), a meta-movie in which she plays herself: "When I first met Maggie"—at the Venice Film Festival in 1994—"I thought she had something incredibly modern, incredibly now. But she also had the specific glow of a movie star, this kind of thing that radiates in film." Over the next three weeks, you can bask in the actress's luminosity at Metrograph, which is screening 20 of her films (a fraction of her output) on 35mm.

By the time of Assayas's initial encounter with Cheung, she was 11 years into an immensely successful career in Hong Kong, where she was born in 1964. Schooled in the UK, she returned to HK at age 18, getting the first runner-up spot in the Miss Hong Kong pageant in 1983, an event that served as her entrée to film. Her breakthrough role was May, the capricious girlfriend in *Police Story* (1985), a high-slapstick actioner starring and directed by Jackie Chan. (As reported in Susan Dominus's November 2004 profile of the actress in the *New York Times Magazine*, Chan remarked that when he first saw Cheung on television, he thought of her as someone who "wouldn't mind me kicking her down a flight of stairs.") She reprised the role in the next two *Police Story* installments, released in 1988 and 1992, and starred in scores of other films during this time, the boom years of the HK film industry; *Police Story 2* was only one of 11 films Cheung made in '88.

That year also marked the beginning of her signal collaboration with the voluptuary maestro Wong Kar-wai. Of the five films they've made, none highlights the actress's incandescence quite like *In the Mood for Love* (2000), a movie whose defining visual element is the slo-mo languid movement of Cheung's cheongsam-clad, exquisitely coifed figure through narrow corridors and dark, rain-slicked streets, and up and down endless flights of stairs. Opening in 1962 in Hong Kong and closing at Angkor Wat, in Cambodia, in 1966, *In the Mood for Love* is a fractured memory piece about an oblique romance between two neighbors in a cramped apartment building, Mrs. Chan (Cheung) and Mr. Chow (Tony Leung), who discover that his wife and her husband are having an affair. "The past is something he could see but not touch," explains an intertitle about Chow; similarly, physical contact with the woman he's growing besotted with—even the brush of fingers—remains tantalizingly elusive. The air electric around her, Cheung's character collapses then and now.

Cheung's extraordinary ability to bring the past to the present (and vice versa) also marks Stanley Kwan's lovely *Center Stage* (1991), a biopic about Ruan Lingyu, the silent-screen divinity of pre-revolutionary Chinese cinema who killed herself at age 24, in 1935. Here Cheung plays (at least) three roles: herself, appearing intermittently in segments in which she and Kwan speak to Ruan scholars and contemporaries; Ruan, both on and off the set; and the characters the icon performed in the various films re-created in Kwan's project. It's not enough to say that Cheung seamlessly moves in and out of these myriad personae. She also does something rarer: she freezes time and thaws it, making bygone eras fluid, lucid, and intoxicating. Enraptured while watching Cheung-as-Ruan at a swank nightclub, elegantly dancing to a samba-playing band, I thought of what Kenneth Tynan once wrote of Greta Garbo: "To watch her is to achieve direct, cleansed perception of something which, like a flower or a fold of silk, is raptly, unassertively and beautifully itself."

In Assayas's limber and funny *Irma Vep*, which he wrote expressly for the actress, Cheung nimbly accomplishes another seemingly impossible, or at least paradoxical, task: demystifying her own superstardom in Asia while also bolstering it for those audience members then unfamiliar with her work (as I was at the time of the film's 1997 release in the US). Arriving in the midst of a chaotic, fractious Paris film office after a 12-hour flight from Hong Kong, Maggie (or, perhaps more accurately, "Maggie") calmly and diligently goes to work as the star of a bedeviled remake of *Les Vampires*, Louis Feuillade's famed 1915 silent serial. Directing the redo is René Vidal, a washed-up Nouvelle Vague director played by that film movement's most paradigmatic star, Jean-Pierre Léaud. "You can be Irma Vep because you have the grace," the unstable auteur tells his leading lady after they watch a clip from *The Heroic Trio* (1993), Johnnie To's wuxia marvel, in which Cheung plays a chopper-riding bounty hunter. Every second that Cheung is on-screen in Assayas's movie bears out René's assessment.

Clean, which Assayas and Cheung made after their brief marriage ended in 2001, was also conceived solely for the actress. She plays Emily Wang, a heroin addict struggling to kick her dope habit, get her life together, and reclaim her young son. For her compassionate, complex portrayal of this imperfect woman, Cheung won the Best Actress award at Cannes in 2004, becoming the first Asian to be so honored.

The victory, as Cheung explained to me when I spoke to her in New York when she was promoting the film, gave her confidence: "Now I dare to think that I can make any choice [in roles]. I've been doing this for 20-something years, so this is a moment when you either start to fade out or become stronger as an actress. Now I feel I can be an actress for a long time, which I didn't dare to think I could be."

But *Clean* is Cheung's last major film to date; she is now primarily focused on composing and recording music. It may be accurate to speak of her movie career in the past tense, but she will always exist in the present perfect.

—*Village Voice*, December 7, 2016

Shelley Duvall

One of the presenting symptoms of my Shelley Duvall fandom is amateur numerology. The actress, among the most totemic and inimitable performers of the New American Cinema, was born on the seventh day of the seventh month of 1949. She made seven films with Robert Altman, the director with whom she remains the most closely affiliated. The greatest of their collaborations, *3 Women*, was released in 1977.

I focus on the dominance of seven in Duvall's life and profession only to confirm what I already believe about occult signifiers: they mean nothing. Despite the lucky number, a hazy sense of misfortune—of a career that ended too soon, or that never quite matched the incandescence evinced in its first years—has lingered over the actress, who has not appeared in a movie since 2002. (An infamous sit-down in 2016 with an ignoble TV host suggested that she has not been well for some time.) Maybe her setbacks were augured by Altman when he spoke to Cliff Jahr of the *Village Voice* for an April 1977 profile of Duvall tied to the release of *3 Women*, her sixth movie with the director. In the piece, Jahr conjectures that the filmmaker "has unique and untransferable rapport with his actors," and Altman seems to concur. "I have harmed a lot of them," he says. "I don't quite understand it. Ronee Blakley, who got an Oscar nomination for *Nashville*"—for her portrayal of an unstable country-music superstar in that brilliant ensemble film from 1975—"has not even been able to get an agent to this day." Later in the article, Altman expresses his deep admiration for Duvall's talents, but his praise is freighted with anxiety about her fate: "Somebody better pay attention to her now, or they're all crazy."

It is impossible not to take notice of Shelley Duvall. With her extremely ectomorphic figure, she calls to mind a walking exclamation point. Her long, Modigliani-like face appears taffy-pulled; the focal points of her amazing visage are her enormous, wide-set brown eyes and her two jutting top incisors. If her striking physicality makes the first impression on the viewer, then her demeanor creates the most lasting one. She is unmistakably fey, but her otherworldliness connotes a planet not too far away from our solar system. Duvall is a delight not just to watch but to listen to; her pellucid voice is filigreed by a Houston drawl that she never filed down.

She was discovered in that Texas city by Altman's emissaries, scouting talent for *Brewster McCloud* (1970). They met Duvall at a party she was throwing with her boyfriend. Charmed by their hostess, the movie men arranged for her to audition for Altman, though she had no idea who the director was (he'd just had a big hit with *MASH*) or what "reading for a part" meant. Altman was convinced that Duvall's naïveté was a ruse. "I decided to shoot a test, so I took her out in the park and put a camera on her and just asked her questions," the filmmaker told David Thompson for the book-length interview *Altman on Altman* (2005). "I was really quite mean to her, as I thought she was an actress. But she wasn't kidding; that was her."

Duvall's untutored wisdom makes her performance one of the few unmitigated pleasures of the antic, exhausting *Brewster McCloud*. Playing Suzanne, a garrulous tour guide at the Astrodome who deflowers and ultimately betrays the flight-obsessed title character (Bud Cort), Duvall, with her Raggedy Ann eyelashes, emerges as an unorthodox femme fatale. "Hi! Are you trying to steal my car?" Suzanne asks Brewster; the actress delivers the line with vivifying, daffy ingenuousness. In her screen debut, she evokes James Baldwin's lapidary assessment of the movie legends who held him rapt as a child: "One does not go to see them act: One goes to watch them *be*."

In pointing out Baldwin's instructive ontological distinction, I don't mean to imply that Duvall, especially in her films with Altman, simply presented her unvarnished self—that she took no care when preparing for her roles other than, say, to memorize her lines. Altman, who gave Duvall a small part as a mail-order bride in the western *McCabe & Mrs. Miller* (1971), *Brewster*'s immediate successor, insisted that she observe the entire production for "acting lessons." She demonstrates a noticeable increase in discipline (particularly with regard to her timing and pauses) in her next project with Altman, the Depression-era-set *Thieves like Us* (1974), in which she plays Keechie, the sweetheart of Bowie, Keith Carradine's on-the-lam bank robber. But even though her acting may be more polished, Duvall's performance style isn't entirely pruned of fascinating idiosyncrasies, such as her strange way of saying "yes"—a word she enunciates with what sounds like a brand-new diphthong—when Bowie asks Keechie if she likes him.

If Suzanne and Keechie are characters brought more vibrantly to life by Duvall's undiluted "essence," then Millie Lammoreaux—the prating, self-regarding employee of a geriatric rehab center she plays in *3 Women*—endures as the apex of her assiduous preparation. Originating in a dream that Altman had, *3 Women* traces the shifting dynamics between childlike Pinky (Sissy Spacek) and Millie, who trains the pigtailed recent arrival to Southern California in the basics of hydrotherapy for the elderly. The two coworkers soon become roommates, sharing Millie's yellow-bathed one-bedroom apartment. Pinky, growing ever more besotted with her new friend, marvels at Millie's professed sophisticated taste, largely shaped by *McCall's* magazine, and at her refined palate, which favors such chemically saturated delicacies as banana pops and penthouse chicken.

"I played her like a Lubitsch comedy—people taking themselves very seriously," Duvall said of Millie in that *Voice* profile. Blithely ignoring the fact that most people find her to be a nattering, desperate fool, Millie may have unshakable confidence in herself, but her certitude never fully masks her fragility, especially in the second half of *3 Women*, when the power balance between Millie and Pinky is inverted. This indelible, richly textured character was largely the creation of Duvall. "Shelley wrote all of [Millie's] letters, all of those recipes, all of her diary stuff. I don't know any writer who could have done it better," Altman told Thompson. (Duvall to Jahr: "Monologues just came out in 15 minutes.")

A few weeks after *3 Women* was released, Duvall could be seen in a bit part in Woody Allen's *Annie Hall*, her only non-Altman film from the '70s (not counting a 1976 PBS adaptation of F. Scott Fitzgerald's "Bernice Bobs Her Hair," in which she starred in the title role). Playing Pam, a witless *Rolling Stone* reporter, Duvall, in the meager screen time allotted her, proves the sole source of buoyancy in a project overpopulated by smug, charmless neurotics, its director-cowriter-star chief among them. We are meant to laugh at Pam's preferred adjective—"The only word for this is *transplendent*"—but Duvall locates the dignity in the dippy journalist's enthusiasms.

At the end of the most storied decade of her career, Duvall was cast in the film for which she might be most widely remembered—and for which she endured tremendous distress. In Stanley Kubrick's *The Shining* (1980), the actress, as Wendy Torrance, the initially sunny mom and helpmate of Jack Nicholson's aspiring novelist, spends the latter half of the film in abject terror; Wendy continually weeps and shrieks as she tries to save herself and her young son from a psychotic paterfamilias. Duvall gives a shattering performance of ceaseless anguish—a traumatized state that mirrors the suffering she experienced in her clashes with Kubrick during *The Shining*'s months-long shoot, some of which are featured in the short making-of documentary by the director's daughter Vivian. (More chilling than anything in *The Shining* is Vivian's footage of Duvall, lying on the floor in between takes, saying, of an undisclosed ailment, "It comes and goes. ... It just got so bad" as a matronly crew member tends to her.)

Duvall's final film with Altman—a live-action version of *Popeye,* in which she stars as Olive Oyl, opposite Robin Williams as the spinach-loving sailor—came out the same year as *The Shining.* "Shelley, I want to give you the role you were born to play!" Altman told the actress. But, paradoxically, in this outsize part, Duvall seems diminished, flattened, as does nearly everyone else in the shambolic funny-pages transfer. Yet the movie, aimed at kids, can be thought of as an oblique prologue to Duvall's signal achievement of not only the '80s but all of her post-Altman work: *Faerie Tale Theatre,* a wonderfully outré anthology television series for children (but with multigenerational appeal) broadcast on Showtime between 1982 and 1987. In addition to creating the program, Duvall executive-produced, hosted, and occasionally starred in *FTT,* which featured a motley group of talents ranging from Mick Jagger to Gena Rowlands as various Brothers Grimm and Hans Christian Andersen principals.

Welcoming viewers to "Rumpelstiltskin," the second episode of the first season, in which she plays the miller's daughter, Duvall offers a quasi-confession: "And, I must admit, as an actress, *Faerie Tale Theatre* also gave me an opportunity for some pretty great roles." When considered more than three decades later, the statement seems to eerily anticipate the imminent attrition of those opportunities. During the 15 years between the end of *FTT* and 2002, when she stopped performing altogether, Duvall's output consisted primarily of small or supporting parts in minor, largely forgotten movies, and assorted TV work. There are some exceptions. Duvall thrills with the few Italian interjections—*Mangia! Simpaticissimo!*—she utters as Countess Gemini in Jane Campion's adaptation of *The Portrait of a Lady* (1996). And she beguiles as Amelia Glahn, a spinster ostrich farmer hopelessly in love with a sadistic mesmerist, in *Twilight of the Ice Nymphs* (1997), a pastel-hued fantasia by cult Canadian auteur Guy Maddin. These late-period Duvall performances, just as much as *3 Women*, return us to Altman's command: *Pay attention to her.*

—*Artforum*, May 2018

Sidney Poitier

In a cover story about his friend Sidney Poitier for the July 23, 1968, issue of *Look,* James Baldwin wrote, "It can become very difficult to remain in touch with all that nourishes you when you have arrived at Sidney's eminence and are in the interesting, delicate, and terrifying position of being part of a system that you know you have to change." Baldwin's essay, published at the zenith of the performer's career, gets at the ineluctable bind that Poitier often found himself in: Hollywood's first major Black star, he was frequently cast as a paragon of moral rectitude, playing martyrs and saintly integrationist heroes, such as the protagonists in two films from 1967, James Clavell's *To Sir, With Love* and Stanley Kramer's *Guess Who's Coming to Dinner.* These characters, and others, exhibit, as Baldwin notes, a "fundamental impulse to decency that ... reassures the white audience."

But the deft, agile, alert actor deepened his roles by—as Baldwin puts it—"smuggling in reality," his gestures and inflections acknowledging the far more complicated and painful realities of Black life. It's precisely this quality that's the focus of the nine-film tribute to Poitier at the Museum of the Moving Image, organized by Mia Mask, a professor at Vassar and the coeditor of the 2015 collection *Poitier Revisited: Reconsidering a Black Icon in the Obama Age.* Significantly, this nonet doesn't include the two movies mentioned above—or Ralph Nelson's *Lilies of the Field* (1963), featuring Poitier as a handyman who builds a chapel for a group of Mitteleuropean nuns, a role for which he became the first African American to win the Academy Award for Best Actor.

Rather, this tightly curated series brings together those titles that best demonstrate the performer's "dangerous electricity that is rare indeed and lights up everything for miles around," in Baldwin's words, including three films that Poitier both directed and starred in.

Born in 1927 in Miami, Poitier grew up in the Bahamas and returned to the Florida city when he was 15. Two years later, he moved to New York, where he joined the American Negro Theater. (Alums of ANT include the actor's future costars Harry Belafonte, Ossie Davis, and Ruby Dee; the latter appeared in five films with Poitier, including Daniel Petrie's 1961 screen adaptation of *A Raisin in the Sun*, in which they reprise the husband-and-wife roles they played in Lorraine Hansberry's landmark 1959 play.) He first appeared on Broadway in 1946 in an all-Black production of *Lysistrata*; in 1950, Poitier made his screen debut in Joseph L. Mankiewicz's *No Way Out* (1950), playing Luther Brooks, a physician at a city hospital who must treat Richard Widmark's racist sociopath and his dying criminal-accomplice brother.

Only 23 at the time, Poitier rivets immediately in this strange hybrid of noir and message movie: impeccably dressed in suit and tie (as the actor would often be on-screen, the attire instantly signaling "respectability"), the young doctor warmly greets the elevator operator, one of the few other Black faces at his place of employment, before changing into his medical scrubs. "I'm not sure of myself yet. ... I think I need a little more time than the others," the intern tells his kindly white supervisor. There's not a trace of self-abasement in Poitier's delivery; the words ring as a calm, honest assessment. Though Luther must exhibit superhuman fortitude, as most Poitier characters had to, *No Way Out* also features scenes of Luther at home, episodes marked by tremendous tenderness between the doctor and his wife, to whom he more nakedly expresses his vulnerability and weariness.

That domestic and marital warmth also permeates the West Harlem apartment shared by Poitier's Tommy Tyler, a dock foreman, and his spouse, Lucy, played by Dee, in Martin Ritt's *Edge of the City* (1957). Yet the central dyad of the film consists of Tommy and Axel (John Cassavetes), a rookie longshoreman plagued by neuroses and looked after by the seasoned stevedore. Among the first movies to center on an interracial friendship, one in which a Black man serves as a mentor to a white one, *Edge of the City* astounds—at least until Tommy's inevitable final-act sacrifice—with Poitier's multilayered depiction of empathy. "It's important to me what happens to you," Tommy tells his anxious pal, who shares his woes with his new confidant late one night at a bar. In this scene and others, Tommy largely remains silent, intent only on listening. Poitier registers profound compassion, in one of the most touching displays of platonic love I've ever seen.

Perhaps the actor's most iconic role, Virgil Tibbs—the Philadelphia-based homicide expert inadvertently on assignment in the Deep South in Norman Jewison's murder mystery *In the Heat of the Night* (1967)—also stays tight-lipped for prolonged periods. Here, though, the silence is a sign of contempt for the bungling peckerwood cops and denizens of Sparta, Mississippi. Once again immaculate in a suit, Poitier's character shows not even a bead of sweat, even in the early-September swelter. On the contrary, Virgil is all tightly controlled, icy fury—a third rail of "dangerous electricity," his power surging in apartheid-era America.

—*Village Voice*, April 6, 2016

Afterword: A Conversation with Erika Balsom

Erika Balsom The word *sex* is in the first sentence of the first two texts in the book: the first on *A Bigger Splash* and the second on *La Piscine*. And in the first instance, it's a sentence all by itself, in capital letters and italicized. So I thought, because you start with that word, I would also start with a question about the role of pleasure and sexuality in your writing.

Melissa Anderson It is something I like to bring attention to, for sure. In the introduction, when I talk about feeling that it wasn't until 2012, at the very earliest, that I began feeling more confident that I had found a style—a large part of that style was foregrounding, as blatantly and as often as possible, the fact that I'm a queer woman responding to cinema. That's a spectatorial position that has not been highlighted all that much, although there are exceptions, of course, like the great B. Ruby Rich. Tamping down that aspect of myself seemed that it would make for really uninteresting criticism. The tricky part has been how to focus on pleasure, how to respond to bodies in a way that is sensual, but never wanting to be lewd or creepy.

EB Which you aren't. Horny sometimes, but not creepy.

MA I think it's also very clear when reading this collection that certain gay male film critics have been a great inspiration. That's because their style is so distinct, and often what makes it so is their extreme horniness. Boyd McDonald is the exemplar of that: he's always writing about the size of asses, the size of bulges. Talking about specific measurements has never really interested me, but, yes, I'm always aware of responding to the human beings looming large before me on a screen.

EB This attitude is an important part of your "acteurist" bent. You use this term to describe your method, and it runs through a lot of the texts. Acteurism could entail being enthralled to celebrity culture. But it seems to me you're interested in stars in this desirous way, and maybe not so interested in celebrity as it exists in our world today. I don't know if this distinction between stars and celebrities is a relevant one for you.

MA It absolutely is. As someone who watches almost no TV, who is not on Instagram or TikTok, my notion of what constitutes a celebrity is very limited. I guess I still operate in a very old-fashioned way of thinking of stars as people who have achieved a certain level of fame thanks to cinema.

EB And who don't exist in our world, maybe—they're not posting pictures of their breakfast on Instagram. They are people that we see only projected on the screen.

MA Right. And because of that, they still have a certain mystique. And speaking of gay male critics, during my very brief time as a graduate student, I read a lot of Richard Dyer, who is one of the most influential scholars when it comes to star studies. Although his writing isn't as puckish as that of someone like Boyd McDonald or Parker Tyler, there's still a style there, and I think it's because there's so much passion in what he's writing about. So in addition to communicating pleasure without being gross or weird, I want the reader to feel a certain amount of passion, whether that's love or hate. That's important to me.

EB You are not afraid of writing negatively. Increasingly, many critics choose to weigh in on the specific things that they want to and mostly that's stuff that they like. Whereas you have some really delicious hit pieces in this collection.

MA Since I'm the one who commissions all the film pieces at *4Columns*, this means I get to decide what I want to review. Often that's movies that have some element that I find compelling. I enter the screening room full of hope. With *The Substance*, for instance—the concept intrigued me; I was curious about the movie as a comeback of sorts for Demi Moore, as a way for her stardom to be rehabilitated. But I despised the movie, and I think one of the critic's fundamental duties is to honor the intensity of her response, even if it's very negative.

EB I also had the feeling, with a few of these pieces, that there are other battles you are fighting a little bit behind the scenes. These are not opinions on specific films but more on specific debates occurring in film culture and the world at large during the period when you were writing these texts, from 2012 to 2024. I wonder if it's worth talking a bit about these 12 years more generally. It's a period of a huge increase in queer representation in mainstream media. A big concern with positive images and a certain kind of politics of representation also takes hold in this time. When I was reading the piece on *Carol* and "The Oscars Made Me Gay," I felt that there were certain battles that you wanted to fight a little bit without addressing them completely directly. I wonder if it's fair to say that you seemed skeptical of a new age of respectability.

MA Absolutely. The notion of "positive images" has always seemed very reductive to me. But, if I'm understanding you correctly, did you sense that, in a few of these pieces, I felt something more strongly than I was willing to let on?

EB No, I think it's about a relationship between the particular and the general. All of these pieces are focused on specific films, most of them on one specific film, and then you have "Star Studies," where you're looking at a star's body of work. So it's not necessarily the place to make huge, opinionated pronouncements on a topic like the politics of representation. But it seems to me that you are more subtly weighing in on those debates. My question is: If this were your "think piece" on these kinds of topics, what might there be to say? You love Boyd McDonald, and you mention that he's not interested in classifying or policing queer representation—and it seems you aren't, either. You have maybe a certain kind of nostalgia for another moment in cinema, such as your love of 1970s American studio movies and how ideologically contradictory they are. That's in the *Play Misty for Me* piece.

MA I'm certainly drawn to those films, those in which you can sense the contradictions at play. When a film remains insoluble in that way, it makes it more indelible. I will never, ever forget my first time watching *Play Misty for Me* or *The Beguiled*, another strange film from 1971.

EB Some contemporary feminist film criticism is very interested in claiming that a movie is good because it's empowering. And that this empowerment could come from positive images, but it could also come from an "unlikable female character," who could then be recuperated as some sort of empowering feminist avatar. I was just so taken by your total disregard for this whole way of approaching movies. Instead, there's a sense that you're more interested in movies that are somehow making felt the mess of human interaction. It's not about necessarily modeling moral values for us. That's not what makes a good movie, in your view.

MA When I sat down to write about *Wonder Woman*, a movie that had been touted for so long as being "empowering," as a movie that would make everyone a feminist, I struggled at first because I just had so little to say. Originally, I had wanted to write about it because I thought, even if this movie is horrible, there would have to be some interesting things to say about it, simply because of its outsize role in the culture at the time. But the movie is just so dull. The most captivating part of the film is the opening segment, when Wonder Woman is a little girl and is being raised on what you could think of—what I thought of—as a lesbian-separatist compound. I had to make some leaps of imagination to be able to write about it. I also devoted a paragraph or two in that 800-word review to more oblique topics, like Wonder Woman enduring for 75 years as a "wildly unstable signifier," whether in her comic-book incarnation, as a *Ms.* magazine cover, and so on. Because if I had taken *Wonder Woman* at its face value, I would have written a deadly boring piece.

EB This idea of bringing in other material made me think about the level of historical research that informs many of these pieces. It feels like there's a lot of close attention to your responses to the actual film. But there's also a kind of educational, informative value in a lot of these texts in terms of film history, which is not always found in more belletristic forms of film reviewing. I wanted to ask about your process: How do you go about doing the background research before you write about something? Do you have a reservoir of material that you draw upon as needed? Or is there targeted reading that you do to prepare?

MA For the past several years, I have kept a commonplace book—an ever-expanding document of quotes or things from books that I really like, ideas that I think are intriguing. Sometimes, when I'm really struggling with how to start a piece, which for me, always takes the most time—

EB It's always the hardest thing. Once you start, then it's like a force that is greater than you.

MA Exactly. It has a momentum of its own. But that first paragraph is excruciating. So sometimes when I'm really stuck, I will look back at this document and think, Oh, here's a quote from Anne Truitt's journals; perhaps I can start with this. Also, my schedule at *4Columns* has given me so much more time to write a piece and do whatever research might be necessary. For example, when I wrote about Sidney Lumet's nutso adaptation of Mary McCarthy's *The Group*, I had the time to read her 400-page novel. But even when I was freelancing and writing what felt like 600 pieces a week, I always tried to incorporate as much historical information as I could, simply because I always found that it made for livelier reviews.

EB It's not only film-historical information, which I think is important. There are certain kinds of critics you read and you have a feeling that they've never stepped outside a movie theater before. In their mind, everything comes back to the cinema, whereas your writing often has a centrifugal force to it. The film is absolutely at the center, but through that, there are lots of other things that can be accessed.

MA I have to give credit for that approach to my friend Nathan Lee. He and I became friends around 2003, when he was a daily critic, working for the since-folded *New York Sun*. He was quite the star, truly the most dynamic daily critic at the time. Our shared homosexuality, I think, brought us together. He was a great model of the kind of film critic who is interested in so many things, whose life isn't simply the cinema and the laptop, who is very interested in art, who reads a lot, who has a very vibrant life. He was also a great model of letting yourself relax and be funny in your writing.

EB Related to that, I wonder if you imagine a reader while writing. Who do you see yourself as writing for? I feel really interpellated by your texts. There's this feeling of complicity, of being invited in, maybe even something conspiratorial about it. Personally, when I write, I don't imagine writing to any type of person in particular. But I know that some writers have an addressee in mind, an ideal reader.

MA Usually I don't. Although when I first started writing film criticism, someone whose wonderful face was in my mind a lot was Wayne Koestenbaum, my adviser in graduate school. But I don't know if I thought of him as a specific addressee. Yet he was another pivotal figure, in that his wide-ranging cultural interests were very inspiring, as was his prodigious word arsenal. This is another reason why I keep a commonplace book: to record all the amazing words I encounter in my reading, which then sometimes appear in my reviews.

EB When reading your work, it doesn't feel like you use a more complicated word when a simpler word would do, which I think is what happens with some lesser writers. In those cases, it feels like the writer is just trying to perform sophistication. In your case, it feels like there's a sparing but extremely sharp use of uncommon words. You're reading the piece, it's going down like water, and then, all of a sudden, something hits like bourbon. It changes the rhythm of reading when you get to a word that's less familiar but that is exactly the word that needs to be there. I noticed your immense and yet restrained fondness for vocabulary.

MA Although you and I don't know each other all that well, perhaps you can sense that I have a big personality. No stage is too small. I am not an actress, but I do have a platform: my Microsoft Word documents. So to drop in a fancy word in a review is perhaps akin to me doing some kind of fancy balletic move onstage.

EB The first part of the book is called "Looking Back." And even outside that section, there are many texts on films from the past. What is the difference for you between writing about new releases and looking at older films? Is there a sense that the responsibility of the critic changes or the role of the critic changes when you're, say, reviewing *Wonder Woman* on week of release versus when you are trying to draw someone's attention to an older film? Or is it all just the landscape of film exhibition in New York City?

MA I think it's all of what you just stated. For the three years that I was at *Time Out New York*, almost everything I wrote about was new releases. When I started freelancing full-time, in early 2009, I wanted to keep as busy as possible and write about as many things as possible, so I cast a very wide net. At this time I began writing for the magnificent David Velasco, who was then the editor of *Artforum* online. He was so receptive to anything that I wanted to write about, even titles playing only in repertory. I could write about something that was screening only once or something that was coming out on DVD. When I was hired as a staff critic at the *Village Voice* in late 2015, they wanted me to have a weekly column in which I could write about whatever I wanted. I said that I wanted the column to focus on repertory cinema, because at that time, New York City repertory film culture was about to undergo this amazing resurgence, and I wanted to call people's attention to that. And at *4Columns*, again, I have tremendous freedom in what I commission—including what I assign to myself. If I look at an upcoming week and there's just absolutely no new release that is even of remote interest to me, I'll write about an older film that's, say, playing at Anthology Film Archives for just for one night but that has some quality that draws me to it, that intrigues me.

EB It's a really noticeable feature of the collection: they're all pieces written between 2012 and 2024 but many of them are about older films. And so there's a question about the relationship between past and present, and what kind of relationship to film history is there in the work of a critic who's covering contemporary developments in cinema. What you mentioned about 2015 and this new golden age of rep cinema in New York—I think there's a very similar narrative in London. For me, one of the most striking features of contemporary cinema, or interesting contemporary cinema now, is this engagement with the past. For some, it might be seen as an indicator of crisis. But I don't see it that way.

MA There's something quite fascinating about reevaluating movies from decades ago. I'm thinking specifically about a piece that I wrote on two older films that were restored and were screened as part of this orgy of commemorative events celebrating the 50th anniversary of Stonewall in 2019. One of those films was *Gay USA*, an amazing documentary from 1977 by Arthur J. Bressan Jr. It's an assembly of footage and interviews from Pride parades, shot mainly in San Francisco but in a few other cities as well. You're seeing all these beautiful young men being interviewed—and AIDS is still a few years away. So while I'm furiously taking notes while watching *Gay USA* at a press screening, I have this horrible realization that a huge percentage of those guys being interviewed, who are so effulgently alive on-screen, are probably dead, have been dead for decades. Sometimes there's something so emotionally and psychologically destabilizing about this kind of retrospectatorship (to use Patrica White's great word), just in terms of being reminded of mortality.

EB That's a very pointed example of something that is always present at the cinema.

MA Yes, the reminder of one's imminent demise. Eros and Thanatos: I'm always struggling with these twinned forces.

EB Are you optimistic about the current state of cinema? The popularity of rep cinema today *could* be seen as some sort of indicator of the bleakness of contemporary cinema and could tie into a bigger argument about the decay or death of cinema. On the other hand, when these screenings of quite obscure films are totally selling out, to me, that feels like a pretty vibrant film culture, even if those films are older films.

MA Yes, I remain optimistic about contemporary cinema, if only for the fact that a film like *Trenque Lauquen*, which premiered in 2022, exists. I remember that I was the only person at the press screening, and the four-plus hours of that film just flew by so quickly. It was an absolute revelation. What a deep pleasure to never know from scene to scene what would happen next, to witness such a profound investment in the depths of fiction. The fact that this film was made gives me hope that there are still enchantments ahead of us.

Erika Balsom is the author of four books, including TEN SKIES *(2021) and* After Uniqueness: A History of Film and Video in Circulation *(2017). Her writing has appeared in publications including* 4Columns, Cahiers du cinéma, e-flux, *and* New Left Review. *She is a reader in film studies at King's College London.*

Acknowledgments

I thank Jake Perlin, with whom I have been discussing movies for 25 years, and Jim Colvill for making this book possible. Thank you to Erika Balsom for the conversation, Ed Halter for the title, and Anna Thorngate for proofreading (and for editing the *Town Bloody Hall* essay).

Thank you to my wonderful colleagues at *4Columns*: Bonnie Chau, Julie Evanoff, Margaret Sundell, and especially Ania Szremski, who edited several pieces in this collection. Thanks to Brian Parks, who edited my *4Columns* pieces from 2017 to 2021.

Thank you to my other editors: Zack Hatfield and Don McMahon at *Artforum*, Michael Miller at *Bookforum*, Alan Scherstuhl at the *Village Voice*, and David Velasco at *Artforum* online.

For their friendship, support, and inspiration, I thank Marina Ancona, Eric Anderson, Liz Brown, Andrew Chan, Nicholas Elliott, Johanna Fateman, Amélie Garin-Davet, Leo Goldsmith, Emily Greenberg, Jennifer Krasinski, Nathan Lee, Dennis Lim, Jean Ma, Lawen Mohtadi, Cara O'Connor, Jeanine Oleson, Lisa Reynolds, Sam Roeck, Teresa Ross Tellechea, Vincent Sallé, Ariel Schrag, Sebene Selassie, Lydia Siegel, Andrea Torres, and Charlotte Wells.

I thank Franklin Gilliam for being my favorite person to go to the movies with, and for so much else.